AMERICA IN THE NINETIES

AMERICA IN THE TWENTIETH CENTURY

John Robert Greene, *Series Editor*

Other titles from America in the Twentieth Century

America in the Twenties
Ronald Allen Goldberg

America in the Thirties
John Olszowka, Marnie M. Sullivan,
Brian R. Sheridan, and Dennis Hickey

America in the Forties
Ronald Allen Goldberg

America in the Fifties
Andrew J. Dunar

America in the Sixties
John Robert Greene

America in the Seventies
Stephanie A. Slocum-Schaffer

AMERICA
IN THE
NINETIES

Nina Esperanza Serrianne

With a Foreword by John Robert Greene

SYRACUSE UNIVERSITY PRESS

Copyright © 2015 by Syracuse University Press
Syracuse, New York 13244-5290

All Rights Reserved

First Edition 2015
15 16 17 18 19 20   6 5 4 3 2 1

∞ The paper used in this publication meets the minimum requirements of the
American National Standard for Information Sciences—Permanence of Paper for
Printed Library Materials, ANSI Z39.48-1992.

For a listing of books published and distributed by Syracuse University Press,
visit www.SyracuseUniversityPress.syr.edu.

ISBN: 978-0-8156-3397-6 (cloth)   978-0-8156-3385-3 (paperback)
978-0-8156-5308-0 (e-book)

Library of Congress Cataloging-in-Publication Data
Available from publisher upon request.

Manufactured in the United States of America

To My Mentors

Nina Esperanza Serrianne holds an MA in history and political science and is currently pursuing a PhD in public policy at George Mason University. She has worked in the nonprofit sector in both statewide advocacy and direct services.

Contents

Foreword

JOHN ROBERT GREENE

"THERE JUST NEVER SEEMS TO BE ENOUGH TIME." "The textbook is so bland, the students won't read it." "Don't *teachers* ever write?" "If I could only find more than one book that I feel good about assigning."

These complaints are endemic to those of us who teach survey American history courses. The book series America in the Twentieth Century was designed to address these issues in a novel fashion that attempts to meet the needs of both student and instructor alike. It uses decades for its organizational schema (admittedly a debatable choice, but it is our experience that chronology, not theme, makes for a better survey course), and each book tackles the main issues of a particular decade in a readable and scholarly fashion. The series editor has chosen authors primarily for their teaching skills—indeed, each book proposal was accompanied by syllabi that show the prospective author's course pedagogy. In fact, contributors have been urged to write these books from their lecture notes and to limit footnote references, which can often distract or intimidate the student reader. In a departure from virtually every textbook series of note, one member of our editorial board is a presently sitting college student, whose comments on the manuscript may well be the most helpful of all. Each chapter ends with a recommended reading list of the authors' favorite books. The list is, admittedly, not exhaustive, but no list of our favorite works ever *is*.

The result is a readable, concise, and scholarly series of books from master teachers who know what works in the college classroom. We offer it to college instructors and their students in hopes that they will, in the words of the Latin maxim, do the one thing that we all in the academy hope that professor and student will do together: "tolle et lege" (take and read).

Preface

EXPERIENCES OF HISTORY are not monolithic. Within each demographic, the social and political context is unique to the individual. This book seeks to give a voice to historically marginalized communities and to provide an overview of the 1990s.

The narrative trajectory begins with the fall of the Berlin Wall in 1989 and concludes with the terrorist attacks of September 11, 2001. The decade after the Cold War and before the war on terror was a unique moment in history for both foreign and domestic policy. The cultural changes of the 1990s must be analyzed within the economic and political milieu of the 1980s. Backlash to the civil rights movement, the conservative revolution, Reaganomics, and the election of Clinton created a decade in which both sides of the political spectrum sought to gain a better footing. New analysis has emerged as events have been revisited for their twentieth anniversaries; and the scholarship on the 1990s continues to develop as we move into the future.

My deepest thanks are extended to Dr. John Robert Greene for his unwavering support as the series editor, my mentor, teacher, and friend.

Thank you to Syracuse University Press for the opportunity to publish this manuscript. Special thanks to Deanna McCay for her assistance, my external peer reviewer for guidance on initial drafts, and my editor Mary Petrusewicz. Additional thanks are extended to those who provided feedback throughout the writing process.

I would like to thank all of the great teachers that have guided me through my education and to specifically acknowledge: the faculty and staff at Cazenovia College who challenged and supported me as an undergraduate and Professors Scott Lemieux and Angela Ledford at the College of Saint Rose, who served on my thesis committee and provided critical intellectual mentoring and recommendations during my graduate education.

Thank you to my family and friends for their unconditional love and support.

Recommended Reading

Haynes Johnson, *The Best of Times: The Boom and Bust Years of America before and after Everything Changed* (Orlando, FL: Mariner Books, 2002), examines the decade as a whole, giving special attention to the scandals and trials of the decade.

AMERICA IN THE NINETIES

Introduction

The End of the 1980s

AFTER DECADES OF Cold War tensions and subsequent hot wars (military conflict with active combat) between the United States and the Soviet Union, President elect George Herbert Walker Bush confidently proclaimed, "for in a man's heart, if not in fact, the day of the dictator is over." During his 1989 inaugural address, he elucidated, "The totalitarian era is passing, its old ideas blown away like leaves from an ancient, lifeless tree. 'A new breeze is blowing.'" Before the end of his first year in office, his prophecy became a reality as the Soviet Union collapsed and the Berlin Wall fell. The year 1989 ushered in a new decade in both American and international politics. The Reagan years (1980–1988) were domestically defined by individualism and power established through personal wealth. Simultaneously, the struggle between capitalism and communism demarcated foreign relations. If Reagan brought "morning to America" in the early 1980s, Bush facilitated the "new breeze" at the end of the decade. As it happened, 1989 was the last year of both the conservative revolution and the Cold War. To the surprise of many, the Bush presidency began a new era of moderate domestic politics, and to the surprise of few, the post–Cold War era.

The conservative revolution of the 1980s was a direct backlash to the progressive social changes of the 1960s. During the 1960s, the Democratic Party gained political momentum and implemented liberal public policies. The assassination of President John F. Kennedy and the vocal student movement set the tone of the country. The American political climate now tended to abandon conservative Republican ideology and supported the new president, Lyndon B. Johnson. Because of this change, conservative Americans sought to restrategize and reclaim the White House. The strategy of the "Rockefeller Republicans" (those following the political ideology of the politician Nelson Rockefeller, often described as the liberal Republicans) focused on the elections they believed Republicans could win. In the wake of Watergate, the end of the Vietnam War, and the counterculture movement of the 1960s, the conservative lobbyists gained an opportunity to restructure the party platform. The new agenda specifically targeted their approaches to fiscal and social issues. As the GOP refocused, many of the social issues raised in the previous decades became bipartisan issues. In the years after the divide between conservative mainstream culture and counterculture, conservatives strove to be the antithesis of the liberal movement. The GOP aimed to fight the "George McGoverns" of politics (the iconic liberal Democratic candidate who lost to Richard Nixon in the 1972 general election). Supported by the evangelical movement of the 1970s, the GOP aimed to repeal the progress in abortion rights, the gay rights movement, the women's movement, gun control legislation, the death penalty, and other social issues. By 1980, the Republican Party successfully created a cohesive platform and regained control of both the Senate and the presidency.

George Bush and Ronald Reagan, then governor of California, began as political adversaries as they both sought the presidency in 1980. During the campaign, Bush tried to learn to appear more likable to the camera, but it was too late. Reagan, a former wealthy movie star, campaigned with charm, excellent communication skills, and the ability to overcome scandals. These attributes awarded him the nickname "the great communicator" and later "the Teflon president." In May 1980, after months of campaigning against each other, Bush resigned the race, leaving the Republican presidential nomination to Reagan. On July 16, 1980, while at the Republican National Convention in Detroit, Reagan selected Bush as the vice presidential nominee to appear on the ballot in November. Bush's inclusion on the ticket was contingent on his embrace of the Reagan platform. Specifically, with the intent to convince voters he was loyal to Reagan, Bush changed his political position to be against abortion. Although he worked hard to persuade voters of his trustworthiness and devotion, many Republicans remained skeptical of his political positioning throughout his career. In the end, the campaigning assuaged the fears of voters, and on November 4, 1980, Reagan-Bush defeated the incumbent Carter-Mondale by a landslide. On January 20, 1981, Bush was sworn in as the nation's vice president.

Reagan's presidency was defined by his socially and fiscally conservative agenda. Throughout both presidential terms, Reagan fulfilled his campaign promises with support from the Senate. Former President Franklin D. Roosevelt inspired Reagan to not only enter politics but also to use his political model for the conservative and Republican agenda. Ironically, the agenda itself was the inverse of FDR's liberal and Democratic agenda; Reagan reversed more New Deal policies than any previous administration. The Reagan administration's policies supported big tax cuts, small government, and were premised on the theory of a "trickle-down effect" of prosperity, which came be to known as Reaganomics. As explained by the historian Michael Schaller in *Reckoning with Reagan: America and Its President in the 1980s*, the philosophy behind Reaganomics was rooted in Reagan's status in the 90 percent income bracket and his desire to eradicate "progressive taxation." His economic plan, "America's New Beginning: A Program for Economic Recovery," was first presented to Congress in February 1981. In addition to tax changes, the plan sought to cut $41 billion from his predecessor President Jimmy Carter's budget and many social programs.

The new financial policies of the Reagan administration, combined with the recession of 1982, created an economic seesaw; consequently, class stratification grew exponentially. According to Reaganomics, theoretically, the tax cuts would create an abundance of wealth among the more affluent classes that would "trickle" down to the poor. This concentration of wealth in the top income bracket has been attributed by scholars to the making of the "1 percent" that now owns the majority of the country's wealth. Although many financial experts and advisers cautioned the president against this approach, Reagan aggressively pursued his financial agenda. As Schaller explained, Reagan met with Congress seventy times during the first four months of his administration to lobby for his tax cuts and increases to the defense budget. Ultimately, he skillfully and successfully negotiated with Congress to ensure that his financial vision was completed.

During Bush's tenure as vice president, he remained devoted to Reagan throughout an assassination attempt, the Iran-Contra affair, and Cold War and hot war negotiations. In October 1987, with the public's support, Bush announced his second bid for the presidency. His reputation with the Reagan administration gave him credibility; however, when juxtaposed with the "great communicator," Bush appeared tepid and at times uncomfortable during his own campaign for office. He was once again challenged to reveal his personality and persuasively articulate his goals to the American people. Bush's political expertise and his popularity was apparent, but he needed to prove that this was sufficient to be elected president. GOP voters were persuaded by the Reagan legacy and the vice president's fidelity. In August 1988, Bush accepted the Republican nomination at the Republican National Convention.

The 1980s was a gilded age of wealth and prosperity, specifically for the upper classes chasing the American dream. In *Sleepwalking through History: America in the Reagan Years*, the Pulitzer Prize winner Haynes Johnson described how America "was passing through a period that increasingly resembled the moral slackness of the spendthrift twenties, a new Gilded Age, and one that, like then, would extract a price for its excesses." This story of wealth and overindulgences was apparent in politics, music, and film. During the apex of the 1980s, the pop singer Madonna's song, "Material Girl," became an anthem for a decade of prosperity for the wealthy. Dressed in homage to Marilyn Monroe's performance of "Diamonds Are a Girl's Best Friend" (1953), Madonna quipped, "Living in a material world / And I am a material girl." This song, coupled with other chart toppers such as Bruce Springsteen's rock anthem "Born in the USA," demonstrated the concurrent narcissism and fervent nationalism in American society during the 1980s. The patriotic platitudes of Springsteen's anthem reiterated the height of American pride under the Reagan-Bush administration.

The national obsession with the lucrative lifestyle of the 1980s was a result of a Machiavellian Wall Street culture and pursuits of the American dream. In *The Presidency of George Bush*, the historian John Robert Greene analyzes how the 1987 movie *Wall Street* captured the essence of the 1980s. The young stockbroker Bud Fox's ambition was to take the fast track to the top by any means necessary and as quickly as possible. Fox found a mentor in the high-powered and opportunistic stockbroker Gordon Gekko—the quintessential Wall Street yuppie. Throughout the movie, Gekko, the anti-hero, preaches his life and business philosophy: "greed is good." As he infamously proclaims during a stockbroker's meeting: "Greed is right, greed works. Greed clarifies, cuts through, and captures the essence of the evolutionary spirit. Greed, in all of its forms—greed for life, for money, for love, knowledge—has marked the upward surge of mankind." Gekko's soliloquy captured the sentiments of the material motivations of the 1980s.

The preoccupation with wealth and affluence was in part a result of the long-term obsession with the American dream, but more important was a symptom of the Cold War culture. The fixation on capitalism and the free market perpetuated American investment in a capitalist society. Regardless of the rise and fall of the stock market, Wall Street firms maintained an authority in the 1980s that represented copious amounts of wealth and power. Throughout the 1980s, access to wealth continued to increase, but in 1987 the economy reached its pinnacle before crashing. As discontentment rose during Bush's term in office, he took the fall for the inevitable decline of the economy.

Across society, the 1980s were a backlash to the counterculture movement and to the progressive legislative changes of the 1960s and 1970s; the free love and drug-dominated counterculture gave way to the decade of conservatism. The 1980s followed on the heels of the sexual liberation movement and the rise of second-wave feminism. The social agenda of the country was more conservative and puritanical. In the early part of the 1980s, there were still moments that were reminiscent of the sexual liberation movement, such as Madonna's or Pat Benatar's music videos aired on the cable television station MTV. As the culture became more conservative and the Republican revolution pushed for traditional values, specifically around gender and marriage, the representation of women in music and movies drifted back to conventional roles.

Additionally, during the 1980s, the glamorous side of sex faded as a new virus took lives. The first cases of Human Immunodeficiency Virus (HIV) and Acquired Immune Deficiency Syndrome (AIDS) were identified in 1981. The quick-spreading and misunderstood virus plagued communities across the United States and the globe, disproportionately impacting minority communities. Since the first five cases were discovered, approximately thirty-four million people have been infected with HIV. This includes more than one million cases in the United States and an estimated half a million deaths; of these, two hundred thousand occurred before the 1990s. In *AIDS in America*, the medical anthropologist Susan Hunter explained that New York City has more HIV infections due to drug use than many developing countries combined. Every thirteen minutes someone in America becomes infected. During the 1980s, views on this rapidly growing disease were commonly rooted in discrimination, homophobia, and confusion. The response from the government was highly intolerant and inactive in preventing or curing the virus. Reagan was supported by religious extremists such as the Reverend Jerry Falwell, who attributed the epidemic to the "wrath of God upon homosexuals." The Reagan administration evaded the issue in a way that the presidents of the 1990s were unable to, as by then the virus was too consuming. As described by Greene in *The Presidency of George Bush*, AIDS was no longer an issue the Reagan administration, or Americans, could ignore. "Because of AIDS, the morality of Reaganism had to confront the very real possibility that one could die from having sex." Unlike during the sexual revolution, casual sex now had a fatal consequence and the epidemic was sweeping the country.

When Bush took office as president in January 1989, the conservative revolution and the rapacious stockbrokers of Wall Street had been dominating America for nearly a decade. As heir to the Reagan legacy, voters anticipated that the vice president would follow in his predecessor's footsteps and continue the trend of conservativism. The popularity of the Reagan administration secured Bush's place as the next president against the Democratic Party challenger Michael Dukakis. Since Bush's days as a young politico, many of his critics denounced him as a RINO—Republican in name only. As a conservative who voted for the Voting Right Act of 1964 and changed his position on abortion, many believed that he was a weak politician or more liberal than he stated. A cover of *Newsweek* magazine hit the stands during the presidential campaign that charged Bush with "fighting the wimp factor." Although the admiration of the Reagan administration was enough to maintain his voting base, Republican voters worried about his presidential style. During his 1988 campaign, Bush was afraid to "go negative" and only adopted a more aggressive campaign style when pushed by his aides. Speaking to his character, he wanted his moral ideology and résumé to speak for itself.

The softer side of Bush that worried voters during the campaign appeared in his first moments in office. His inaugural speech began as an ode to the Reagan years. Considerable portions of his discourse reiterated his support for the policies of the Reagan administration, including criticisms of welfare, support of family values and the anti-abortion movement, and a call to action for activism on the part of the youth and the elderly. However, a glimpse of the forthcoming Bush presidency and departure from his campaign strategy was captured when he called on Americans "to make kinder the face of the nation and gentler the face of the world." Although Bush proved to be a hawkish president on the international front, his domestic policies led to much criticism and eventually debased his career.

The first two years in office, Bush disassociated himself from the Reagan legacy and established his own prestige. Although Reagan left office with the highest approval rating since FDR, the factions of the Democratic and Republican government needed bipartisan collaboration. This was integral to moving forward with new legislation and to address the impending financial crisis. Bush reflected in *All the Best, George Bush: My Life in Letters and Other Writings* that he knew success would require him to work closely with the Democratic-controlled Congress. During Bush's inauguration speech, he set the tone for bipartisan partnership when he labeled the incoming era "the age of the offered hand" and extended his hand to those across the aisle in a gesture to create a bipartisan movement. Although Bush ran an aggressive election campaign, once elected, he returned to his imperturbable political style.

When Bush transitioned to the White House in January 1989, he broke from the Reagan administration by appointing new members to his cabinet. During Bush's campaign, he established his right-hand men in the Republican Party and trusted them to guide him through his presidency. Reagan loyalists and appointed staff viewed this as Bush's first step to abandon the Republican Party. Greene described this political decision as an "ideological house cleaning." He elaborated, "Reagan appointees were shown the door in a way that made it look like a Democrat was coming into office." Among Bush's transition team was his most influential appointee, John Sununu, his chief of staff. Whereas Bush was known for being diplomatic and soft, Sununu was aggressive and relentless. In *The Modern Presidency*, the political scientist James Pfiffner described him as "Bush's pit bull." Despite being saturated in politics from a young age, Bush was inclined to take a soft approach to policymaking. Sununu's antagonistic approach to politics allowed both the president and his staff to play into the "good cop/bad cop" dynamic that was inherent in the administration. Pfiffner expounded that Sununu's more conservative politics also helped retain the Republican voting base during the early years of the Bush presidency. Although Sununu pushed Bush to the Right politically, the president's commitment to his own agenda, not the Reagan agenda, set him up for immense criticism. As his term progressed, almost fulfilling the critical prediction, Bush became the "soft" version of himself for which he was berated.

The economic calamity of the Bush administration was inevitable. During Reagan's time in office, the federal debt more than tripled; by January 1989, the debt amounted to over $2.7 trillion dollars. Although the rich continued to profit and to gain prosperity, Reaganomics created instability in the economy. Greene noted Reagan's impact on the Bush administration: "In his seemingly sincere attempt to turn the clock back to a time when values were simpler and America's place in the world was strong and secure, Reagan unleashed a host of demons that plagued his successor." Reagan believed that "high taxes and excess spending" needed to be fixed. However, his economic plan backfired when the deficit grew under Reaganomics. Additionally, the interest on the debt increased from $69 billion when Reagan took office to $169 billion when Bush took office eight years later. Unfortunately, the consequences of Reagan administration policies came at the worst time for the new president. Johnson wrote that in the first weeks of Bush's term in office, "the unpaid bills of the eighties were coming due" and the new president was faced with the consequences. The tax cuts and fiscal policies of the Reagan administration created a volatile economy that resulted in the economic recession, which beleaguered the Bush administration. The recession specifically burdened Bush during the 1992 campaign.

Bush's succession was impacted by international politics. As a result of the animosity with the Soviet Union and Communist countries, the foreign policy agenda of the Reagan administration concentrated on the Cold

War and subsequent hot wars. The administration took an aggressive stance on both the Cold War and the Berlin Wall. Throughout the 1980s, Reagan accelerated a heavily anticommunist agenda and spoke at length about bringing capitalism to Soviet countries and the world. The Cold War caused Americans to feel fear and hostility for decades. For the duration of the Cold War, America and the Soviet Union engaged in "us versus them" rhetoric, which perpetuated a malevolent relationship between the two super powers.

The cultural and political divisions of the Cold War were literally embodied in the Berlin Wall. The guarded wall was erected in 1961 to cut off East Germany from West Germany, obstructing emigration and separating pro- and anti-Soviet states. Countries around the world had been pushing for a unified Germany. The United States and England were apprehensive about what unification meant for international relations, but Mikhail Gorbachev, General Secretary of the Communist Party of the Soviet Union (1985–1991), ultimately decided it was best for his country and the Pan-European vision to tear down the tangible barrier. As Bush predicted in his inaugural speech, the Cold War was coming to an end. After forty years, the symbolic end of the war came on November 9, 1989, when Gorbachev gave the order to tear the wall down. Overnight, international relations changed. At home and in Washington politics, the collapse was viewed as triumph for the United States and capitalism abroad.

As the Wall fell, Bush's popularity among the American people soared. Bush was criticized for not partaking in a more aggressive stance against the end of the Cold War. Consistent with his character, he was publically humble; he famously stated that he would not "dance on the wall" as it fell. He was slighted for his lack of enthusiasm during this historic moment. A reporter asked him, "you do not seem elated. . . . I am wondering if you are thinking of the problems." The president candidly responded, "I am not an emotional kind of guy." Bush's public hesitation was in part due to concern about what an overly patriotic and bellicose reaction from the United States might spark. At the time, it was uncertain what would unfold globally as the Wall crumbled. The muted response from Bush was intentional in an effort to appear diplomatic and to not incite backlash against the United States. With the fall of the Berlin Wall, the United States and capitalism led in an era of new global politics.

The Reagan administration and the events of the 1980s determined the context of the 1990s. Bush was affected by the decisions of his predecessor. On the domestic front he continued to negotiate the economic calamity as the recession continued. During the 1980s, as an extension of the Cold War, the United States became involved in hot wars across the globe. Additionally and unbeknownst to the American people, during the Iraq-Iran War from 1980 to 1988, the United States government supported Iraq and its leader Saddam Hussein. The Reagan administration was plagued with the scandal of illegally shipping arms to Iran during the conflict. Simultaneously, the United States also sent confidential information and arms to Iraq. As the *New York Times* reported on January 26, 1992, "In the end, officials acknowledged, American arms, technology and intelligence helped Iraq avert defeat and eventually grow, with much help from the Soviet Union later, into the regional power that invaded Kuwait in August 1990." The support of Hussein from the Reagan-Bush administration only precipitated the dictatorship; the strengthened power of the Iraqi leader became problematic during Bush's first year in office. The challenges and successes of the Bush administration were rooted in the policy decisions of the Reagan administration. The conflict in Iraq and the faltering economy provided Bush with both his legacy and the albatross of his career.

Recommended Reading

A great and lengthy introduction to the 1980s can be found in Haynes Johnson's *Sleepwalking through History: America in the Reagan Years* (New York: W. W. Norton, 2003). The recent editions are not only a national best-seller but also connect the Reagan years to the current and consequential issues of the twenty-first century. For more on the Reagan administration, see the Reagan scholar Michael Schaller's *Reckoning with Reagan: America and Its President in the 1980s* (Oxford: Oxford University Press, 1994). Addressing the AIDS crisis in America is the internationally acclaimed book by Randy Shilts, *And the Band Played On: Politics, People, and the AIDS Epidemic, 20th Anniversary Edition* (New York: St. Martin's Press, 2007). Tony Kushner's play and TV miniseries *Angels in America* provides a look into the early struggles with the virus.

1

America in the Gulf and Bush's Limited Domestic Agenda, 1990–1992

DURING GEORGE H. W. BUSH'S acceptance speech at the Republican National Convention in 1988, he acknowledged the various qualities of both himself and the presidency. He admitted to being a quiet and personal man. Additionally, he defined the presidency as a protector and advocate of the American people. He addressed foreign policy, concerns of war, democracy, and diplomacy while advocating for a "policy of peace through strength." He appealed to the American people for their continued support in the post-Reagan years and outlined his position on the war on drugs, capital punishment, and pollution. He asserted, "[a] president must be many things." Bush was a leader abroad in the post–Cold War era, began and ended wars, and attempted to rectify the tumultuous economy he inherited, all while maintaining a "limited" domestic agenda.

Throughout Bush's presidency, his foreign policy successes were far reaching and global. From his first day in office addressing the Cold War conflict, Bush positioned himself to be victorious internationally. After many years of struggling to navigate the U.S. relationship with the Soviet Union, Bush led America into a new era of global power and foreign relations. The war on drugs, the Cold War, and the hot wars led the president into nontraditional battles, where the United States was ultimately triumphant. Bush was scrutinized by both political parties for his domestic decisions, but he flourished with global politics.

Beyond the Cold War, Bush's early days in office addressed the international war on drugs; he engaged in military action against the Panamanian dictator and international kingpin Manuel Noriega. As vice president, Bush assembled a coalition of government and military agencies known as the South Florida Drug Task Force to help fight the international war on drugs, specifically drug entry into the United States in Miami. The trafficking of cocaine by Noriega and the Colombian politician Pablo Escobar contributed to the rise of cocaine consumption in the 1980s and international drug smuggling. Bush's decision to invade Panama and overthrow Noriega was in retaliation for the murder of a United States Navy seaman and the beating of two witnesses. As Bush committed to military action, he reflected to Brent Scowcroft in a letter about new intelligence, "Reading this, I am convinced more than ever we should try to extricate Noriega. Let's go." In an effort to hold Noriega accountable for drug trafficking, in December 1989, the United States sent in troops to find and apprehend him. The troops were unable to capture the dictator; the consequential violence killed twenty-three Americans and hundreds of Panamanian civilians. After two weeks of fighting, Noriega surrendered to the Drug Enforcement Administration (DEA) on January 3, 1990. Bush rang in the second year of his presidency with a victory in the war on drugs as Noriega was sent to a prison in Miami. The Bush administration was a militaristic titan abroad; within weeks of Noriega's demise, Bush was contending with another post–Cold War dictator, this time in Iraq.

The 1990s began a new era of international relationships and it was necessary for America to assess its role as a global leader and its budget. In the post–Cold War years, the allocation of the budget dedicated to Cold War protections was questioned. The procurement budget dropped from $126 billion to $39 billion between 1985 and the beginning of the Gulf War. The Gulf War presented President Bush with the opportunity to engage the Soviets as allies and build a new vision. The rhetoric of "one war to end all wars" and the collaboration of countries for one cause invoked for many former President Woodrow Wilson's hope for World War I and the League of Nations. More important, the question that arose after the fall of the Berlin Wall was what does safety and security look like in a post–Cold War world?

The Gulf War was the first test in international relations after the Cold War ended. The United States encountered the challenges of reestablishing allies, identifying enemies, and clarifying the volatile relationship with the Iraqi leader Saddam Hussein. The Bush administration reviewed the policies of the Reagan administration toward Iraq, the impact of these conflicts on the United States, and the financial support provided by the American government. In 1987, under Reagan, the United States provided Iraq with a $1 billion dollar loan; this was the largest loan of its kind to any nation in the world. A portion of this loan was used for resources for the military execution of the Kurds—a primarily Muslim population centered in a geographical area inclusive of eastern Turkey, northern Iraq, western Iran, eastern Syria, Armenia, and Azerbaijan. The United States did not want to criticize Saddam and opted instead to continue supporting the dictator. Samantha Power explained in *A Problem from Hell: America and the Age of Genocide* that the Bush administration sustained this funding and in January 1990 Bush overrode Congress by extending the line of credit by nearly $200 million. The economies were integral to one another, emboldening the United States to ignore the human rights violations.

Because the agriculture sectors were intrinsic to one another, if U.S. policymakers ostracized Iraq because of violence it would damage the United States economy. During the 1980s, Iraq was the ninth largest purchaser of U.S. farm products. They imported one million tons of wheat annually and consumed about 25 percent of rice production. When Congress was deciding the future of funding for Iraq, this deeply influenced politicians from agricultural states and their agendas. The dependent nature of the relationship led to the continuance of billions of dollars in aid to Iraq and a climate of perceived collaboration; in reality the heavy reliance on U.S. funding was devastating the Iraq economy. The economic situation only exacerbated conflicts in the area when Saddam used the economic disparities facing his country as an excuse to invade Kuwait in August 1990 and continue his execution of the Kurds. Ultimately, ignoring the volatile nature of Saddam's leadership placed issues of global security on the table. Responding to violence against Kuwait by the Iraqi government, the U.S. military launched Operations Desert Storm and Desert Shield and engaged America in war abroad. However, unlike Bush's vision and Wilsonian rhetoric, it would not be the last war of its kind.

The alliance between the United States and Iraq evolved drastically in the late 1980s and early 1990s. Initially, the United States explicitly ignored the ethnic and social conflicts in Iraq and turned a blind eye to the genocide of the Kurds enabled by U.S. dollars. In 1989, despite the mass violence Saddam committed against his own people, President Bush signed National Security Directive 26 (NSD-26) to continue funding to Iraq. As Power concluded, "normal relations between the United States and Iraq would serve longer-term interests [of the United States] and promote more stability in both the Gulf and the Middle East." Additionally, Greene explained in *The Presidency of George Bush*, the business relationship between the United States and Saddam placed the Bush administration in a position where it was not willing to openly criticize the Iraqi leader.

For more than two decades, the United States avoided acknowledging the systematic killing of the Kurds by the Iraqi government. During 1987, Iraqi offenses against the Kurds intensified and the zenith of the genocide occurred during February and September of 1988; these acts of horror came to be known as the "Anfal Campaign" or the "Kurdish Genocide." When Saddam employed poisonous gases to push tens of thousands of Kurds into Turkey, the United States condemned the atrocities with a slap on the wrist. The neglect of the Reagan administration became a problem for the Bush administration when Saddam threatened the global community. The chemical weapons that Saddam used against his own people specifically became a concern internationally during his infamous "Burn Israel" speech. When feeling imperiled by Israel, Saddam threatened that if Israel were to attack his country, "By God, we will make fire eat up half of Israel." Bush's position on Iraq shifted during his time in office. At first Bush viewed Saddam as a strategic dilemma; however, by the end of the war, he adopted the issue of what to do about Saddam as America's "moral crusade." Although as president Bush ignored human rights violations and genocide in other parts of the world, he was vocal about the rape and murder of Iraqi citizens. It was not long before the president gave speeches and press conferences that referred to Saddam as "worse than Hitler."

On August 2, 1990, Saddam ordered 140,000 Iraqi troops and 18,000 tanks to invade Kuwait. Scholars have attributed the decision to invade Kuwait to the economic decline of Iraq after America placed funding on hold. The oil reserves seized by Saddam in the invasion were originally discovered in the 1930s and grew exponentially after Kuwait was liberated from Great Britain in 1961. Approximately the size of New York State, at the time of the invasion, Kuwait was home to 10 percent of the world's oil and an army of 16,000. By invading Kuwait, Saddam took control of 20 percent of the world's oil reserve. This worried the officials in the U.S. State Department because of the proximity of Kuwait to Saudi Arabia. If Saddam expanded his control to Saudi Arabia, he would control 50 percent of the world's oil. The fear of Saddam's expanding power motivated Bush to quickly assign troops to arrive in the region by August 6, 1990. Bush ignored pushback on utilizing troops to protect Saudi resources from Colin Powell, national security adviser (1987–1989), chairman of the Joint Chiefs of Staff (1989–1993), and future secretary of state under President George W. Bush (2001–2005). The president announced to the press that American troops would be deployed to defend the American "friends" in the Persian Gulf and support the withdrawal of Saddam's troops from Kuwait. By the end of August, Bush called up the reserves and approximately 80,000 international coalition troops were deployed to Saudi Arabia.

The invasion into Iraq presented Bush with the opportunity to demonstrate to the American people and the world community his clout as commander in chief. Taking an aggressive stance against Saddam Hussein allowed the typically placid president to demonstrate his capacity to navigate foreign policy. According to the Gallup Poll, Bush maintained approval ratings in the sixties when the crisis and impending war began. When troops were deployed, the American public backed the war at around 70 percent. After the invasion, nearly three-quarters of Americans supported the president; this jump in the polls sustained him until he dropped over 20 percentage points in a few short months, one of the worst slides in the modern presidency. The cynicism about the economy was palpable and the growing burden on American people impacted his popularity.

The day after the invasion by Iraq was unparalleled in U.S. history because of the alliance it created between the United States and the Soviet

Union. For the first time since the Cold War, the two world powers stood together for the purpose of condemning the government actions of Iraq and calling for an international response. The invasion of U.S. troops was strengthened by the support of a broad coalition of thirty-four international allies. The Security Council and the majority of countries around the world employed economic sanctions against Baghdad to cripple Saddam's power. Additionally, the Security Council approved twelve resolutions that supported severing the supply of arms to Baghdad. The affable alliance between the coalition countries represented a new era of global politics but also a united global front against Saddam.

The troop deployment intended to stop Saddam from invading Saudi Arabia and potentially gaining control of the majority of the world's oil. Based on an amicable diplomatic relationship with Saudi Arabia since the 1930s, Bush called on King Fahd of Saudi Arabia to provide a safe haven for American troops, members of the Kuwait government, and many of the refugee citizens. The decision of the king to welcome the U.S. military into his country cost him politically with members of his government and with the terrorist group Al-Qaeda. Some scholars have argued that one of the political consequences of Saudi support to America was the rise of the international terrorist Osama Bin Laden and consequently September 11. Saddam responded to the involvement of the United States by declaring "jihad" or holy war against America and Israel. During a *New York Times* interview reported on October 30, 1990, Saddam declared, "whoever shall commit aggression against Iraq shall turn out to be the loser." Additionally, he blamed the recent decision of U.S. military intervention on Margaret "the Iron Lady" Thatcher, Great Britain's prime minister (1979–1990), and officials in Israel. The public animosity between Saddam and the Western counties contributed to the growing tensions as the United States predictably moved toward military intervention.

The majority of the Bush administration determined that the plan for military intervention in Iraq, known as Operation Desert Storm, could not occur without calling up large numbers of army reserves. However, this strategy was met with opposition from many government officials. Sununu argued with Powell that without calling the reserves Saddam could still be defeated. However, Powell was unwavering in his position on this tactic and supported the deployment of troops only with a guarantee of tens of thousands. Powell's fear was rooted in the Vietnam Syndrome, the fear of deploying American troops with great force into an endless or unwinnable war. Paradoxically, in the deployment for Operation Desert Storm this would be the first time the reserves were called since the Tet Offensive of 1968. Many viewed Powell's stubbornness as simply oppositional. He believed that before American lives were put on the line every aspect had to be considered. In his autobiography, *My American Journey*, Powell reflected, true to his principles, that "war is a deadly game; and I do not believe in spending the lives of Americans lightly." The rationale for calling up the reserves was to avoid a situation similar to the prolonged Vietnam War. However, the original two hundred thousand requested troops later expanded to five hundred thousand. Although peers in the administration challenged Powell's proposal, he stood firm in his recommendation and did not ignore the impact deployment would have on the lives of Americans. Powell was not an antiwar chairman of the Joint Chiefs of Staff and ultimately his desire to protect families and individual lives gave way to the decision to deploy. Some saw the impact that deployment would disproportionately have on military families and advocated for the draft to be reinstated if an army of such great proportions was necessary. Bush's final decision was to call more than a quarter million people from the reserves to fight Saddam.

In October 1990, Congress pushed back against the president's deployment of troops. Bush worried about continuing strong international collaborations and the stability of the global coalition. Bush met with the members of his cabinet on October 30, 1990. During the meeting, the War Council decided to deploy the troops to the Middle East. With the congressional elections the following week, the administration delayed the announcement until after the election, and the troops were officially called on November 8, 1990. This was a bold decision by the president. Consequently, he was presented with a letter from Congress that demanded the War Powers Clause (Article I, Section 8, Clause 11) in the Constitution be adhered to properly. Eighty-one members of Congress explained to the president that "recent reports and briefings indicate that the United States has shifted from a defensive to an offensive posture and that war may be imminent. We believe that the consequences would be catastrophic—resulting in the massive loss of lives, including 10,000 to 50,000 Americans. This could only be described as war. Under the U.S. Constitution, only Congress can declare war."

Members of the House and Senate wanted the Executive Branch to allot more time for the sanction to work before calling the reserves and declaring war. During this time, the sanctions were in fact effective against the Iraqi leader. Although Saddam was in control of 20 percent of the world's oil supplies, the restrictions from the United Nations left him with no ability to sell it. Despite the limitations on executive prerogative enumerated in the Constitution, Bush did not believe that he had to report to Congress and wait for its permission on the issue of war making.

Peers within the administration supported the president's belief that turning to Congress to declare war eroded the powers of the presidency. Richard "Dick" Cheney, the secretary of defense (1989–1993) and future vice president under George W. Bush (2001–2009), was vocal about his support of the president to move forward without the consent of Congress. He believed if Bush backed down it would weaken the presidency and the powers of the Executive Branch. Additionally, Cheney supported Bush's argument against adhering to the War Powers Clause by looking back in history to also compare Saddam to Hitler; he argued that in the weeks and months after Pearl Harbor, Hitler would have been able to take over Europe if the president had deferred to Congress to declare war. Although Cheney's position on presidential power was more extreme than most, his premise was supported by the actions of the current administration and the members of the preceding one. Additionally, although troops had been deployed for more than sixty days to a war zone, with the support of his administration Bush continued to argue that American troops were not in "immediate danger." The constitutional debate over who had the power to take the country to war had not concluded and troops continued to remain on the ground.

Congress was not ready to relinquish the power granted to it by the Constitution. This issue was complicated not only by the morality of calling up the largest number of the reserves since Vietnam but also by the paradox that following the Constitution meant opposing the president. Congress wanted the issue to dissipate. When Bush made public his plan to call up the reserves, the confrontation between the branches became inevitable. The president faced opposition from members of the Senate across the political spectrum, ranging from Senator Ted Kennedy to Senator Dick Luger. Most members of Congress were not challenging the war but were arguing the constitutionality of the president's decisions. Luger, one of the great leaders of moderate Republicanism, stepped away from his party to call on his lame duck colleagues to vote on declaring war abroad. Concurrently, Bush reached out to his allies, but even Senator Robert Byrd of West Virginia advised the president to follow the lead of Congress and the Constitution.

As Congress reviewed the information and decided to vote on the declaration of war, the Bush administration set its own deadline, January 15, 1991, for Saddam to remove his forces from Kuwait. Although Bush had support from the United Nations, the lawsuit from Congress and the dispute over the War Powers Clause forced him to remain accountable to the other branches of government. However, the decision of Congress to vote on declaring war came after the president made the military decisions. Luckily for him, they were one and the same; Congress voted to support the president's deployment of troops to Iraq. On January 15, the day proposed for Saddam to leave Kuwait, Bush signed National Security Directive 54 and "initiat[ed] military hostilities against Iraq." The directive stated the aims of the war: "(a) To effect immediate, complete, and unconditional withdrawal of all Iraqi forces from Kuwait. (b) To restore Kuwait's legitimate government. (c) To protect the lives of American citizens abroad. (d) To promote security and stability of the Persian Gulf." This was the moment when the initiative in Iraq shifted from Operation Desert Shield to Operation Desert Storm.

On January 17, 1991, at 3 am Baghdad time, the United States and its allied forces began the air attacks against Saddam; the five and a half weeks of bombing provided Americans with an advantage over the Iraqi army. On February 1, Cheney threatened that if Saddam were to use chemical or unconventional weapons against American troops, the United States would retaliate. By the first week in February, Powell's tactic of extreme force was apparent with the presence of over a half million U.S. troops deployed to the Gulf. The air strikes against Saddam continued as citizens and historical landmarks became casualties of the war; one bombing campaign alone killed over four hundred people. On February 22, President Bush gave Saddam an ultimatum to withdraw his troops within twenty-four hours or the American government would deploy ground forces to push him out of Kuwait. When the Iraqi leader ignored this threat, allied ground troops were deployed.

The ground campaign of the operation began on February 24, 1991. In response to the intensification of the war, Saddam fired off Scud missiles and hit U.S. barracks in Saudi Arabia, killing twenty-eight U.S. soldiers. With a quick turn of events, U.S. troops and the international coalition ground forces entered Kuwait city and engaged in combat with the Iraqi Republican Guard. In just 40 minutes, three hundred Iraqi tanks were hit and one American life was lost; the quick ground battle met its intended goals. The allies in the coalition suspended their operations and a cease-fire was implemented 100 hours after the mission began. American troops lost 148 soldiers in action and 458 were wounded, 92 coalition soldiers were killed, and approximately 22,000 Iraqis were killed. The mission was viewed as complete and the Bush administration moved to end the war without removing Saddam from power.

After the cease-fire, the war was not over for Iraqi civilians. During the war, the Kurds relied on the presence of American support in Kuwait for protection. A detrimental consequence of the cease-fire for non-Americans was the absence of a ban on Iraqi military helicopters; this allowed for violence to continue even though the ground troops were forced out of Kuwait. For Americans, the brevity of the war allowed for a clear end date and for the agenda to stay within the limits set by the Security Council. With the leader that Bush had likened to Hitler still in power, pulling out the troops was inevitably controversial. As Greene explained, the intent was never to implement a regime change, the aim was to remove Saddam from Kuwait and restore power to Kuwait. Now that Saddam's power was limited again to Iraq, he was no longer threatening or controlling 50 percent of the world's oil, and therefore the decision to end the war was final.

On March 6, 1991, Bush announced, in a joint session of Congress, that the war in the Gulf was over; Kuwait was liberated with very little loss of American lives. Americans were enamored with the troops in the weeks after Operation Desert Storm. As David Halberstam observed in *War in Time of Peace: Bush, Clinton, and the Generals*, "the country fell in love with the troops and their amazingly swift victory. Everyone loves being on the side of the victor. But the war was without real resonance." The approval of the war and support of the troops was easy when the weight of the war was primarily absent. Unlike the Vietnam War, the Gulf War did not generate feelings of bereavement, but rather sentiments of success.

The American people's temporary amicable feelings toward the war gave way to real concerns about the economy. The first responses to the Gulf War allowed the country to feel as though it had disengaged from the Vietnam Syndrome and could engage in quick and efficient combat missions abroad. Fears of a Vietnam-like quagmire returned when the high of the Gulf War victory passed. With conflict brewing in Bosnia, the multifaceted nature of foreign policy became increasingly complex. Once again, American policy-makers felt apprehensive and apathetic about deploying troops abroad.

In the wake of the Gulf War, the president's approval rating skyrocketed to an unprecedented 90 percent, demonstrating a decidedly improved acceptance of the president than before the war. However, his celebrity status was short lived and by October his approval had declined to 59 percent. After the midterm elections, which shaped several of his executive decisions, his approval plummeted further to 50 percent. The decline in ratings over the second part of the president's term came as a shock to Bush. From his perspective, his list of achievements spoke for themselves. He had ended the Cold War, reformed the U.S. relationship with Russia as Boris Yeltsin assumed power in 1991, and removed Saddam from Kuwait. On the foreign policy front, Bush was believed to be invincible. From academia to popular culture, Bush's legacy in American and global history appeared indisputable. However, the Cold War had lasted for decades, and subsequently the new victory in Iraq and Kuwait had left Americans feeling saturated by war. It was clear that Americans wanted their economic and domestic needs addressed.

Although Bush was aggressive in the international arena, he failed to bring the same passion and success to domestic politics. His hawkish personality as commander in chief created a strange dichotomy as the press and his own party continued to hound him for being weak on domestic issues. At the beginning of the 1990s, after having been in office for a year, Bush was faced with a multitude of challenges: the deployment of troops, conflicts within the Republican and Democratic parties, and the impending 1992 election.

Bush's presidency was inevitably complicated by his predecessor's legacy. Any deviation from the Reagan agenda unavoidably upset the majority of his electoral base and provided ammunition to his critics, specifically the Far Right. By his own accord, Bush separated himself almost entirely from Reagan's legacy and the plan of the conservative revolution. Bush invested in domestic policies to create his own reputation, perpetuating the perception that he was a traitor to his own party. Problematically, the Republicans did not want a new agenda and the middle- and working-class voters wanted someone who understood their strife. Bush placed what he believed was best for the country over party politics, and therefore created a lasting detriment to his political career.

The affluence of the 1980s was the bane of the Bush administration. Under the Reagan administration, the rich had never been richer. However, the inevitable trajectory of Reaganomics set the heir to the Reagan administration up for economic failure and disappointment from the American people. The economic recession during the Bush years was a repercussion of the policies of the Reagan administration. Affluent citizens, who experienced an abundance of wealth under the Reagan administration, were financially hurt in the recession and were consequently disgruntled. Additionally, lower-class Americans who never benefited from the trickle-down economics of the Reagan administration continued to suffer at an accelerated rate as the economy continued to decline. When Bush advocated for and implemented the "tax revenue increases" he had vociferously campaigned against, he knew this would potentially end his opportunity for a second term. This act of political courage placed the needs of the country over his rapidly approaching reelection.

While Bush and his cabinet approached international conflicts with the Powell doctrine of extreme force, Sununu's agenda for domestic policies was the antithesis of this. Sununu worked to implement a "limited agenda" on the domestic front. Bush intentionally placed his attention on the international concerns of the administration, while only addressing a skeletal amount of domestic concerns. Initially, Sununu reported to the *New York Times* in a December 14, 1988 article that the limited agenda was for the transitional period of the administration to "to get things moving through the system rather quickly." However, the approach to the benchmark issues of education, the environment, and military spending all carried into the four years of Bush's presidency. Sununu's original sentiment was remnant in the struggle between domestic and foreign policy as the economy tanked and wars began abroad. Additionally, the domestic agenda of the Bush administration incited vociferous criticism when his policies became increasingly inconsistent with the Reagan administration and the desires of his base of support. The decision to put domestic issues on the periphery of the administration earned Bush criticism and cost him the reelection. Despite the denunciation of both parties for his domestic agenda, Bush produced some historic legislation during his time in office. The Bush presidency will never be remembered for its domestic successes, specifically because of the deviation from the Reagan administration and because they paled in comparison to the Gulf War.

Bush's domestic legacy was embodied in the 1990 Americans with Disabilities Act (ADA): new pioneering legislation that provided unprecedented protections to disabled Americans. Although Bush had a complicated relationship with many minority groups, he consistently advocated for those with physical and developmental disabilities. Scholars have surmised that the loss of his daughter Robin to leukemia at the age of three motivated the president to protect those struggling with developmental and intellectual impairments. Protecting Americans with disabilities was Bush's campaign promise and passing the legislation fulfilled his word to the American people. As explained by the historian Edward Berkowitz in *Principle over Politics?: The Domestic Policy of George H. W. Bush*, early polling data demonstrated that Bush's strong and genuine support for the bill was one of the topics that swayed Democratic voters to cast a ballot for a Republican president during the election.

The innovative legislation was the first comprehensive bill to provide protections for Americans living with disabilities. All-inclusive in scope, the bill addressed issues ranging from discrimination in employment to access to public facilities. Bush leveraged support in Congress simply by the nature of the bill. Unlike other politically loaded social issues, Bush successfully attracted the support of Republican voters. In a high-profile op-ed in the *New York Times*, James Brady, the White House press secretary under Ronald Reagan and vice chairman of the National Organization on Disability, became the fiscal voice advocating for passage of the historic legislation. He began by acknowledging that "astonishingly, it is legal under Federal law for a restaurant to refuse to serve a mentally retarded person, for a theater to deny admission to someone with cerebral palsy, for a dry cleaner to refuse service to someone who is deaf or blind." He recognized the bill was originally created under the Reagan administration, an accomplishment of which both he and the president were proud as it came to fruition.

Laying out the challenges and discrimination facing this community, Brady explained that at the time, of the thirty-seven million Americans living with a disability, "66 percent of working-age adults with disabilities are unemployed and dependent on Federal subsidies." Brady argued that outlawing discrimination and providing jobs for disabled Americans was more fiscally responsible and a way to "strengthen our national economy." The Republican motivation for supporting the bill was multifaceted. As civil rights was on the table with the impending Civil Rights Act of 1991, the bill became heavily partisan, racially loaded, and a wedge issue between the parties.

Under President Bush, for the first time in American history, Americans living with disabilities would be afforded new and unprecedented protections; worldwide, the act was the first of its kind. The final version of the ADA prohibited discrimination "on the basis of disability" in "employment, State and local government, public accommodations, commercial facilities, transportation, and telecommunications." Although the act was not fully implemented for two years, the Equal Employment Opportunity Commission (EEOC) worked quickly to create new regulations and standards to hold businesses accountable. Employers with fifteen employees or less were not subject to the regulations; also employers were not responsible for accommodations when they placed an "undue hardship" on the operations of a business. The term "undue hardship" was defined by the EEOC as "an action requiring significant difficulty or expense when considered in light of factors such as an employer's size, financial resources, and the nature and structure of its operation." These necessary changes have continued to protect individuals with disabilities in the decades since its implementation.

Under the ADA, employers became responsible for creating equal employment opportunities. Much in the way the Civil Rights Act of 1964 changed discrimination against other minority groups, the ADA provided federal laws and regulations to protect those living with disabilities. In Bush's speech on the south lawn of the White House on July 26, 1990, he inferred parallels between the words of the Declaration of Independence and the historic legislation, and he concluded: "[the ADA] brings us closer to that day when no Americans will ever again be deprived of their basic guarantees of life, liberty, and the pursuit of happiness." In *Principle over Politics?* Berkowitz notes that when the president signed the legislation into law, he drew an analogy between the newly implemented Act and the fall of the Berlin Wall by declaring, "Let the shameful wall of exclusion finally come tumbling down." The legislation was important not only for its innovative protections to the disabled community but also for salvaging the reputation of a president who had more blunders than domestic successes.

The ADA served as the most prominent and successful domestic legislation of the Bush administration. Berkowitz explained in *Principle over Politics?* that one of the missed opportunities with the ADA from a political standpoint was the inability of the Bush administration to capitalize on the political dividend. Bush needed domestic successes to sustain his political career in office; the ADA had the potential to provide him with that political capital. However, other issues, including wars abroad and the economy, would quickly overshadow this domestic success.

As was intended in Bush's "limited agenda," environmental policies were addressed; however, Bush estranged himself further from the Reagan legacy when he proposed revisions to the Clean Air Act, an environmental law passed under Nixon that Reagan had been explicitly against renewing. Building off the successes of the Clear Air Act of 1977, the Clean Air Act Amendments of 1990 focused on air quality and impacts on the stratospheric ozone layer. Despite the advocacy against it from Reagan and the GOP, in 1989, as president, Bush proposed broad revisions to the initial act. To further enhance the bill, the modifications were created from proposals to Congress in the 1980s. The new proposal focused on three major environmental issues: acid rain, urban air pollution, and toxic air emissions. Not only did Bush focus on the effects of these pollutants on the environment but he also drew attention to the health implication for Americans. To resolve the differences in the House and Senate bill, a joint conference committee convened from July to October 1990. Although the recommendations from the conference were ultimately omitted, the bill continued to move through Congress. The House passed the bill 401–21 and the Senate followed by passing it 89-11; both versions reflected the majority of the president's supplications. Additionally, the bill was strengthened when the House and Senate bills added research and development provisions. The new legislation represented a progressive move forward for environmental legislation and was the first governmental step toward addressing "clean" energy sources and cutting dependency on oil—topics that would gain momentum in later years.

Among many other things, this legislation held companies accountable to develop "cleaner" and more fuel-efficient cars. Highly influenced by the energy crisis of the 1970s, policymakers wanted to take action on concerns around access to resources and on environmental issues. The act brought with it not only a renewed interest in creating electric cars but also in maintaining a culture in which fuel mileage and pollution were manageable. A second law in California passed by the Californian Air Resources Board (CARB) implemented a Zero Emissions Vehicle (ZEV) mandate. In the 1990s, new models from Nissan, Toyota, and other leading car manufacturers began producing energy efficient models. The electric cars produced very little exhaust and took small amounts of fuel to run. Although a few decades later hybrid cars would become popular, the push to promote the electric car and reduce dependency on gas was met with great opposition from car companies. On November 15, 1990, Bush signed the new version of the Clean Air Act, further creating a wedge between his legacy and Reagan's.

Looking to the future of America, Bush sought to implement a strategy that would change education long term, but most important, before the end of the decade. In 1991, Bush devised a nine-year strategy to move the United States into the next century. Unlike Bush's other domestic decisions, his goal for education was one of the areas in which he worked to fulfill the Reagan agenda. He introduced "America 2000," which proposed "to improve learning and teaching by providing a national framework for education reform" through standardized testing and national standards. The program had two areas of focus: the topics covered (English, math, science, history, and geography) and the age groups targeted (testing administered in fourth, eighth, and twelfth grade). Additionally, the legislative proposal addressed the debate over public and private schooling. Bush's vision for education in America needed support from the House and Senate.

Initially, both political parties warmly welcomed the suggestion of education reform; however, this approval was ephemeral. Bush's first obstacle with his education bill was the Democrat-controlled Congress. Bush attempted to draw bipartisan support to the bill in an effort to see it succeed. Bipartisan support became complicated when Democrats supported the bill but had their own demands as well. Senators Claiborne Pell and Edward Kennedy directed the bill through the Committee on Labor and Human Resources in an attempt to use the bill to fit their own agenda. Both advocacy groups and Congress pushed back against the movement for reform, the most contentious point being the testing provisions.

The standardized tests designated in the bill discriminate against poor and minority students, who studies have shown perform at lower levels on standardized tests. Although significantly more research that supports this claim has been produced in the decades since Bush proposed "America 2000," the evidence was still available in the early 1990s. Specifically, a three-year and $1 million study in collaboration with the National Science Foundation and Boston College's Center for the Study of Testing, Evaluation, and Educational Policy received a lot of attention as the bill was being debated. The *New York Times* reported, "The study found that tests profoundly shape what teachers teach because of the enormous pressure to improve students' test scores." More important, the article addressed the issue of how this approach only teaches for what is tested and does not develop critical thinking and analysis skills. Additionally, schools with heavy minority populations were found to be at a disadvantage due to a lack of resources provided to those schools; however, the students were held to the same standards. Regardless of the findings and the criticism, the bill continued to move forward with support from the president.

Criticisms of the bill came not only from the Left; the Republicans also cautiously critiqued their president. For politicians on the Right, the issue of state's rights outweighed the concerns of individual students; they questioned if the bill gave too much power to the federal government and if it was unconstitutional. The scholar Martin Sharp explained in *Principle over Politics?* that the Constitution does not explicitly address education, but that the Tenth Amendment states that power not delegated to the United States is reserved to the states or to the people—therefore making education an issue for each state. Granting power to the federal government for education did not sit well with Republicans, but they were cautious about condemning an already domestically weak president. The bill was revised many times as both the House and the Senate negotiated its provisions. Much to the president's chagrin, the bill continued to weaken around the time of the election and it was clear that it was stuck in the Senate. Bush let the bill die and committed to renegotiations during his second term—an opportunity never afforded to him.

The domestic agenda of the Bush administration resulted in calamity after calamity as the 1992 election drew closer. Although the president avoided a full-blown scandal like the Iran-Contra affair during his term in office, his presidency was not without embarrassments. Domestically, for every step Bush took forward, he took more steps backward as his popularity waned. Additionally, Bush was faced with the reality that he was losing his base of support. Conservatives hated the domestic successes that he did have and were angry about his deviation from the Reagan agenda. The same political affiliations with the Reagan administration that won him the 1988 election cost him the reelection. He was believed to be increasingly out of touch. Bush attempted to ride his popularity from the Gulf War through to the election year, but his attempt was futile.

Recommended Reading

For a look at Bush's personal letters and documents in what is perhaps his closest book to a memoir, see George H. W. Bush, *All the Best, George Bush: My Life in Letters and Other Writings* (New York: Scribner's, 1999). For a concise overview of the Bush administration, John Robert Greene, *The Presidency of George Bush* (Lawrence: University Press of Kansas, 1999). A multiauthor perspective on the domestic policies of the Bush administration is given in Richard Himelfarb and Rosanna Perotti, eds., *Principle over Politics?: The Domestic Policy of the George H. W. Bush Presidency* (Westport, CT: Preager Publishers, 2004).

2

The 1992 Campaign, Why Bush Lost, and How Clinton Won

HOW DID A SITTING PRESIDENT with an 89 percent approval rating lose an election? President Bush ended the Cold War and won a war in Iraq against the dictator Saddam Hussein, yet when Americans went to the polls they supported a young governor from Arkansas with 43 percent of the votes. As the success of the Gulf War faded, Democrats did not identify with the president, and paradoxically, Republicans believed the president's moderate politics and RINO actions aligned more with the Democratic Party. Bush's political successes derived from his foreign policy strengths. Consequently, the people were frustrated with his domestic policy decisions and deviation from the Reagan administration's legacy, and exhausted by the faltering economy. The famous political scientist Aaron Wildavsky noted that there are "two presidencies," "domestic" and "foreign." Although he published "The Two Presidencies" in the late 1960s, Wildavsky contended that "since World War II, presidents have had much greater success in controlling the nation's defense and foreign policies than dominating its domestic policies." Although written decades before Bush held the presidency, this was specifically the problem that he faced in the post–Gulf War years. His 89 percent approval rating could not withstand his domestic policy decisions, specifically around fiscally conservative social issues.

In 1988 when Bush campaigned for his first term, his political adviser, Lee Atwater, encouraged him to run a more aggressive campaign. Bush infamously told the American voters, "Read my lips, no new taxes." This promise would become the burden of his reelection campaign. In June 1990, Bush had been deadlocked with Congress for weeks on budget issues and subsequently faced challenges with both Democrats and Republicans. After extensive discussions, it appeared that a compromise had been reached and that members of both parties were on board. In a formal press conference, Bush announced that tax revenue increases would be included in the final version. When he first decided to rescind his campaign promise and compromise with the Democrats on tax revenue increases, he knew it could end his political career but believed in the bipartisan support of the bill. Although Speaker of the House Newt Gingrich gave the president his word in support of the new agenda, he ultimately spoke out publically against Bush's decision. When Bush broke his campaign promise, his rapidly growing conservative base felt betrayed; when his reelection campaign began, those sentiments had not dissipated.

The media and the political parties took the opportunity to expose the reversal of Bush's position. The *New York Post* published a picture of the president with the caption, "Read My Lips . . . I Lied." This jab captured the sentiment of Bush's Republican base as they became progressively disgruntled with the president. Many saw the tax compromise as the ultimate betrayal of the Reagan legacy and the conservative tax agenda of the 1980s. Many voters believed this was another strategy by Bush to move to the center and act as a moderate. Republicans felt cheated, and most important, they did not believe the president was remorseful in his decision. The tax debacle followed other decisions Bush had made to compromise his position in the Republican Party. In March 1989, only months after taking office, Bush reversed his campaign position on semi-automatic weapons when he announced a temporary, made permanent, ban on imports of semi-automatic rifles. As gun control was one of the most controversial issues in American culture, conservatives and gun advocates wanted to know that the president would protect their interests. The discontent and feelings of betrayal began to brew and the Republicans questioned if they wanted to support their incumbent in the next election cycle.

President Bush's alienation of voters caused him to lose the election long before November 1992. The isolation of working-class Americans was a specific result of the failing economy. Additionally, middle-class Americans felt abandoned by the president and thought he was out of touch. Although Atwater, the architect of Bush's presidential campaign, worked to make Bush's Ivy League personality more accessible to the average American, Bush was unable to prove to the American people that he understood their financial struggles. Bush saw an opportunity to connect to the middle class during the 1992 National Grocers Association convention. While browsing the exhibitions, Bush encountered a mock check-out lane, which included an electronic scanner. The president's "amazement" with technology only underscored his disconnect from the everyday experiences of the average American. The *New York Times* reported that the president "grabbed a quart of milk, a light bulb and a bag of candy and ran them over an electronic scanner. The look of wonder flickered across his face again as he saw the item and price registered on the cash register screen." Bush's genuine disconnect with something as basic as a grocery store scanner that had been in common use for over a decade only emphasized how out of touch he was.

The White House spokesperson defended the president and stated that he had been grocery shopping at his vacation home in Kennebunkport, Maine, but it was too late. Bush attempted to remedy the situation, but continued to act as his own worst enemy. He struggled to balance these embarrassments by calling attention to his policy successes. This effort to overcorrect his political blunder proved to be his biggest weakness as a presidential candidate. Domestically, the promise of innovative legislation did not matter against the calamity of the hikes in taxes and the plummeting economy. The end of the Cold War and Bush's accomplishments in the Gulf were a thing of the past to voters. Despite his attempts to attract blue collar and Reagan Democrats, Bush had alienated too many factions of his voting base and Americans were anxious about his stance on domestic issues. The middle-class moderate voters forgave him for not being an intensely conservative president, but they could not pardon him for the recession, which impacted them personally. Women voters were vital to capturing the election, but Bush had alienated many women with his 1991 nomination of Clarence Thomas to the Supreme Court. When Thurgood Marshall, the first black man to sit on the Supreme Court, resigned, Clarence Thomas quickly became the president's choice to fill the vacated seat. Arguably the largest sexual harassment scandal in American history came after the nomination of Thomas. As news of sexual harassment leaked to the press, Anita Hill, the former aid to the nominee, brought her accusations against Thomas to the public's attention. Hill was labeled heretical and her character was questioned on national television and in front of the Senate Judiciary Committee. Bush stood by Thomas and praised his reputation at the swearing-in ceremony. After the humiliation of Hill and the president's support for Thomas, women voters turned away from Bush. Having already changed position on the issue of abortion, he now lost additional support after his failure to stand firm on the issue of sexual harassment.

When it came time to vote in November 1992, the demographic of women voters was still reeling from the Thomas nomination. It should have been easy for Bush to appeal to female constituents, since he was running against Bill Clinton, who was accused of sexual harassment and extramarital affairs. However, the pre-presidential sex scandals of the Clinton campaign were pallid in comparison with Thomas's offenses. Bush's nomination in light of his support for Thomas came across as impudent regarding the rights of women, whereas Clinton's transgressions were viewed as less crude and a personal matter. Hillary Rodham Clinton voiced support for her husband, which not only saved his campaign but also greatly challenged Bush. The president could not compete with the Clintons as a cohesive unit. There was no equivalent to Hillary's defense of her husband to amend the damage done by Thomas's nomination. The stark comparison between sexual harassment and sexual infidelity was clear to female voters. Although this did not exempt Clinton from criticism, it gave him the upper hand in the campaign. Despite the Clinton sex scandals that emerged throughout the 1992 campaign and Bush's strong commitment to family values, women voters surprisingly continued to trust Clinton but not Bush.

In 1988, Bush's key to success was his energetic campaign consultant and former chair of the Republican National Committee, Lee Atwater. Unlike the young Machiavellian Republican, Bush did not believe in attack campaign strategies. Bush believed that his political agenda and successes should speak for themselves and that it was not necessary to criticize his opponent. His strong personal ethos was a liability in political campaigning. During the 1988 campaign, however, Atwater directed Bush to take a cheap shot at Dukakis, which consequently won Bush the campaign and ushered in a new era of political strategy. Tragically, in 1991 Atwater was diagnosed with a brain tumor at age forty and succumbed to it within a year. The unexpected loss of the architect of his first campaign left Bush without the incentive to attack his opponent; Bush detested using negative strategies and was not a natural campaigner as was his 1992 opponent. Clinton loved to campaign and was adored by the cameras. Atwater had recognized this difference between the candidates and had set into motion an attack campaign on a bad real estate deal that haunted Clinton for the rest of the decade.

Many conservatives speculated that the absence of Atwater cost Bush the 1992 election. After Atwater's death, no one ever truly took his place in politics. Although it is impossible to analyze what did not happen, it is fair to speculate that Bush did not know how to sell himself without Atwater's guidance. Atwater could make the American people see the Ivy League educated Texan as accessible, despite his elitist background. Bush's personable characteristics were not evident in the 1992 campaign. James Baker, Bush's chief of staff, took over the reelection campaign, but without Atwater's aptitude for campaign-trail strategy, the president's appeal to the American people fell flat. He appeared detached and uninterested in his own bid for reelection. When juxtaposed with Clinton's ardor for campaigning, Bush appeared weak and the American people noticed it.

White House Chief of Staff John Sununu was another iconic Republican absent during the president's reelection campaign. Labeled the "pit bull" by news outlets and political analysts, Sununu had more enemies than allies in Washington. Many Republican strategists blamed the recession and other calamities of the Bush administration on Sununu. It was speculated that Bush could run a more effective reelection campaign without him. In December 1991, Sununu announced his resignation as the president's right-hand man. Sununu was the face for many of the poor domestic policy decisions within the administration, but the reality was that many Americans identified these unpopular decisions with the president. In his resignation, the chief aide to the president clarified that he worried his role in the administration would "be a drag" on the president's reelection campaign. Publically, he told reporters, "I knew the rules of the game when I came to town. He's going into a campaign. He doesn't need the extra political target that folks would be shooting at." Many saw Sununu's rancorous personality as a liability to the presidency. During the termination of his tenure, Sununu had walked a fine line between outwardly bashing the president and giving him his support for future endeavors, including reelection.

Although Sununu was not the campaign strategist that Atwater was, he knew how to push the president to campaign in a direction he was not so willing to go on his own. In later interviews, Sununu revealed he wanted the president to be less diplomatic in politics and more aggressive toward his opponents both inside and outside of the Republican Party. The aide's resignation impacted the workings of the administration; however, Bush was his own worst enemy, not Sununu.

Regardless of Bush's success in the Gulf, the fractioning of the Republican Party led conservative voters to look for an alternative presidential candidate. The conservative titan Pat Buchanan announced his candidacy for the presidency after Bush had launched his reelection campaign. As a former senior adviser to Nixon and Reagan, Buchanan had long established himself as a strong voice for the Right. His disapproval of the president's policies provided an outlet for the Far Right sector of the Republican Party to vent its frustrations about Bush's swing to moderate and centrist policies. Facing a challenger within his own party was an embarrassment to the incumbent president. In the New Hampshire primary, Buchanan demonstrated his strength by winning 37 percent of the votes. As the election campaigns continued, Buchanan's staunch conservative ideology made Bush appear increasingly moderate. The GOP wanted to elect a conservative Republican and continue the political legacy of the 1980s; from his first day in office, Bush proved that he was not that politico.

Although Buchanan was not a serious threat to Bush's reelection campaign, his challenge to the sitting president was of symbolic importance in a volatile election year; his conservative politics made the president look weak as he attempted to win reelection. Buchanan continued to run a negative campaign against Bush and damage the presidency. When it became apparent that Bush would be the nominee, other members of the Republican Party called on Buchanan to back down.

Bush won the nomination, but Buchanan's retrogressive ideology continued to make the president appear moderate and weak to the conservatives. After abandoning his bid for the presidency, Buchanan became most famous for his "culture wars" speech at the 1992 Republican National Convention. Although he was no longer challenging the incumbent, his speech paid homage to the "Reagan doctrine" and called on Republicans to fight against "homosexual rights" and the "radical feminist agenda." Buchanan never made it to the ballot on the Republican ticket, but the disgruntled conservatives were not ready to give in to the potential moderate agenda of a second term for the president. It was only a matter of time before third-party challenger Ross Perot entered the race. The apparent dissatisfaction with the two-party system began in 1988 and created the opportunity for Perot to run as a third-party candidate in 1992. In *The Presidency of George Bush*, the historian John Robert Greene expounded that the "groundswell" for Perot began in the 1988 election when the public voted in smaller numbers and there was great discontent with the candidate choices. On Election Day in 1988, two-thirds of Americans wished another candidate had been present on the ballot.

This sentiment was still present in the 1992 election. Perot, a self-made billionaire in the technology sector with roots in the Texas oil industry, was the most successful third-party candidate since Theodore "Teddy" Roosevelt in 1912. Much like Roosevelt, Perot presented voters with an alternative to the two-party ticket and quickly gained popularity as a result. He sold himself as a reformer and alternative to the politics of Washington. Unlike his opponents, the political neophyte had to establish himself as a presidential candidate. The absence of political experience gave Perot a fresh platform from which to elucidate his ideas; however, this also meant that he had no experience outside of business from which he could draw. With $65 million of his own wealth, Perot was not at a loss for financial resources. His greatest challenge was to get out of his own way. Public enthusiasm and voter support quickly dissipated because of Perot's erratic campaign. Perot's greatest weakness in the election was his sporadic campaign style. The Texan launched his campaign for the executive office while appearing on CNN's *Larry King Live* on February 20, 1992. King questioned Perot about the circumstances under which he would run for president. Perot's first answer focused on the two-party system. He told King, "I will not run as either a Democrat or Republican, because I will not sell out to anybody but to the American people, and I will sell out to them." When King asked him if he would run as an independent, Perot responded by challenging voters to register him in "all fifty states." Perot said his campaign was a new direction in politics that would quell the worries of voters. Although his political ideology was not centrist in nature, he believed he could appeal to members of both the Left and the Right who felt abandoned by their parties. This was logical, as his interview came after Buchanan's resignation of his campaign for president. However, Perot had not announced an official bid for the presidency.

It was not until July 1992 that Perot made his first official announcement of the race for president, and he did so by pronouncing his withdrawal. After a few months, while the other candidates accepted their respective parties' nominations, Perot abstained from campaigning. On October 1, a month before Election Day, Perot decided to officially announce his run for office. His "in and out" style of politics had caused many potential voters to lose interest in his candidacy. In an election year, with a crumbling economy and the need for reform pushed on both ends of the political spectrum, voters were seeking a spokesperson for their issues. When Election Day came, despite his erratic campaign style, Perot won 19 percent of the popular vote. Many Republicans attributed the loss of both Bush and Perot to the splitting of votes between the candidates; however, there are no data to support this claim. Subsequent research has demonstrated that Perot took votes away from each candidate equally.

Bush could not escape his own legacy during the campaign; he was haunted by his own history. The last Friday before the election, Bush was thrown a curve ball when the report from the Iran-Contra scandal of the Reagan years was published. The criminal association of the Reagan administration, stemming from the arms-for-hostage deal with Iran in 1985, was the last kind of publicity that Bush wanted just days before the election. Throughout the years of investigation, Bush stood by his story that he was not involved in key meetings tied to the scandal. Just days before the election, new evidence surfaced placing Bush in incriminating meetings, which he had previously adamantly denied. Clinton seized this last opportunity to attack Bush's already impaired credibility. Bush hoped to save his campaign by ignoring the confrontation from Clinton, but the effort was futile.

It is hard to fathom how a president with vast support during the majority of his presidency could lose the reelection; the reality of the 1992 election is that Bush defeated himself. The election was decided when the Right felt abandoned by the moderate domestic policies of the Bush administration and deviation from the Reagan agenda. While leading the country into war, Bush maintained high approval ratings, but neither side of the aisle was satisfied with his domestic policy decisions. The Republicans believed the president jettisoned their agenda and the Democrats wanted their own candidate in the executive office. Because of this, Bush lost his constituents before Clinton was a nominee. Prominent Republican strategists believed that the recession would recover before the election, and that this combined with the popularity of the war would win the election for the president. In reality, these issues only produced the Clinton campaign. Some scholars have blamed the blasé vice president, Dan Quayle, for not adding more vitality to the ticket, but data show the challenge lay with Bush. The economy and the alienation of multitudes of voters was the nail in the coffin of the Bush campaign. Bush was unable to "get out of his own way" during the 1992 campaign. His historically high numbers from the Gulf War did not translate into domestic issues and he could not convince the American people to give him another term.

The presidential nominee Bill Clinton did not win the election as much as Bush lost the election. Clinton's strongest campaign talking point used the recession against the incumbent President Bush. During the fall, Clinton pushed far ahead of Bush in the polls, but the deal closer of the election occurred during the second presidential debate in October. A young woman asked the two men, "How has the national debt personally affected each of your lives? And if it hasn't, how can you honestly find an economic cure for the common people if you have no experience in what is ailing them?" Bush tripped over the question and asked for clarification, making it immediately clear to the audience that he did not understand the sentiments of the inquiry. Digging himself deeper into the hole, Bush asked her to "help him understand." When it was Clinton's turn to answer, he began to enumerate the ways in which he saw the recession impacting the people of his state and those around him. In this moment, Clinton demonstrated his understanding of the recession and the need to refocus on domestic policies. As Clinton was answering the question, Bush looked at his watch, sending the message that he was disengaged from the problems of Americans. This was the real moment Bush lost the election.

Clinton began the 1992 campaign as the underdog and challenger to the president. His charismatic personality and rags-to-riches story won the hearts of Americans as he blazed through the campaign trail. Clinton's journey to the presidency was tortuous because of the absence of his opponent and the tabloid obsession with his personal life. His diverse background made him a versatile candidate; his southern background and liberal ideology helped him capture both the North and the South. A poor upbringing and Ivy League education made him appealing to several different educational and socioeconomic demographics. Despite being labeled a womanizer and adulterer by the press, he connected to voters in a way that Bush never could.

Clinton, formerly William (Bill) Jefferson Blythe III, was born in Hope, Arkansas, on August 19, 1946 to Virginia Cassidy Blythe. Three months before his birth, his father, William Jefferson Blythe II, was tragically killed in a car accident. During his early years, Bill lived with his grandparents while his mother completed her nursing degree. In his memoir, *In My Life*, Bill attributed growing up with his grandparents' progressive views of integration in the segregated South to his passion for civil rights. Bill's mother returned to Hope when he was four years old and the same year met the automobile salesman Roger Clinton. Shortly after, the two were married and the family moved to Hot Springs, Arkansas. Roger's abuse of the family forced Clinton to balance a traumatic home life and the challenges that come with being a teenager. In 1956, a new member of the family was born, Roger Clinton Jr. Wanting to have the same name as his half brother and mother, Clinton legally changed his last name from Blythe to Clinton.

As a teenager, Clinton devoted himself to schoolwork. In his senior year of high school, he was selected to travel to Washington, DC, to be a part of Boys Nation, a special youth leadership conference. While in Washington, the young leaders were invited to the White House. In the rose garden, Clinton shook the hand of President John F. Kennedy (JFK). The meeting had a lasting impact on Clinton, who, inspired by the heroism of JFK, committed himself to a life of public service. Searching for a school that was both affordable and prestigious, Clinton selected Georgetown University and majored in international affairs. During his undergraduate years, Clinton interned with Arkansas Senator J. William Fulbright, providing him with both the hands-on experience of Washington politics and a reaffirmation of his career choice. In 1968, Clinton graduated from Georgetown and was selected for a Rhodes scholarship at Oxford University in England.

Upon his return to the United States, he began law school at Yale University. Throughout his time at Yale he remained engaged in political issues, including passionately campaigning for the 1972 liberal presidential candidate, George McGovern. It was also at Yale that he met his future wife and political partner, Hillary Diane Rodham. After graduating from law school, Clinton returned to Arkansas to teach at the University of Arkansas at Fayetteville. Hillary moved to Washington to work as a member of the "impeachment inquiry staff" for the House Committee on the Judiciary during the Watergate investigation—which looked into the June 1972 break-in of the Democratic National Committee at the Watergate Hotel by President Richard Nixon. When Nixon resigned from office, Hillary's job ended; she moved to Arkansas to start her life with her law school sweetheart. The same year, Bill Clinton was presented with his first opportunity to run for office.

In 1974, just six months out of Yale Law School, Clinton ran for the United States House of Representatives seat in Arkansas' Third Congressional District. Ultimately, Clinton was defeated in his first campaign for Congress but maintained his fervent desire for a career in public office. Proving himself to be the next big thing in Arkansas politics, he was elected Arkansas Attorney General in 1976. However, Clinton set his eyes on the governorship, and in 1978 he was elected governor of Arkansas with 60 percent of the vote. His early political success was impeded by the loss of a second term to Frank White, who used Clinton's youth and education against him.

Fulfilling his future name, the Comeback Kid, Clinton took the hit and returned to politics as a stronger politician. Hillary took control of his reelection campaign and rebranded the public image of the couple. Knowing her public role as his wife, she underwent personal changes to make the family more appealing to constituents. She got a new haircut and took her husband's last name to silence critics, and she worked hard on the gubernatorial campaign. The people voted Clinton back into office four years later, where he remained until he was elected to the presidency.

During the Democratic primaries, Clinton was faced with the challenge of proving to the American people that he was the most qualified and competent contender for the position. Clinton first set his eyes on the presidency in 1988, but quickly put everything on hold when rumors of extramarital affairs surfaced and threatened to stymie the campaign. When he recommitted to running in 1992, he first needed to establish himself in the primaries. As related in *A Complicated Man: The Life of Bill Clinton as Told by Those Who Know Him*, the eyes of the country were on the governor from New York, Mario Cuomo, as Democrats across America wondered if he would run. Cuomo was a more established politician and titan in the Democratic Party. Initially, some of Clinton's advisers discouraged him from running in 1992 because he would be competing against an incumbent president who was still riding a high approval rating from the Persian Gulf War. It was still not evident that Clinton would win the nomination in the days before the New Hampshire primary. Constituents were still learning the name of the new politician, but when allegations of Clinton's sexual indiscretions surfaced, overnight scandal made the young politico a household name. The sex scandals of the Clinton campaign demonstrated his resilience as a candidate, but his reputation for being a womanizer has beleaguered his political career.

In January 1992, the campaign began to unravel. The first attack came from the tabloid *Star*, claiming that Clinton had engaged in affairs with five women. Many dismissed the allegations as nothing more than gossip from a grocery store tabloid. Shortly after, Gennifer Flowers, an Arkansas state employee and lounge singer came forward claiming to have had a twelve-year affair with the candidate. The allegations were quickly taken more seriously when Flowers produced taped phone conversations with Clinton. To address the public relations calamity, Bill and Hillary appeared together on CBS's *60 Minutes*, which aired immediately after the Super Bowl. Over fifty million people tuned in to watch the couple defend their marriage to the public. Many scholars and campaign aides have credited Hillary with turning Bill's campaign around and saving his political career. In the interview, Hillary convinced the American public that she was standing by her husband, and they should too. The Clintons both wanted the White House and Hillary was determined to help her husband win the presidency.

When the Flowers scandal had quieted, the *New York Times* reported, "unless the other shoe drops to make him look like a liar, Clinton is looking more like the Democrat's nominee." To Clinton's surprise, the other shoe did drop and it happened a week before the New Hampshire primary.

On February 6, the *Wall Street Journal* published an article on a letter that had surfaced from Clinton's second year as a Rhodes scholar. In the letter, twenty-three-year-old Clinton wrote to Colonel Holmes, who ran the Army Reserve Officers' Training Corps (ROTC) program at the University of Arkansas: "First, I want to thank you, not just for saving me from the draft, but for being so kind and decent to me last summer, when I was as low as I have ever been." As questions regarding his draft dodging quickly spread, Clinton worked fast to provide a rationale for his action. He had first gained exemption from the draft through educational deferment, but the law then abolished graduate deferments; however, graduate students were allowed to complete their current term. When Clinton left for England, he was eligible for the draft and knew that he might be called. He knew that many close friends were receiving draft notices and was aware that he might be next.

During the spring term, the letter finally came and Clinton was able to finish his semester. In *My Life*, he recalled that he concluded that the best option for him was to enroll in law school and join ROTC at the University of Arkansas. In July, both programs accepted him, but with the stipulation that he would go on active duty after he graduated from law school. In addition, Clinton explained that knowing another person was being drafted in his place caused him much guilt. He therefore withdrew his deferment status, placing himself back in the draft pool. The same month, Nixon announced that graduate students would be granted deferment for the entire current school year, not just the semester; this guaranteed Clinton another school year. Clinton explained that it was not with foresight of this law that he had opted out of the ROTC and back into the draft.

The media was not interested in this explanation and Clinton was criticized for his character and was labeled a draft dodger. The campaign staff quickly responded with another attempt to revamp the image of the campaign and the candidate. Clinton conducted public interviews to appeal to the people and clarify the contents of the letter. Polling revealed that the redemptive strategy of the campaign staff was effective in creating the image of "a man from Hope" and that he had shown the public he was a person that could overcome scandal. This strategy was successful for a few weeks and he earned his nickname, the Comeback Kid, but by the end of March Clinton was under siege for another controversy.

The *New York Times* reported on March 30, 1992 that Clinton had admitted to experimenting with marijuana when he was in England as a Rhodes scholar. Clinton had attempted to downplay the situation by telling the reporters, "I didn't inhale and I didn't try it again." He also attempted to save face by stating that he had never tried any other illegal drugs after that one experiment while abroad. Additionally, he clarified, he had never broken a state law. Drawing attention to the other politicians, Clinton pointed out that admitting to experimenting with marijuana had not hurt Clarence Thomas in his nomination to the Supreme Court. Using his opponent's words against him, he reminded the public that Bush had declared Thomas' use of it in college "a minor matter." Ultimately the new scandal wore off and Clinton was able to move forward riding on his new image of "the Comeback Kid."

During the controversy, the *New York Times* reported that marijuana was not an issue that the American public was much concerned with, as opposed to draft dodging or extramarital affairs; 82 percent of registered voters surveyed by NBC News and the *Wall Street Journal* reported that "smoking marijuana in college" should not disqualify someone from becoming president. More important, the American people decided that they would much rather focus on the real issue at hand, the recession. The campaign trail and road to the presidency was not an easy one for Clinton, but it demonstrated the resiliency of his political career. Scandals that would be the demise of most politicians became for Clinton hurdles that he overcame. Clinton earned the nickname "the Comeback Kid" for good reason. Like Reagan, who was known as the "Teflon president," Clinton could bounce back from scandal and humiliation—a talent that has sustained him throughout his political career.

For Clinton, the issue in the campaign for the presidency was not his political competency, but his character. Although he was a young candidate with less experience than his political adversary, Clinton projected a sense of competence and ability. It was his questionable morals that bothered voters, and Clinton's greatest challenge was proving to the American people that he was trustworthy. He was able to convince many women voters that he loved his wife and, more important, could handle domestic issues, like the economy, more efficiently than Bush.

The campaign took every opportunity to provide newspapers and television stations substantial policy material to distract from the stories of sexual scandal. Knowing Bush would be his opponent, between the 1988 and 1992 election cycles Clinton evaluated Bush's political strategy and where he could be hit the hardest. Clinton emphasized that he was a fresh face after the Reagan legacy and that he could meet the needs of the American people. Whereas Bush used the term "liberal" as a slur, Clinton owned it as the answer to the domestic calamities of the Bush administration. Working as a team, Hillary and Bill knew from the beginning their strategy would be to attack Bush where he was weakest—the economy. Although the Clinton campaign strategy was clear, they could not have predicted the political curve balls to come.

Clinton had a connection to the American people that Bush did not. His charisma, diverse background, and ability to relate to the American people prevented voters from viewing him as elitist and made him appealing. Even though both men were Ivy League educated, Clinton showed the American people that he knew their struggles, their aspirations, and understood the American dream. Clinton related to the voters and demonstrated empathy. As he met with potential constituents at rallies and campaign events, people believed they were understood and heard. When speaking at a Manhattan nightclub early in the campaign, Bob Rafsky, from the AIDS activist group Act Up, confronted Clinton about the government's lack of action regarding the fatal disease. Clinton responded by stating "I feel your pain." This became his famous line, and when he said it, people did not feel that they were being duped or mollified, but that he truly cared. Paul Begala, the political consultant and adviser, told the historian Michael Takiff in *A Complicated Man*, "Empathy is the most important characteristic we can have in a president." When juxtaposed with Bush's obtuseness in the debates and at the grocery store scanner, Clinton was perceived to understand and care about the American people. Clinton capitalized on many of Bush's ineptitudes; demonstrating his compassion for the plight of plebeian Americans during the recession gave voters a vested interest in his victory.

Clinton engaged in a competitive campaign and advanced from underdog to president. After winning the New Hampshire primary, Clinton quickly gained momentum and support in the states that followed. In June

1992, he defeated other Democratic candidates, specifically, the governor of California, Jerry Brown, and won the California primary. With this success he surpassed the number of delegates required to win the nomination. When it was apparent that Clinton would be the presidential candidate, he moved ahead to select a running mate. A week before the Democratic National Convention, Clinton announced that he had selected Albert Arnold "Al" Gore Jr., a Senator from Tennessee. Gore was first elected to the House of Representatives from 1977 to 1985, and served until he won a seat in the Senate. His military experience, financial background, and Harvard degree complemented Clinton's draft scandal and concentration on improving the economy. A Southern Baptist with a progressive social philosophy, Gore brought to the table foreign policy experience and a strong record on environmental issues. Clinton carefully selected his running mate to both compensate for his own weaknesses and bring credibility to the ticket. Gore's enduring marriage and clean-cut image went with the campaign's emphasis on family values, which was necessary to combat the controversy surrounding Clinton's personal life.

Perhaps most important, Gore was a fellow southerner and his presence on the ticket helped to deliver the South. Dynamic together, both Democrats and Republicans viewed the candidates as a youthful liberal duo. As a moderate, Gore sought the presidential nomination in 1988 but declined to run in 1992. Gore understood Clinton's advocacy of centrist policies, and like the president, spent his years as vice president moving to the center on issues. Much like the juxtaposition of Bush and Clinton, when compared with the impassive vice president Dan Quayle, Gore appeared energetic and evocative.

At the Democratic National Convention, with a nod to Mario Cuomo and rhetoric focused on the future of America, Clinton formally accepted the nomination on the Democratic ticket for the presidency. His speech paid homage to the middle class and he reiterated his commitment to them if elected to presidency. He strengthened his campaign against Bush by contrasting the failing economy against U.S. successes abroad: "just as we have won the Cold War abroad, we are losing the battles for economic opportunity and social justice here at home." He recognized his own weaknesses, mainly those of character, and acknowledged that many voters still did not trust him. His campaign team worked hard to rebrand his image so potential voters would find him more trustworthy. Clinton confronted the question voters were asking—why should I trust you?—and he told listeners, "tonight, as plainly as I can, I want to tell you who I am, what I believe, and where I want to lead America." Additionally, in this speech he won women voters by thanking his mother and wife, vocally supporting families, and vowing to protect *Roe v. Wade*. The doubts of Americans were addressed in this speech and it allayed the last of the fears. Most important, he spoke about the economy and drew attention to the fallibilities of the Reagan legacy. With Clinton's vice presidential pick and the 1970s rock anthem "Don't Stop Thinking about Tomorrow" for the campaign theme, the Comeback Kid was ready to move full speed ahead to the presidency.

Clinton succeeded in his bid for the presidency not only because of Bush's unengaged campaign but also because he was able to move to the center. Ironically, it was centrist policies that cost Bush his political base but gained Clinton national support. Throughout his campaign, Clinton aimed to win back the blue collar and Reagan Democrats. Although he embraced both the Left and the Center, he pulled together voting demographics that Bush was unable to because of the only issue that mattered in 1992—the economy. With this tactic, Clinton reshaped the Democratic Party.

On election night, the Democratic Party was filled with optimism. Throughout the campaign, Clinton pitched his administration as the beginning of a new era and Democrats were ebullient about the prospect for change. When voters went to the ballot, Clinton won the election with 43 percent of the vote. Clinton and Gore replaced Theodore Roosevelt and Charles Fairbanks as the youngest presidential team to ever serve in the White House. The Clinton administration ended twelve years of Republican-dominated politics and ushered in two terms of a moderate presidency.

Recommended Reading

James Pfiffner, *The Modern Presidency* (Boston: Cengage Learning, 2005), examines the politics of the presidency, including election politics.

3

The Domestic Clinton,
1993–1996

THE CLINTON ADMINISTRATION proved to have one of the worst transitions to office in the modern presidency. Although the new president had an innate knack for politics, his experience had not fully prepared him for the White House. The political scientist James Pfiffner explained in *The Modern Presidency* that Clinton was the first Democratic president to enter the White House acutely aware that he needed the assistance of a chief of staff to get the job done. Looking for someone he trusted, Clinton turned to Thomas "Mack" McLarty, his childhood friend and previous political adviser. However, Pfiffner aptly noted that in McLarty's year and a half in office, he spent more time as an "ambassador" for the president and less time creating structure within the office. The structure of the Oval Office was crucial because of the paucity of experience among staff. Clinton utilized the young volunteers and employees who worked on his campaign, but their dearth of political experience in executive office politics exacerbated the difficulty of the transition. Additionally, Clinton's own lack of experience in executive politics set him up for many failures, both domestic and foreign, in his first few years. Clinton was heavily criticized for running the White House as if he was still on the campaign trail.

Some members of the Clinton administration have described this time of transition as pure chaos. The president was learning his job duties, as was his staff. During a PBS *Frontline* interview, Secretary of Labor Robert Reich was asked about the description in his memoirs of the transition being "hell." Reich answered, "You know, you get a lot of campaign workers, most of them very competent people, but they all begin to dream about being in the White House, in the administration. . . . Most have never been in government, particularly when Democrats have been out of government." Reich explained that 1993 was a transition year—not only to a new presidency but also a new Democratic Party.

Both the Democratic Party and the president struggled to find out who they were in the new administration and political climate. The Republicans had dominated Washington for the twelve years prior, and in 1992 the Democrats attempted to regain their footing. The agenda and challenges were new and different from the last time they held the White House. Part of navigating the role of the new Democratic Party was taking a definitive position on the liberal versus conservative battle over social issues. Clinton drew heat from both parties and his constituents when he retracted the nomination of Lani Guinier for assistant attorney general for civil rights. He did so because she was "too liberal" and was particularly vocal on issues of voting reform. Consistent with the rest of his presidency, Clinton chose to move toward the center. In addition to restructuring the political party and constructing the administration, Clinton faced the challenge of negotiating the financial crisis, specifically, balancing the budget and fixing the deficit.

The first few years of the Clinton administration were defined by the failure to reform health care and the extreme focus on fixing the budget. The budget and moderate policies dominated the political landscape of the 1990s. The first two years working with Congress proved difficult, in part because of the scattered agenda of the administration, but also because of the complex relationship between the branches of government. Clinton joined with Congress on his more moderate bills, most notably the Family Medical Leave Act (FMLA) of 1993. However, challenges with Congress and the chaos of Clinton's own agenda left him at many times relying on executive orders for achievements. As explained by Michael Les Benedict in *The Blessings of Liberty: A Concise History of the Constitution of the United States*, the tumultuous relationship between this presidency and the Congress eroded the system of checks and balances between the branches of government. In the first years of the Clinton administration, the fiscal climate forced Congress and the president into negotiation.

Throughout the campaign and the beginning of Clinton's term in office, he spoke strongly against the Republican's fiscal agenda of the previous decade. He argued that the Republicans had twelve years to prove their economic plan, and they proved that it did not work. He called for the "aggressive reduction of the federal budget" and aimed to balance the budget immediately. In Clinton's first year in office, the economy took precedent over all other policy decisions, including health care—which had been a personal agenda item of the Clintons. Clinton knew that to salvage his reputation after the transitional calamity he would have to fix the economy. In finding a budget deal to amend the deficit and the recession, Clinton attempted to appease everyone on the political spectrum, including the liberal Democrat and lion of the Senate Edward "Ted" M. Kennedy and the Republican Party icon and future speaker of the house Newt Gingrich. Clinton finally submitted a five-year plan to reduce the deficit, inclusive of spending cuts and increases in taxes. According to Pfiffner, the proposal was well on its way to a vote when Clinton interrupted the process and introduced a less than $20 billion stimulus package, prompting a filibuster on the bill from Congressional Republicans. Ultimately, the administration passed the budget proposal without a single Republican vote, but not without last-minute political challenges as Congressional members vacillated on their positions.

Only one vote was needed to pass the deficit reduction bill in the House. At the last minute, the new swing-state representative Marjorie Margolies-Mezvinsky, the first Democrat to be elected to Pennsylvania's 13th District since 1916, unexpectedly changed her vote to a no. Although other members of the House, specifically Democrats, had opted to vote against the bill, White House officials knew that passing the budget bill was contingent on Margolies-Mezvinsky's vote and negotiated to keep her support. In a move that cost her reelection in a Republican district, Margolies-Mezvinsky amended her vote to support the president and the bill passed with 218 votes in the House. When the bill came to the Senate floor, it again depended on one vote; this time, Vice President Gore was the tiebreaker in a 50-50 Senate vote. Margolies-Mezvinsky reflected in an interview years later with PBS's *Frontline* that this was the moment that began Clinton's economic legacy. She explained, "I think that most people who look at that period, the 90s, as being so strong financially and ending up with that extraordinary surplus. . . . I think most folks who know anything about finance will say that's where it started. That was the day that it started." The vote on the deficit reduction bill began the apparent economic improvements of the 1990s; this was why voters had supported Clinton in the election, in response to the Bush recession.

Clinton wanted health care reform to be his legacy, but he first had to confront other social issues that he had unintentionally forced on the table; one issue was gays in the military, which the president had addressed even before assuming office. Since Clinton remained in campaign mode into the first year of his administration, he answered many questions from the press as if he were still a candidate and not the president elect. In Michael Takiff's *A Complicated Man*, Michael Dukakis relates how the issue of gays in the military came to the fore. Shortly before taking office, on Veteran's Day weekend after the 1992 election, Thomas Friedman of the *New York Times* asked Clinton about gays in the military. Clinton replied candidly, "I don't think people ought to be discriminated against on the basis of sexual orientation." "Including the military?" asked Friedman. "Including the military," responded Clinton. Immediately, the *New York Times* reported that the president was supporting lifting the ban of gays in the military. Clinton had a few weeks until his inauguration to contrive a solution for the issue he had inadvertently placed on the table.

Presidents before Clinton were challenged to integrate the military. Harry Truman was faced with the issue of racial integration. The *New York Times* commented that whereas Truman had utilized his executive power to end racial segregation, Clinton deferred to General Colin Powell. Powell was vocal about his explicit opposition to the inclusion of gays in the military. Additionally, Clinton had to navigate the hostility he encountered from the U.S. military after the allegations of draft dodging during the campaign. With no military experience, Clinton had to prove to the military that he deserved the position of commander in chief. The worst transition in the modern presidency only further damaged Clinton's credibility on military issues.

After the *New York Times* report, the Clinton administration quickly strategized to accommodate the new agenda item. "Don't Ask, Don't Tell" (DADT) was announced on July 19, 1993. The policy was reminiscent of the "separate but equal" solution for integrating whites and blacks and did not address the deeper issues of discrimination. The early decision to support the policy and its implementation set the tone for Clinton's already rocky relationship with the military.

In addition to navigating a relationship with the military, Clinton struggled with Congress on the issue of integrating the gay, lesbian, and bisexual community into military service. As the executive moved forward on the issue, the legislature threatened to become involved; specifically, Senator Bob Dole, the future presidential candidate from Kansas, menacingly stated that he would consequently propose an amendment to the Family Medical Leave Act. By expressing his conservative opinion, Dole positioned himself, before the next election, as the opposition to Clinton with an anti-gay and socially conservative agenda. In an attempt to persuade voters, Dole used Clinton's stance on DADT to argue that the president was following a socially liberal agenda. However, the Left did not concur with Dole's assertions; they believed Clinton had abandoned an agenda that supported equality. Ultimately, DADT did not satisfy liberals or conservatives, foreshadowing many of the reactions to future policy decisions of the Clinton administration.

Clinton had always intended his legacy to be a comprehensive health care bill. As pointed out by Takiff, when Clinton accepted the nomination from the Democratic Party, he emphasized his belief that health care is a right and not a privilege. The Clintons originally planned to push a health care bill through within the first hundred days in office. At Clinton's first State of the Union address, he highlighted the links between health care and deficit reduction, thus connecting his personal legislative agenda and the concern of the country. However, when the Clintons first started pushing for reform and the timeline became clear, many political strategists said that it was not the right political climate, it was unobtainable, and that they should wait before proceeding. Even other Democrats in the Senate expressed to Hillary privately their concern about acquiring the votes needed from Democrats. However, the Clintons ignored these recommendations and concerns and pushed forward at full force.

As the First Lady, Hillary took the lead on the Clinton Health Care Task Force at the president's appointment. Created by the Clinton administration, the goal of the task force was to see the Clintons' health care vision through on their timetable. Hillary had been a champion for issues impacting women, children, and families; heading the Health Care Task Force was an extension of this previous work. Despite her determination to see the bill through, the agenda item became a political calamity.

In 1992, nearly thirty-seven million Americans were uninsured, the majority of whom were working-class families and children. The recession and the increasing loss of jobs during the Bush administration also created a fear among the insured of losing both their health insurance and their jobs; this only encouraged the Clintons to stay on their intrepid course and timetable. Hillary believed in the need for health care reform not only as a solution to many public health issues but also as a solution for the ever-looming deficit. The task force produced a document of their findings and the 1,300-page blueprint for a new law to reform the health care system. The task force and the Clinton administration envisioned a health care system that utilized the private-sector economy to drive down the cost of insurance, and it would have universal access to health care for all Americans.

The debate over health care reform created factions in both political parties. Although Clinton was voted into office as a moderate Democrat, the political climate of the post–Reagan-Bush years on Capitol Hill and in the country was still largely dominated by Reaganites. Health care was not a priority for Republicans; additionally, many Representatives and their constituents believed in small government and opposed the proposals of the task force strictly on this basis. Members of Congress vocally debated the role of government in health care, specifically the size of the government. Moreover, Democrats were not united on the idea of health care reform, making it more difficult for the Clinton administration to sell its agenda. In her memoirs, *Living History*, Hillary recalled that politicians threatened a filibuster if the bill got to the Senate floor. Seeking political guidance, Hillary turned to Majority Leader Senator George Mitchell for assistance on placating Congress. Following Mitchell's direction to convince the members on Clinton's staff and Congress to include health care reform as part of a budget reconciliation strategy, Hillary recalled feeling optimistic about the challenge, but she did not anticipate the backlash from opposition groups.

In late February, the health care reform momentum decelerated when three opposition groups sued the task force, claiming that as the First Lady, and "not technically a government employee," Hillary could not legally be involved in either the task force or any subsequent meetings. Other opposition groups created television advertisements that fed into the media hype and targeted "Hillarycare." The ads vilified the bill and the beleaguered president and First Lady, claiming they were against the American people. Chris Jennings, the senior White House adviser on health care, articulated to Takiff in *A Complicated Man* that the frenzy was exacerbated by the image already created of the Clintons as sleazy, hippy, and untrustworthy. In the midst of the media and legal hype over the health care debate, Hillary's father suffered a stroke, which took her away from Washington until his death in April 1993. When Hillary returned, she and other task force members continued to meet with members of Congress, but the momentum for health care reform had declined. The bill never made it to a vote and by May, the Clinton Health Care Task Force was officially dissolved. Other members of the Clinton administration, such as Jennings, continued to work on the issue behind the scenes, but not with the same voracity of the task force. The loss was devastating to the administration, and specifically to Hillary.

The Clinton administration counteracted the overwhelming defeat of their health care reform project by focusing on moderate policy change in education, family, and other more accessible topics so that the bills could be pushed through Congress more easily. This strategy resulted in some of the greatest achievements of the Clinton administration. Specifically responding to the failure of the health care legislation, Clinton diligently appealed to his voting base with agenda items to enhance the lives of families and children. In tandem with the health care bill, the Clinton administration was already working on the FMLA.

Effective August 3, 1993, the FMLA provided protections for workers, specifically mothers, by making a legal basic entitlement for incapacity due to pregnancy, the care of a child after birth, the care of a spouse or child with a serious health condition, or a serious health condition that prevents employees from performing their job. The bill assured an employee twelve weeks of paid or unpaid job-protected leave from work. Military families received additional entitlements: an employee's spouse, child, or parent on active duty and on deployment to a foreign country was granted a twelve-week leave for qualifying exigencies. Eligible employees were granted a twenty-six-week leave period to care for a service member. During an employee's leave, the employer was required to maintain the employee's health plan, whether the leave was paid or unpaid. The FMLA guaranteed employees that they could resume their position and salary when they returned to work. It permitted workers flexibility and ensured their protection. The Clintons' health care reforms had failed, but the initiative to help women and families had not; they succeeded in including a health care provision in the FMLA.

The Clinton administration concentrated on issues that impacted all Americans, specifically middle-class voters who supported moderate political ideologies. Clinton moved the FMLA and other policy decisions forward because they appealed to constituents in the Center. He was aware that the more moderate his agenda, the more votes and support he had in Congress. The president knew that he could push centrist bills, both new and previously proposed, through Congress with bipartisan support.

To support his law-and-order rhetoric, in November 1993 Clinton advanced the Brady Handgun Violence Prevention Act, also known as the Brady bill. The legislation had been originally proposed in 1987 after the assassination attempt on then-president Ronald Reagan and named after James Brady, who was shot during the attempt. The bill established federal legislation for a five-day waiting period and required criminal background checks on persons seeking to purchase handguns. Previously, when the bill was sent to the floor for a vote it was killed in the House. After seven long years, the bill passed in both the House and the Senate, allowing Clinton to sign it into law. Although the debate over gun control was controversial, and some conservatives knew they would lose their voting base, the 103rd Congress voted to approve the bill.

The following year when the Brady law went into effect, it specifically impacted the thirty-two states that previously did not have background check restrictions. When the bill was passed, the majority of Americans agreed with Clinton's position on gun control. Studies from the Pew Research Center demonstrated that in 1993, 57 percent of Americans agreed that it was more important to "control gun ownership" than to "protect the right of gun owners." Additional Pew Research studies demonstrated that firearm deaths peaked in 1993 before consistently declining in every year since; by 2010, the number of firearm deaths was 49 percent lower than in 1993.

Throughout the years since the Brady bill passed, the emotionally loaded issue of gun control continues to be disputed.

The first two years of the Clinton administration saw many policy failures and successes, ranging from gun control to health care reform. In *The Modern Presidency*, Pfiffner analyzed the combination of minor victories and major defeats of the administration between 1993 and 1994 and attributed it primarily to the political climate. As he explained, "Clinton was elected with [a] 43 percent plurality, he ran behind most members of Congress, he had fewer Democrats in Congress than other recent Democrats, and his party lost seats in the election. Combine those with a very ambitious policy agenda and you have a prescription for high conflict and low success." Clinton took the inevitable impediments in stride and continued to push for his more moderate policy plans.

Hillary was repeatedly criticized during the Clinton administration, but specifically in regard to health care reform. Taking a step back, Hillary responded to the health care debacle by writing her first book, *It Takes a Village*. The book addressed the political issues the administration was working through with Congress, primarily social issues impacting women and children. As Clinton regained the support of constituents, his approval in the polls skyrocketed. Hillary, however, who had championed the health care reform debacle, did not experience the same revival in public support. This was only the beginning of Hillary's polarizing role in politics.

Hillary was an anomalous First Lady with her bold personality and influence on the president. Other First Ladies worked to aid and guide their husband's agendas, but Hillary was the first to be given an office in the West Wing. She had twenty staffers and even a residential speechwriter. Hillary reflected in *Living History* that her office and staff were known as "Hillaryland." The most innovative change was that the First Lady and her staff members were fully integrated into the daily operations of the West Wing and the agenda of the Clinton administration, and they attended senior staff meetings. This inclusion led to one of the greatest criticisms the Clintons faced around the prominent role of the First Lady. When he was elected governor and president, the voters supported "two for the price of one," but once in the White House, the public was uncomfortable with her power. The country became more interested in her during an emerging scandal around legal work she had done in the late 1970s.

In July 1994, still attempting to quell the chaos from the transition and the media's unrelenting canards, Clinton replaced his chief of staff, McLarty, with Leon Panetta, Director of Office Management and Budget. Panetta's priorities included a restructuring of the administration, which still included inexperienced staffers who had campaigned for Clinton. The policy agenda was chaotic. In an attempt to refocus the administration, Panetta restructured the day-to-day organization of the White House and meetings with the president. One of the most prevalent changes was access to the president; Panetta limited contact between staff and Clinton, specifically aiming to eradicate the "walk-in" culture of the Oval Office. Some scholars have credited Panetta's changes to the subsequent achievements of the administration. Pfiffner asserts that Panetta's successes were due in part not only to his assertive personality but also to Clinton's willingness to delegate more authority to his chief of staff. Panetta not only had more power over the staff but also maintained an authoritative role with Congress. Panetta's reorganization allowed the administration to develop a more lucid vision of its policy agenda and it was subsequently more successful in achieving its unambiguous goals.

In 1994, the Clinton administration created and passed the largest crime bill in American history. In an effort to appeal to both parties, Clinton proposed the Violent Crime Control and Law Enforcement Act of 1994, a moderate policy that was both an aggressive approach to "law and order" and progressive legislation for families. The bill provided funding for over one hundred thousand new police officers and $6.1 billion for prevention programs. The Federal Bureau of Investigation (FBI), Drug Enforcement Administration (DEA), Immigration and Naturalization Service (INS), and other branches of the Justice Department were awarded an additional $2.6 billion to address crime. Controversially, the bill also contributed $9.7 billion in new funding for prisons.

Following on the success of the Brady bill, perhaps the most conspicuous component of this bill was the assault weapons bans that prohibited the manufacture of nineteen different "military-style" assault weapons, in addition to those with "combat features," "copy-cat models," or high-capacity magazines that exceeded ten rounds. Looking to focus on issues pertaining to domestic violence, guns were also addressed in the section of the bill that prohibited the sale of firearms to a person with a restraining order for family violence. For some representatives, the section of the bill that additionally restricted the sales of guns was contentious because of the previous political risk many Democrats had taken when they voted for the Brady bill. They worried about their constituents and keeping their Congressional seats during the next election cycle. This new bill also sought to expand the offenses that were punishable by the death penalty; create new penalties for drug trafficking—specifically, those committed by gangs; and enhance penalties for crimes relating to illegal immigration—including $1.2 billion for border control, deportations, asylum reform, and a tracking center, and an additional $1.8 billion to reimburse states for the incarceration of illegal immigrants. With this new bill, juveniles over the age of thirteen who had committed serious crimes were now prosecuted as adults, and sex offenders were required by federal law to register in their state for ten years as sex offenders after their release from prison.

Most important, this bill contained the Violence Against Women Act (VAWA). VAWA was landmark legislation that addressed sexual and domestic violence; specifically, legal protections, legal and criminal justice responses, and community prevention. It created new federal crimes as well as funding for rape crisis programs and domestic violence shelters. The bipartisan bill was historic and created unprecedented protections for victims of sexual and domestic violence. The renewal of VAWA in subsequent years has continued to provide funding to prevent and end the epidemic of gender-based violence in America.

The political landscape of the United States was transformed with the 1994 midterm elections; the changes in representatives elected to office dictated the politics of the second half of the 1990s and six out of the eight years of the Clinton administration. Led by the political veteran and Speaker of the House Newt Gingrich, the agenda of Republican incumbents and those newly elected fixated almost exclusively on being "anti-Clinton." After the 1992 election the party was left factioned and defeated. When the Clinton administration began to gain momentum and organization, it provided the Republicans with issues to unify themselves against. In an interview with

Takiff, Scott Reed, the former executive director of the Republican National Convention, attributed the solidarity of the Republican Party during the midterm election to the consensus over its hatred for the health care bill. The hot-button topics easily impassioned those on both sides of the aisle and the GOP saw this as a chance to rally its base. The politicians played on the fears of the American public that the Clintons could not be trusted and the belief that health care legislation was beyond the scope of presidential power. The Republican political strategies of the midterm elections paid off as the party began to regain power.

In September 1994, just months before the election, Newt Gingrich announced a "Contract with America," the Republicans' final push to activate their voter base. Introduced during a rally at Capitol Hill, the aim of the contract was to enumerate the legislative agenda of the GOP. Among other things, it sought to "bring an end to big government." The contract included a pledge from members of the Republican Party stating that the 104th Congress would introduce ten pieces of legislation within the first hundred days of the new session. The topics of the legislation ranged from a response to the fiscal crisis to pornography, and covered both fiscal and social concerns. The legislative agenda was determined by a polling process that analyzed what issues 60 percent or more of voters would support. Many of the issues, specifically crimes and tax credits, overlapped with bills that Clinton would later put forward because they were popular with both the constituents and Congress. Based largely on the agenda of the Reagan administration, Gingrich and his allies tapped into the demographic of Reaganite Republicans and their votes. The "contract" drew media attention to a previously trounced party just before the election. However, in the data that have been analyzed since, there is no proof that the new agenda actually persuaded voters.

In 1994, the Democrats were in a weak position because of the cohesiveness and organization of the Republican Party. Many Democrats struggled to distance themselves from some of the policy calamities of the early Clinton administration; the Brady bill, for example, caused some Democrats to lose their more moderate bases of support. Clinton was forced to campaign for his administration and presidency in a midterm election year. The Democrats won strong in 1992 with the help of cable station MTV and the youth vote; however, the midterm election was not as attractive for the Democratic voting base and created lower support and turnout at the polls. Additionally, the GOP was organized, energized, and ready to win. Preparing for the midterm election, Clinton gave speeches and met with constituents in order to keep the American people engaged in his presidency. This engagement with the public served as a reminder of his domestic accomplishments, specifically the changes in the economy, despite the reality that the transition had been disastrous.

Ultimately, Democratic Party appeals to the people were not enough on Election Day and the Republicans swept the vote in what has since been labeled the "Republican revolution." The results of the 1994 midterm election were historic; not one Republican incumbent lost a seat, and the party won back fifty-four House seats and eight Senate seats. This marked the first time since January 1955 that the Republicans controlled the House. Additionally, the Republican revolution was victorious in numerous gubernatorial races; twelve Democratic governors lost their seats to new Republican challengers. A moderate Democrat was running the White House, but the U.S. government was now largely conservative.

In 1993, Clinton appointed the women's rights activist and U.S. Court of Appeals Judge Ruth Bader Ginsburg to the Supreme Court to fill Justice Byron White's seat. But even with the new liberal appointee, the court remained in a conservative deadlock. With a conservative activist Supreme Court and Republicans controlling both the House and the Senate for the first time since 1952, the presidency entered a new era of challenges. In 1994, the GOP was ready for a political comeback.

Clinton knew that he had to respond to the massive congressional defeat. Unbeknownst to the White House staff, Clinton turned to the political strategist Dick Morris for outside advice. Clinton trusted Morris, not only because of their longtime friendship but also because he had advised Clinton on and off since 1978. Morris had a well-known reputation for polemic opinions and strategies. During the interim years of assisting Clinton, Morris worked for several Republican politicians, which exacerbated his already untrustworthy reputation. Wanting to keep Morris's advisory role a secret from his staff, Clinton referred to his confidant by the code name "Charlie." Morris was responsible for defining the second half of the first term of the Clinton administration (1994–1996) and ultimately much of Clinton's legacy.

Morris's goal was to rebrand the administration in time for reelection in 1996. Irrespective of winning his first term, Clinton, with his moderate approach, political scandals, and tumultuous policy agenda, was something of an enigma to the American people. Morris wanted to give him an image that would appeal to the majority of voters. Conflicts between insiders and outsiders in the executive office grew as Morris and Panetta clashed over their role and vision for the Clinton administration. Each time Clinton deferred to Morris, Panetta lost influence in the White House. Panetta had no knowledge of Morris, and Morris was not an administration employee, so the policy agenda became increasingly chaotic with competing and inconsistent guidance. It was not until nearly six months after the midterm election that Panetta became aware of Morris's influence on the president and Morris was more formally included in the workings of the administration.

Morris discerned the needs of the American people and thereby built Clinton's image. Responding to the reactions over the active role of the First Lady, Morris recommended that Hillary reduce the visibility of her influence and remain active only behind the scenes. Many voters believed that if Hillary appeared strong, Bill must be the weak one in their marriage and therefore a weak president. Hillary agreed to this political strategy; stepping away from the health care initiative, she focused on her book and other side projects. Despite Morris's efforts, the American public was never comfortable with Hillary as the First Lady. Eleanor Roosevelt, also a complex figure in her time, was the last visible First Lady in the White House. Although some people adored Hillary's headbands and tenacity, she remained a conundrum and most constituents were never completely content with her. She spent the rest of the Clinton administration negotiating her role as wife, mother, First Lady, and political activist.

After the 1994 midterm elections, Clinton lost control over his relationship with Congress. The GOP focused on cutting Medicaid and Medicare programs in order to help balance the budget, regardless of opposition from the public. The president and Congress were unwilling to compromise on each other's budget proposals. In late September 1995, as reported by the *New York Times*, Gingrich publically threatened to send the United States into default if the president did not balance the budget on the Republicans' terms. He stated, "I don't care what the price is. . . . I don't care if we have no executive offices and no bonds for 60 days—not this time." Clinton was unwilling to give in to political threats or relinquish his agenda for the budget. Americans nervously paid attention, knowing the impact that a shutdown would have on their personal lives, especially those who were employed by the government. Additionally, the financial sector was acutely aware of the financial impact a shutdown would have on the national and international markets. As reported by the *New York Times*, Gingrich vowed to "hold the federal debt limit hostage"; as a result of not agreeing on a compromise, "the government will be unable to meet many of the payments due in November for Social Security, military pay and interest on the Federal Government's $4.9 trillion in debt."

In October 1995, the budget still unbalanced, the government faced a shutdown. Both parties offered budget proposals, but neither side was willing to compromise; consequently, they chose a shutdown. The government officially shut down for six days in October; as a result, over one million government workers went on furlough. In part, the refusal to come to an agreement was over the issue of government programs. Two of the emergency spending bills presented to Clinton proposed raising the cost of Medicaid premiums and cutting a variety of federal programs. Although Clinton moved to the center on many issues, initially he was not willing to compromise with Republicans on their proposed cuts to social programs. From the beginning, the president made it clear to his staff and the public that he would reject the proposals put forward by the Republicans in an effort to protect his agenda.

The frozen jobs impacted the impending 1996 election, as voters and the media continued to witnesses the politicians' refusal to compromise. While the Republican nominee Bob Dole, a World War II veteran and the Senate Majority leader from Kansas, was on the ballot to run against Clinton, Gingrich was running the Republican Party. Dole knew Gingrich's decision to proceed with the shutdown would be the catalyst for Clinton's reelection. Stuck playing the political game of staying loyal to his party while disagreeing with its decision, Dole decided to use his own congressional power to try to avoid the impending government closing. Moving forward, the presidential hopeful looked to his fellow congressional allies to gather the votes necessary to put an end to the imminent government shutdown and furlough. He knew that without continuing the budget negotiations, the regular appropriations could never be passed.

Nearly a week into the shutdown, Clinton signed a continuing resolution that allowed the budget negotiations to continue and the government to remain open, thus assuaging the impact of the furloughs on workers. However, the unwillingness of both parties to reach an agreement only delayed further negotiations. By November, approximately 40 percent of nondefense workforces were still temporarily laid off. The Republicans drafted another budget proposal to the president in December, and Clinton vetoed it. Although the Republicans controlled both the House and the Senate, they did not have the necessary votes to override a presidential veto. Subsequently the government shut down for twenty-one days, the longest government shutdown in American history.

Clinton was not concerned with popularity or polls but in sticking to what he believed was right; he was determined to protect social programs and reduce the deficit. With the same resolve, the Republicans did not want to abandon their plan to balance the budget in seven years. Chris Jennings told Takiff in *A Complicated Man* that the budget negotiations were also the Republicans' way of pushing the GOP health care agenda, which proposed to cut $270 billion from Medicaid and $180 billion from Medicare over the course of five years. Additionally, the Republicans proposed tax cuts of $240 billion for the wealthy within the same five years. These schemes only provided Clinton with more ammunition not to compromise, which ultimately allowed him to achieve his budget goals. Knowing that positive public opinion was imperative to campaign success, Clinton benefited from the shutdown as his approval ratings skyrocketed. The shutdown reflected unfavorably on Congress. Clinton had turned the crisis into a victory for himself.

It was not until August 1997 that the negotiations were finally settled and Clinton signed the Balanced Budget Act of 1997. Despite Clinton's resistance, the final bill included some reductions to Medicare. Additionally, it also included middle-class tax relief and an increase in taxes for wealthy Americans. Amounting to nearly $152 billion, the budget cuts mostly impacted college students and families with children. The administration did not have the full support of the Democrats in the House. Nearly a quarter of the House Democrats voted against the proposal, including the Minority leader Dick Gephardt. The final bill proposed a fully balanced budget by 2002. Although Morris had looked to change Clinton's image, the president's actions—hard on the economy and soft in the wake of tragedy—created the perception that the American people could trust their president and move past the scandals.

On April 19, 1995, Americans experienced the most serious domestic terrorist attack in American history. The twenty-six-year-old ex-Army soldier Timothy McVeigh bombed the Alfred P. Murrah Federal Building in downtown Oklahoma City, killing 149 workers and 19 children. The building housed offices for Social Security, the Secret Service, the Drug Enforcement Administration, and other federal agencies, including a daycare center. Shortly before 9 am, McVeigh parked a rented yellow Ryder truck in front of the U.S. federal government office building. The truck was filled with a homemade bomb that McVeigh had created from a mix of agricultural fertilizer, fuel, and a variety of chemicals. After lighting the fuse, McVeigh abandoned the locked truck and took off in a getaway car. The bomb destroyed most of the building, as well as more than three hundred buildings in the surrounding area. McVeigh's motivation for the bombing was anger over the Waco siege in Texas in 1993. The compound of an extremist religious group possessing firearms and drugs came under fire from the FBI, resulting in the deaths of seventy-six adults and children. Two days later, on April 21, 1995, McVeigh was apprehended for the bombing. To the surprise of the FBI, McVeigh had already been arrested. Approximately an hour and a half after the bombing, the police pulled a car over after it was spotted missing its plates. The driver, McVeigh, was discovered with a concealed weapon and was subsequently taken into custody.

Clinton's response to the Oklahoma City bombing consoled the people and demonstrated his leadership skills. During the 1992 campaign, his kindness and empathy contributed to his election to office, and now in office he showed the same qualities again. Takiff called him the "comforter in chief" because of the way he handled the situation. In a press conference, Clinton referred to the attack on "innocent children and defenseless citizens" as an "act of cowardice" and "evil." He pledged to work with the U.S. government to respond to the bombing and to investigate. Before it was discovered that the attack came from McVeigh, an American citizen, many believed it was the work of the international terrorist organization Al-Qaeda. Only two years earlier in 1993, the World Trade Center was bombed when parked trucks detonated, killing six. Given the similarity in method, many initially assumed that the Oklahoma bombing was an attack by Al-Qaeda. McVeigh was tried and executed for the crime six years after the bombing, on June 11, 2001. The tragic bombing was a pivotal moment for Clinton that refuted the old perception of him as a sketchy politician, and he gained popularity as the people grew to trust him as a leader.

Clinton's political strengths lay in the domestic sphere; welfare reform was a leading agenda item since his days on the campaign trail. Welfare was consistently a priority for both Democrats and Republicans, but the parties had a drastically different vision for reform. The budget negotiations drew attention to the issue of public assistance programs, and welfare proposals now made their way to the president's desk. The first bill was proposed in June 1994 with the aim of placing time restraints on access to benefits. The program was called "Welfare to Work" because of the two-year limitation, by which time a recipient had to find employment. The lifetime limit for welfare benefits would be five years. According to Takiff, Clinton's first draft of the bill budgeted $9.3 billion for "job training, child care, and job subsidies." Because of the president's contentious relationship with Congress over health care and despite his moderate policies, Clinton was unable to gain support in the House or the Senate. After the changes of the 1994 midterm election, this was his last chance before the 104th Congress took power and implemented its own agenda.

When the Republicans won the House and the Senate, a new agenda for welfare was crafted. Opting to slash over $69 million in aid to families, the new Republican Congress passed two different reform bills and Clinton used his veto power against both. To counter the proposals, Clinton crafted a third option. The final bill was a compromise with the Republicans and most of the conciliation came from the executive office. As Takiff described, Clinton believed that he would be able to amend the cuts to food stamps and the denial of benefits to immigrants. Many on Clinton's advisory staff urged him to wait to approve the bill until the administration had what it wanted and warned that passing the bill would be a political disaster. However, the man who had the ear of the president was still Dick Morris. Taking Morris's advice, and ignoring his staff's, the president passed the bill. Contrary to the apprehensions of Clinton's staff, Morris believed that the bill could give Clinton a bump up in the ratings for the upcoming presidential election just a few months away. Clinton had known that he would have to pick his battles with the Republicans and welfare turned out to not be one of them. In *Why Americans Hate Welfare*, the political scientist Martin Gilens explained that under the new bill states would still create their own limitations on receiving welfare benefits. Passage of the bill created chaos in state agencies, as it took years for each state to restructure its welfare programs.

The bill created the largest reform in welfare since the establishment of the program during the Great Depression in the 1930s. On August 22, 1996, Clinton signed into law the new welfare reform bill; and just as he had pledged in his initial campaign, the final bill ended welfare as Americans had known it. The government would no longer provide the federal aid that it had for sixty-one years to people who had lost their jobs. Clinton received backlash from both his own staff and the Left for signing the conservative version of the law. Contrary to the political claims of the administration, Clinton did not end welfare, he only changed it. Many of the people required to find work at the end of the two-year or five-year requirement were unable to obtain employment and instead qualified for disability. Although the data showed welfare numbers declining, the recipients mostly moved from one government program to another or just slipped through the cracks and disappeared.

After the debacle of the transition to office and the setback of the Republican revolution, it was not inevitable that Clinton would win another term in the 1996 election. Reminiscent of the Republicans in 1992, there were many concerns from Clinton staffers and aids that another Democrat would run against the president in the primaries. Clinton knew this would be an issue when he campaigned during the 1994 election (a nonpresidential election year) in an attempt to keep his voting base of support. Articulating his vision for the future, and relying on fundraisers and his charisma, Clinton successfully secured his place in the Democratic Party. Clinton set the tone for his second shot at the presidency when he pledged to "build a bridge to the twenty-first century," thereby demonstrating to the people his forward-looking policies and agenda. Once nominated at the 1996 Democratic National Convention in Chicago, Clinton maintained a steady lead over the Republican nominee Bob Dole.

After the government shutdown Clinton's popularity increased, and the Republicans were now eager to reverse their drop in the polls. Unlike the 1992 campaign strategy, the Republican Party was careful to select a moderate candidate rather than Far Right to counter Clinton's new appeal to the center. This strategy was apparent when Dole won the primaries against more extreme conservatives such as Pat Buchanan, Steve Forbes, Lamar Alexander, and Alan Keyes. However, Dole was described by the media as an ardent fiscal hawk and he presented a strong argument for fiscal conservatives and Reaganite social values.

Congressman Jack Kemp was selected as Dole's vice presidential nominee. He was described by the *Washington Post* as "the ex-quarterback, congressman, one-time vice-presidential nominee and self-described 'bleeding-heart conservative.'" The ticket was comprised of self-proclaimed "American heroes." Projecting an "all-American" image and proposing an agenda focused on family values and smaller government, the Dole-Kemp ticket attempted to bring voters back to the Republican Party. However, these two older faces on the Republican ticket were harshly juxtaposed with the young incumbents in the White House. When they were contrasted, voters viewed Dole as old and Clinton as younger and more in touch with the people. Dole referred to his campaign as "restoring the American Dream," but it ultimately fell short with voters.

In a flash of déjà vu from the 1992 election, Ross Perot entered the 1996 election as a third-party candidate, this time as a contender representing the Reform Party, which he had founded the previous year. Unfortunately for Perot, his 1992 success and popularity did not carry over into the 1996 election and he was unable to repeat the large numbers of support. Although both Democrats and Republicans focused on the moderate constituent bases of support, voters were unmoved by the campaigns. Election Day voter turnout was the lowest since the 1924 election. The energy of the 1992 election had since waned and the MTV generation that elected Clinton in the wake of the Republican revolution went to the polls in much lower numbers.

Overall the apathy and low voting turnout contributed to both Clinton and Dole carrying votes along partisan lines. Andrew Kohut, the director of the Pew Research Center for the People and the Press, explained to the *New York Times* in the week after the election, "every one of the performers in the election got lower ratings than they did in '92, and even in '88." However, after the election, 53 percent of Americans reported being pleased with Clinton's reelection.

Once again, Clinton reasserted his reputation as the Comeback Kid and captured enough votes to remain in the White House. Just two years earlier his political career had been declared dead, but in 1996 he rebounded with another term in office. Clinton was reelected on November 6, 1996 with 49 percent of the popular vote and 70 percent of the electoral vote (379 votes). Dole finished second with 41 percent of the vote and Perot obtained 8 percent of the vote. Although Dole and Perot both ran their campaigns on the public's fear that the Clintons could not be trusted, the American people gave the Clintons the benefit of the doubt at the polls. The House and Senate remained controlled by the GOP, but the Democrats celebrated Clinton as the first Democrat to win a second term since FDR.

The policy agenda for the second term of the Clinton administration was inevitably a moderate one. Clinton knew he had won the election by leaning to the middle and continued to support bills that had bipartisan appeal. With four more years ahead of him, he remained committed to domestic progress. Clinton's staff changed as members of his cabinet stepped down, but the strategy of supporting centrist policies remained the same. In 1997, Panetta resigned as chief of staff and Clinton brought on Erskine Bowles, an investment banker who had been involved in the administration since the beginning. Bowles served for two years and during that time continued Panetta's legacy of order and structure. The 1996–2000 term of the Clinton administration was comprised of more high-profile scandals and policy decisions, both at home and abroad, than the first term could have ever predicted.

Recommended Reading

The best book on the Clinton administration is Michael Takiff's oral history, *A Complicated Man: The Life of Bill Clinton as Told by Those Who Know Him*

(New Haven, CT: Yale University Press, 2010). Bill Clinton, *My Life* (New York: Knopf, 2004), is the first memoir by the former president and provides a firsthand account of his term in office. Hillary Clinton's first memoir, *Living History* (New York: Simon & Schuster, 2003), focuses primarily on her experience in the White House.

4

The United States and Genocide

THE 1990S were primarily an age of genocide; the crisis that transpired in Somalia, to be discussed shortly, was a distraction. The United States was faced with a plethora of options regarding the foreign policy agenda under both Bush and Clinton. As with many post–Cold War era conflicts, officials who shaped U.S. foreign policy cited the heavy losses in Vietnam as a reason to avoid deploying American troops to any country abroad. Both the Vietnam Syndrome and Machiavellian-inspired Realism Theory, which holds that nation-states are motivated by national interests to increase their own power, shaped the philosophy of the Bush and Clinton administrations. On December 4, 1992, troops were deployed to Somalia because of a concern for U.S. interests, but the deployment was portrayed as a humanitarian relief effort. Ultimately, the Somali military operation in October 1993 killed nineteen American soldiers and two thousand Somali citizens. The foreign policy decision in Somalia was a brief moment in American history but shaped the next decade of policy abroad.

The relationship between the United States and Somalia was long, complicated, and rooted in the Cold War. The volatile relations between tribal clans in Somalia culminated in a civil war that engulfed the country in 1988. Contrary to popular opinion, the violence in Somalia was not genocide, but carnage between tribes of equal power. The difference between the conflict in Somalia and the genocides that occurred in in Bosnia, Rwanda, and Kosovo was the systematic extermination of an ethnic group. Early in their relationship, the United States backed the Somali leader Siad Barre when he seized power in 1969 during a coup that killed the elected president Abdi

Rashid Ali Shermarke. Although Barre declared Somalia a Socialist country in 1970, the United States continued to support the leader until 1991, when he fled the country after being ousted from office. In the absence of leadership, General Mohammed Farah Aidid assumed power and became the de facto ruler of Somalia. As described by scholars, although an oppressor had fled the country, one warlord had replaced another. The violent change in leadership resulted in the deaths of nearly one thousand people a week.

The deployment of U.S troops to Somalia was rooted in the hot war aftermath of the Cold War. As far back as colonialism, domestic interference by an outside Western country created increasingly complex relationships between both the tribes and the colonizers. Tribal leaders in Somalia were aware of the Cold War investments of the United States in countries abroad. It was in America's economic interest and aligned with the previous foreign-policy support of Somalia to provide aid to the country. Throughout the Cold War, Somalia's volatile relationship with the Soviet Union inevitably created a capricious relationship with the American government. As late as the 1980s, the United States provided military and economic aid to Somalia. This was done at an astonishing pace compared with other countries in Africa, and during a time when Cold War tensions were fought through ground wars around the globe. Under the Bush administration, the United States poured an enormous amount of military aid into Somalia with the intent to arm and support the Somali people. Additionally, U.S. officials campaigned for "country building" or "democratic diplomacy" abroad. The agenda at the United Nations changed with the new Secretary General, the Egyptian politician and diplomat Boutros Boutros-Ghali (1992–1996), and the new course of action was to unarm the Somali people.

President Bush changed the foreign policy agenda not only for the remaining months of his administration but also for the Clinton administration when he deployed twenty-eight thousand troops near Mogadishu. Powell urged the United States to stay out of the conflict in Somalia, and references to the Vietnam Syndrome were present in all such advice. Bush ignored his advisers and on August 14 ordered a "limited intervention," thus disregarding Powell's doctrine of extreme force. However, this strategy allowed Bush to deploy troops to where the U.S. interests lay—Somalia, not Bosnia.

The Bush administration stated that the mission was solely for humanitarian reasons and that it was sending personnel and resources strictly for
relief efforts. By 1991, widespread drought had deprived Somalia of resources.
Famine and death were on the rise, and consequently the conflict between
tribes escalated. The extreme drought caused the price of food to increase;
as a result, starvation and malnutrition plagued citizens. According to the
Brookings Institute, by the end of 1992, 1.5 million people faced "imminent" starvation. If Somali citizens left their homes, they were subjected to
tribal violence; however, staying inside meant a lack of resources and dying of
hunger. The famine in Somalia impacted U.S. economic interests because of
the close relationship of American oil giants to the oil resources in Somalia
and the instability arising. Before troops left for Africa, the media picked
up on this new policy decision. The price to pay for the media attention to
the famine in Somalia was the neglect of the Bosnian genocide happening
in tandem.

Powell believed that as many as half a million lives could be saved from
Aidid's violence and the consequential tribal wars, but he refused to support
any deployment without a clear strategy for withdrawal. After Powell's directive and with approval from Bush, U.S. troops were officially deployed in July
1992. To address concerns regarding the Vietnam Syndrome, Bush placed
the troops on a timeline for a minimum tour overseas. The plan required
American troops to establish power, after which they would be replaced by
UN troops. This strategy was considered to be in line with the Powell Doctrine, often defined by scholars as "the application of overwhelming force."
By the fall, it was apparent the situation in Somalia was worsening and the
timeline would have to be amended. Because of the dearth of assistance from
America after U.S. troops were pulled out, Brent Scowcroft, national security adviser in the Bush administration, worried that food delivery would not
provide sufficient relief to the people of Somalia.

The decision to deploy troops to Somalia rather than Bosnia, where mass
genocide was occurring, originated in former Cold War relationships and
the American focus on economic interests. In *War in Time of Peace*, David
Halberstam aptly summed up the decision to take action in Somalia: "For a
variety of reasons Somalia was the better choice, and the mission, though in
a more distant country, appears containable and offers the easiest possibility

of extraction." An investment in Somalia was made during the Cold War and the Bush administration was unwilling to ignore it.

Bush's decision to deploy troops changed the campaign agenda of the Clinton administration. During the 1992 campaign, Bush slighted Clinton for his inexperience with foreign policy. After the election, Clinton's ability to lead the troops as commander in chief, specifically after Bush's successes in the Persian Gulf War, led to speculation that as a new president Clinton would inevitably "stumble" in regard to foreign policy. This prediction came to fruition.

The misstep came in Somalia, which dictated the foreign policy of the Clinton administration in other pockets of the world. Because of the change in America's foreign policy agenda in the months before taking office, Clinton was given very little choice but to have Somalia be the first order of foreign-policy business. Yet on this crucial global issue and others, he spouted hollow rhetoric and struggled to find his footing. Somalia was one of the most important events of the 1990s because it set the precedent for the rest of the decade, both in policy decisions and Clinton's obstinate relationship with the military.

In January 1993, according to Bush's timeline for Somalia, the United Nations was positioned to assume leadership of the mission and grant the United States a reprieve. According to Halberstam, this is where everything went wrong. The already problematical relationship between Clinton and the U.S. military became more difficult as the conflict in Somalia became increasingly uncontainable. Changes in both the U.S. and the UN administrations caused chaos and altered the course of the original timeline. The flaws in U.S. policy were attributed to the lack of structure and engagement from leaders. According to Halberstam, Boutros-Ghali thought the American response was inevitably weakened because "Bush was back in Texas, Powell was on his way out of the Joint Chiefs, and Clinton's mind was on other matters." These factors led to a scattered and weak approach from the United States.

Under Boutros-Ghali, the Egyptian agenda influenced the mission of the United Nations. Since Boutros-Ghali and Barre were close allies, the relationship between Boutros-Ghali and Aidid was deeply personal. Boutros-Ghali profited from leaving Somalia with a new political system, specifically

one that benefited Egypt, rather than food and humanitarian aid. By changing the power structure of the government and the tribes, Boutros-Ghali
could advance the interests of Egypt's constituents. President Bush and
Boutros-Ghali disagreed over their vision for Somalia. The *New York Times*
reported that "the Bush Administration and Mr. Boutros-Ghali have been
at odds over the goals of the mission, with the Secretary General calling for
troops to disarm the weapons-strewn nation and the American command
insisting that its role is to safeguard food convoys." However, much like
Boutros-Ghali, the United States had political motivations for wanting to
protect the Somali people.

As the United States expanded its military forces into the civil war–
torn country of Somalia, the rhetoric of the Security Council reflected the
old "country building" notion of previous decades. Historically, the U.S.
deployment of its military abroad has had a controversial "democracy-build-
ing" agenda. The historian William Appleman Williams and the Wiscon-
sin school of historians examined the United States' approach to democracy
building internationally as a way of securing U.S. interests by creating and
supporting puppet governments. Their scholarship emphasizes the role that
capitalism plays in U.S. foreign policy and the economic motivation of policymakers. When President Clinton's U.N. Ambassador, Madeleine Albright,
spoke to the UN Security Council in 1993, she mirrored the language of
many of her predecessors and committed the United States to "restoring"
Somalia. This vision included the traditional rhetoric of "country building"
and imagined a new democratic Somalia. Halberstam argued in *War in Time
of Peace* that the agenda presented by Albright diverted from the original
mission of humanitarian aid. The chaos of the deployment to Somalia, the
lack of focus and coherent agenda by all councils involved, and the domestic-
policy distractions of the Clinton administration, when coupled with the
increasing violence of the tribal wars, created an inevitable catastrophe.

The situation in Somalia became increasingly contentious the longer
U.S. troops remained. On June 5, 1993, the United Nations announced a
weapons inspection and Aidid retaliated by attacking the Pakistani troops
that had been sent by the United Nations to replace 2,600 U.S. marines.
Halberstam identified this first of many attacks between the Somali forces
and the U.S./UN military and the constant retaliation as the "cycle of

violence." During the next few months, mass deaths occurred as the two forces continued to retaliate against each other. Both the Somali and Western forces sought to classically dehumanize each other. In war and genocide, when thinking about opponents, each side removes human attributes, allowing opponents to be viewed only as enemies and not as people with families and lives. The Clinton administration made it clear that the "enemy" was no longer hunger or sickness. Replacing humanitarian aid, the priority became ousting Aidid. By mid-June, a warrant had been issued for Aidid's arrest with a reward of $25,000, and plans to capture the leader were underway.

The cycle of violence reached its apex when Aidid's forces attacked U.S. Rangers in the First Battle of Mogadishu, more commonly known as Black Hawk Down. In the days before the attack on the U.S. Rangers, the U.S. military assailed a house in which tribal elders were meeting. In the first assault American helicopters launched an anti-tank missile at the building full of civilians, followed by an attack from ground troops to finish off any survivors. This mission was purportedly to capture Aidid as he was meeting with top officials and was structured like other assignments for Army Rangers and Delta Forces. Anticipating a 90-minute mission, the military officials did not carry water and night goggles. Unexpectedly, Somali militia ambushed the Americans and shot down two U.S. helicopters. When the first helicopter was shot down, the prepared ground convoy attempted to assist the injured soldiers. However, heavy fire trapped the Rangers in the alleys of the buildings. Meanwhile, a half mile away a second helicopter was shot down, killing two Delta Forces operators, and the pilot was taken hostage. The firefight continued for 17 hours and eighteen American lives were lost. The morning of October 4, 1993, a rescue convoy saved the Americans, but the story was not finished. When a video of a naked U.S. Ranger being dragged through the streets of Mogadishu was broadcast on every news station in America, an unprecedented wave of anti-Somali sentiment ran rampant.

In the days after Black Hawk Down, President Clinton opted to withdraw troops from Somalia. By dispatching new short-term reinforcement troops to the region, Clinton was able to begin implementing a plan to fully withdraw troops by March 31, 1994. Because of the recent events, the decision to deploy more troops abroad before bringing them all home created uproar in both the public and congressional spheres. In the months before the U.S. troops returned home, the violence of Black Hawk Down created a shift in American attention: suddenly Somalia was a front-page story. With the search for Aidid abandoned, within months the U.S. mission formally ended and UN peacekeepers left the following year.

The mission in Somalia was largely a failure because of the loss of American lives and a muddled agenda. The deployment of troops did not solve the humanitarian needs of hunger or poverty, and the U.S/UN involvement did not settle the changes in government. Halberstam argues that the United States believed that Aidid was the creator of Somali violence and chaos, when in reality he was a reflection of it. The situations in Bosnia and Rwanda were explicit acts of genocide, designed to systematically eliminate ethnic groups. Some scholars have cited the violence in Somalia as the reason for U.S. noninvolvement in peacekeeping and humanitarian missions in Bosnia and Rwanda during their respective genocides.

U.S. foreign policy in the 1990s was shaped by the multiple genocides occurring abroad. When analyzing the American and UN approaches to genocide, it is most important to note that policymakers often handled the atrocities as if they were faults in diplomacy. Yet genocide is a conscious decision and not a situation that can be resolved by negotiations. Contrary to popular belief, genocide is not an accident, nor is it inevitable, and there are no global regions that are predisposed to violence and ethnic cleansing. Genocide is always a series of horrific decisions made by leaders and is never spontaneous; it originates from racism and discrimination. The details are different, but the roots of the violence are the same.

The laws to restrict the Bosnians and Rwandans were similar to those imposed on the Jews during World War II. The violence in Bosnia, Rwanda, and Kosovo was not about tribal warfare or civil war, but about power and the systematic elimination a class of people. Genocide plagued the twentieth century. After the Holocaust, international laws were implemented to hold perpetrators of genocide accountable. However, the United States found a loophole to international law and only had to evade labeling violence as genocide to avoid taking action. In the last century, there has been no year when mass killings and genocide were not occurring somewhere in the world. The unceasing murders were fueled by the inaction of the global community and the United States as a global leader. There was the misperception that in order to take action against genocide, the Powell Doctrine of extreme force had to be implemented; however, these types of ultimatums were not necessary.

During the 1990s, America struggled to stabilize its policy abroad. The collapse of the Soviet Union in 1991 created an inevitable set of geographical and political problems; specifically, the geographical division of government and power was violent and bitter for Bosnia. Slovenia and Macedonia established their independence with little or no bloodshed, whereas Croatia lapsed into mass war during the fight for freedom. Bosnia and Herzegovina were quickly consumed by mass violence from the Bosnian Serbs led by the Serbian president Slobodan Milošević. Many experts predicted that Bosnia would be a potential area of conflict when Yugoslavia was divided in the post–Cold War years. In 1991, the demographics of Bosnia reflected a multiethnic, multicultural region of Yugoslavia. The population of 43 percent Bosnians, 35 percent Muslims, and 18 percent Roman Catholic Croats was the most heterogeneous of any of the republics in Yugoslavia.

Contrary to the opinion of many scholars, the conflict in Bosnia did not occur suddenly. As Samantha Power stated in *A Problem from Hell*, the war arrived, it did not erupt. She explains that in February 1991, Deputy Secretary of State Lawrence Eagleburger (under Bush) traveled to Bosnia to follow up on reports of sadism in the area. Eagleburger's familiarity and expertise with the Balkan region extended back to his years as U.S. ambassador to Yugoslavia from 1977 to 1981 and his partnership with Henry Kissinger in the 1980s. Some level of conflict between the Bosnian Muslims, Croats, and Serbians was anticipated by many of the Bush officials; however, when Eagleburger arrived, he was greeted by brutality and mass death. The magnitude of the slaughter by Milošević against a specific class of people demonstrated to Eagleburger the enormity of a conflict that would only escalate. Upon the deputy secretary's return, explains Power, he reported to Jim Hooper, the deputy director of the Office of East Europe and Yugoslav affairs, "now that I've been there, I think you were being much too optimistic. It is going to be bloody as hell." Unfortunately, his prognosis was accurate.

Inspired by centuries of ethnic tensions, Serbian President Slobodan Milošević led the systematic killings in Bosnia. Most important, the Serbian officials knew the global community would not hold them accountable. The perceived inevitability of ethnic violence became an excuse for international policymakers to evade the genocide. To defend their positions, they cited sources that claimed the conflict would never quell because violence was an inherent quality of the native people. Almost as predictable was the response from the United States. Many officials did not support the needs of other countries if the situation did not concern U.S. interests. This attitude remained consistent from the Bush to the Clinton administrations.

Much like Hitler and other architects of genocide, Milošević was elected to his position of power. He first took office in the Serb parliament in 1989 and appealed to the people through his charisma. Milošević was described by Secretary of State Madeleine Albright as a "ruthless opportunist"; he saw an opening in politics left by the death of the Yugoslavian leader Josip Broz Tito and proceeded to climb the ranks of the Communist Party. A Machiavellian approach to politics was not the only tactic that Milošević had taken from his predecessor. He also learned from Tito the exploitive and "heavy-handed" approach to creating deep racial divides, specifically between the Bosnians and the Croats. Milošević was personable and charming. Like Hitler, his rhetoric was racially loaded, appealed to the fears of the people, and never explicitly delineated his intention to create death camps for Bosnian Muslims.

Milošević's plan to eliminate an ethnic group was similar to previous genocides and the global community was no stranger to the systematic killing of citizens. Within the first seven months of the war against the Muslims, ten thousand civilians were murdered and seven hundred thousand were displaced from their homes. American policy officials sat idly as terror spread through the former Yugoslavia. The question on the minds of the public and members of both the Bush and Clinton administrations was, how do these human rights violations intersect with American policy? Or more crudely, why is this an issue for the American people and government? The American government concluded that initiating intervention was not the responsibility of Americans, but of the entire global community.

The topography of the post–Soviet Union territory influenced each ethnic group as the genocide progressed. As explained by Power, the geography and demographics of the region created a dynamic whereby the violent Serbs were supported by Serbia, the victimized Croats had the support of Croatia, and because of a lack of international protection, the brutalized Bosnian Muslims were victims of ethnic cleansing. No matter what direction Bosnia took in the future, the Muslim community would suffer. If Bosnia remained a republic, the Serbs would continue to receive better jobs and education opportunities, whereas the Muslims and Croats would continue to face physical and social abuses. If Bosnia left the republic, its Muslims would have no protection. With the support of global allies, Bosnia could leave the republic and declare independence from the Serbs. To leave without support of the international community, or at least a few specific countries, the Croats and the Serbs would draw on additional resources from Serbia and Croatia, and the Muslim community would be left with nothing. As could have been predicted, a full-scale genocide of Bosnian citizens occurred before the United States and the United Nations intervened. Initially the violence was viewed as a European problem that should be settled by Europeans. The world community and the Bush administration adopted the same view.

The actions, or lack thereof, by the global community allowed the genocide to grow and spread. Albright criticized the initial approach by the United States and others by explaining, "diplomats arranged cease fires that didn't stick and predicted an end to the violence that did not come." The failure of policy continued to be blamed on the ethnic diversity of the region and the discriminatory belief that the violence was inherent to the region and the culture. These patronizing attitudes ignored history and disregarded centuries during which various ethnicities in the region had intermarried and lived together in peace, creating families that existed contrary to Milošević's ideal of ethnic purity. The perspectives of foreign policy officials on the conflict in Bosnia mirrored official policy during the tragedies of the Holocaust. The systematic killing of a group of people by Milošević was reminiscent of the fate of Hitler's victims in the Third Reich. During both the Holocaust and Milošević's reign of terror, the U.S. policy and attitude toward trains carrying citizens to death camps and the extermination of ethnic groups was lackadaisical and even apathetic.

The experience in Vietnam of fighting a war that could not be won was still fresh for many U.S. policy officials, and the administration was apprehensive to deploy U.S. troops to Bosnia to stop the genocide. Their fear

dominated foreign policy decisions regarding Bosnia and the result was apathy and inactive policy reports. Serb officials, aware of the concerns of the
American government, capitalized on and exploited its fears. The Bosnian
Serb leader Rodovan Karadžić stated, "The United States sends two thousand Marines, then they have to send ten thousand more to save the two
thousand . . . this is the best way to have another Vietnam." During a Security Council debate regarding the deployment of troops to Bosnia, much like
in the Gulf War, Powell argued that the troops should be sent at full force or
not at all. Frustrated with Powell's argument to withhold troops, Albright
revealed in her memoir that she quipped to him, "exactly what are you saving this great army for?" Irrespective of differing opinions of officials in the
Clinton administration, the troops remained stationary.

During the Bush and Clinton administrations, the lack of agenda can
partially be attributed to the inability of either administration to have a uniform strategy to the genocide. Power believed the approaches to the Bosnian
genocide could be divided into three camps: dissenters who favored U.S.
intervention, senior policymakers opposed to intervention and the deployment of ground troops, and those who supported bombing but assumed it
would never happen. Power explained that the Bush and Clinton administration evaded labeling the mass slaughter of Bosnian Muslims "genocide"
because of the legal responsibility. Using the term "ethnic cleansing" allowed
for both Bush and Clinton to distance themselves from the atrocities. By
labeling the violence "ethnic cleansing" and declaring it to be a mutual ethnic conflict, the global community escaped responsibility.

The idea of the violence as ethnic conflict or a civil war was supported by
press conferences; Scowcroft explained that he believed there was a difference
between ethnic cleansing and civil conflicts. Scholars have observed that the
narrative from the media and the government presented three different stories of the violence: it was a tragedy and they were empathetic to the victims,
it was a consequence of the breakup of Yugoslavia, and, like Vietnam, it was
an unwinnable internal conflict that could not be stopped by U.S. military
intervention without huge losses. Propaganda by the government and media
influenced public opinion and support of the situation abroad. Power cited a
poll that demonstrated the shift in opinion contingent on the morally loaded
label "genocide": "54 percent of Americans favored military intervention in

Bosnia, that figure rose to 80 percent when those surveyed were told that an independent commission had found genocide under way." The international law constructed in 1948 around the term "genocide" was created to protect those experiencing the violence. However, this legal protection evolved into a disagreement regarding the events and a way for the American government to avoid direct interventionist policies in Bosnia and later in Rwanda.

The strategies deployed for Bosnia were symbolic and devoid of action. In 1991 the United Nations, supported by the Bush administration, declared an arms embargo against the Serbs. The Serbs did not view the arms embargo against Milošević as a legitimate threat. The Serbs' access to resources and weapons made the embargo a worthless ultimatum. They continued to resupply their weapons stock through Belgrade, the capitol of Serbia. The Croats received help from Zagreb, the capitol of Croatia, and also escaped the restrictions of the embargo. Bosnian Muslims were left with no protection or way to circumvent the embargo. Without follow-through from the United States or the United Nations, Milošević was willing to ignore any potential consequences.

Much like the situation in Somalia and other countries, the United States and the United Nations attempted to use diplomacy with a leader who, as Power puts it, was undiplomatic and committing genocide. This strategy was as effective as it would have been for the United States to try to make diplomatic compromises with Hitler about Auschwitz or Dachau. By isolating Milošević through the embargo, Bush believed it would effectively end the violence. Contrary to Bush's intentions, the arms embargo only decreased access to weapons for Bosnians and increased violence from the armed Serbs. Since the U.S. government remained an inactive bystander, its actions supported the rape camps, work camps, and genocide of the Serbs. In April 1992, the executive office made clear its agenda to support symbolic measures. The hollow threats had dire consequences. As the war continued, the Serbs planned attacks knowing that the West would not respond or protect the area.

In May 1992, the accounts of Bosnian Muslims sealed in boxcars and sent to work and rape camps were exposed to the public. Regardless of the descriptions that invoked the Holocaust, the Bush administration did not comment on or condemn the atrocities. The violence was unrelenting; by

July, ten thousand Bosnians were fleeing their homes daily to seek refuge. Advanced technology allowed the State Department to investigate the camps via satellite. Power cited a disturbing account from Jon Western, an analyst in the State Department's Bureau of Intelligence and Research, who explained that the United States had the ability to predict which villages would be targeted by Milošević's forces next simply by watching the satellite imagery. Most disconcerting was the reality that U.S. forces were given no directions or policy initiatives to follow. Consequently, they were forced to watch the murders unfold and were only ordered to report after the lives were lost.

The parallels between Nazi death camps and the Bosnian camps were felt by the international community, and the images of Bosnian Muslims deported on trains to those camps invoked the same feelings of terror as did the Nazi deportations. The international Jewish community openly addressed the genocidal violence. On April 10, 1992, President Bush met with Yitzhak Rabin, the prime minister of Israel, about Serb violence. Rabin believed Serb violence was reminiscent of Nazi violence. Public opinion was represented viscerally when thousands of Jewish American protesters gathered in Washington during Rabin's visit to show their outrage over the apathy and inaction of American policy.

Throughout the genocide in Bosnia, the Bush administration remained committed to U.S. economic interests. Powell refused to budge from his position of no funding for humanitarian aid, deployment of U.S. ground troops, or airstrike assistance. The administration's uncompromising position was complicated by the unwillingness of the Republicans to take any chances during an election year. Power quoted Scowcroft articulating the Powell Doctrine, the Vietnam Syndrome, and the concept of "nation building" in one statement: "We could never satisfy ourselves that the amount of involvement we thought it would take was justified in terms of the U.S. interest involved. . . . We were heavily national-interest oriented, and Bosnia was of national-interest concern only if the war broke out in Kosovo, risking the involvement of our allies in a wider world war. If it stayed contained to Bosnia, it might have been horrible, but it did not affect us." The statement was prophetic, as the United States did not intervene in Bosnia until Kosovo was under attack.

The Bush administration was presented with innumerable opportunities to take action. When Americans were first granted access to the Bosnian camps, the world obtained the first look inside the horrors of the genocide. The extreme images of the death and rape camps gave the media and American policymakers a chance to take action against Milošević. The Bush administration announced in a press conference that they would "not rest until [they] gained access to any and all detention camps." However, access to the camps proved to be futile because it exposed the atrocities but prompted no policy changes. On August 13, 1992, the U.S. and UN Security Council committed to delivering humanitarian aid through "all necessary measures," but the president once again declined the request for troops.

In Bush's last days in office, he took steps to recognize the genocide. On December 18, 1992, after months of debating the specific language to be used regarding the violence, the United States concurred with the UN assessment that ethnic cleansing was in fact a form of genocide. By the time this important decision was made, it was the holiday recess and the new administration would commence the following week. On the last day of the Bush presidency, the administration's assistant secretary of human rights, Patricia Diaz Dennis, made clear to the American people that the abuses in Bosnia were acts that "bordered" on the legal term "genocide." Her assessment was too little, too late. The Clinton administration was handed a foreign policy disaster with the crisis in Somalia and failed to pick up where Dennis left off. It would be years before action was taken on Bosnia.

Clinton had capitalized on Bush's inaction regarding Serbian death camps during the election. On the campaign trail, he had enumerated the policies he believed most effective for military action, specifically air strikes, against the Serbs. However, when he reached the White House, he placed his priorities elsewhere and abandoned these campaign commitments. As with many other issues, as Power observed, it was as if Clinton remained in campaign mode while in office and spoke a "good game." He condemned Serb violence, but failed to pass related policies for years into his presidency. Scholars and administration officials have revealed since that in the first months, the focus of the foreign policy agenda was to analyze the inherited crisis in Somalia. Although the administration remained largely apathetic politically on the Bosnia crisis, Albright stood out as a dissenter against a policy from the beginning. Albright's fierce support for the Bosnians was in part due to her family's personal Czechoslovakian heritage. As the twentieth United States ambassador to the United Nations, her unique position in the administration gave her access to foreign officials and the international community.

Whereas Bush adhered strictly to the Powell Doctrine, Clinton labeled his approach "interventionist." He favored tight economic sanctions, humanitarian aid, and, during the 1992 campaign, a bombing operation. However, economic sanctions ultimately sustained Serbian access to outside resources and did not provide support to the Bosnian Muslims. The hawkish candidate from the 1992 campaign election rallies gave way to a president concerned with domestic policy, specifically his own agenda of passing health care legislation. Clinton faced the conundrum of addressing the needs of both constituents at home and citizens around the globe. During evaluations of the potential strategies for the Clinton administration, Secretary of State Warren Christopher said he did not believe there were many plausible options for the United States.

Clinton's national security adviser, Tony Lake, joined the new administration. Upon arrival, Lake was eager to take action against injustice and protect human rights. Much like the previous administration, Lake was concerned about involving the United States in an unwinnable war. Albright once said that Lake "had the Vietnam bug in his ear." But Lake soon relinquished his ideas about a Vietnam syndrome repeating in Bosnia. Lake and Albright advocated for action in Bosnia because of the potential impact on security issues in Europe that would influence U.S. interests. Thanks to Lake and Albright, the belief in protecting American interests broadened to extend beyond direct economic interests, specifically oil. The first nine months of the Clinton administration were shaped heavily by the foreign policy agenda of the Bush administration, not only because of ongoing policies in Somalia but also because Powell still served as chairman of the Joint Chiefs. Throughout, Powell's position on using overwhelming force remained unwavering. He believed the deployment would take tens of thousands of men and women, billions of dollars, the loss of many lives, and endless war. His beliefs starkly contrasted with Albright's idea to learn from the lessons of Vietnam and help the Bosnian victims. Albright was in the minority regarding the provision of extensive aid and protection to the Bosnian Muslims. It was in the U.S. diplomat Richard Holbrooke that Albright found an ally.

Within the administration, there were differing opinions on the arms embargo and the direction America should take regarding Bosnia. The embargo became a bargaining power for the United States and the United Nations. Even though the embargo was not as restrictive as the United States would have preferred, Milošević wanted the embargo lifted. Albright explained in her memoir that the United States hoped the embargo would force the violent leader to reach an agreement with the United States. Opinions of what policy actions should be taken challenged the divided administration; by not taking action, the Clinton administration allowed the genocidal actions of Milošević to continue. U.S. officials hoped that bringing Milošević to the table would lead to granting independence to Bosnia and Herzegovina. The United Nations believed Milošević would recognize this opportunity to negotiate and provide the United States the opportunity to suspend sanctions. Hundreds of thousands of lives were lost before the Clinton administration learned this lesson.

The most recognizable policy of the Clinton administration toward Bosnia was the "lift and strike" policy proposed by Vice President Gore, Lake, and Albright. This policy would end the embargo on arms shipment to Sarajevo, the capital of Bosnia and Herzegovina, while threatening air strikes. It provided an opportunity for the Serbs to relinquish the violence and the Bosnians to fight back and gain protections. When Clinton agreed to this plan he sent Christopher abroad to strengthen European support. However, the Europeans were ambivalent about the safety of officials and the level of UN involvement. Scholars have noted that Christopher's diplomatic campaign was not aligned with his personal desires and his lack of enthusiasm was obvious. As Albright stated, "How could we persuade others if we could not persuade ourselves." The Clinton administration maintained its distance from the genocide as it worked to establish itself abroad.

Whereas Bush had focused on reelection strategies and recovering popularity, Christopher knew the Clinton administration needed to repair its credibility with the American public. During a tumultuous transition and the blunder in Somalia, Christopher did not want to risk the reputation of the administration and believed that inaction would be the more reputable option. The diplomatic campaign against Milošević attempted to establish Clinton as a reliable global leader committed to protecting human rights. However, the details of the policy demonstrated the hollowness of the threats and economic sanctions. The crises in Bosnia continued unchecked and Milošević's violence showed no signs of subsiding. As much as Americans attempted to ignore it, the genocide was not going away. The violence resulted in one of the bloodiest mass killings in history.

In 1995, the United Nations designated the Bosnian town of Srebrenica as one of three remaining safe havens for Bosnian Muslims. Many speculated that if the refugees were relocated to one place the Serbs would inevitably attack that location. On July 6, 1995, Srebrenica fell to the Serbs and within five days Milošević's forces murdered eight thousand people. Given the safe haven's location, a valley, the attack was even deadlier. When the Serbs began shelling, they held the advantage against the powerless Bosnians. The women and children were separated from the men and boys over the age of twelve. During the genocide, the Serb forces focused on sending women to rape camps and killing adolescent and adult males. Thousands of bodies were dumped into mass graves and covered. When questioned, the Serbs denied any knowledge of the murders and speculated that the men and boys were hiding in the woods or with their families. Initially, the White House was slow to respond to the genocide, but the loss of eight thousand lives in 120 hours proved to be the turning point for the United States and NATO.

Hearing rumors of the executions, Albright requested the CIA provide more information. Two weeks later, Albright received satellite photos that exposed a soccer field full of bodies. The pictures, along with the stories of witnesses, constructed a credible narrative for the Srebrenica massacre. On August 10, 1995, the Security Council met and, using both interviews and the photos, Albright presented to her colleagues the reality of the genocide in Bosnia. Unlike previous meetings about the Bosnian genocide, the brutality in Srebrenica finally shifted the agenda toward an active American policy. After the meeting, Albright advocated for "no more duel-key nonsense from the UN"; in other words, no more hesitancy about using NATO air forces. Clinton made a commitment to no longer acquiesce in genocide. Although it would be years before the United States truly took relevant action to stop Milošević, the initial step was a UN memorandum to hold the Serbs accountable if they attacked the two remaining safe areas.

In the aftermath of Srebrenica, Albright pitched a new strategy to the president: the notion was that if American troops would inevitably end up in Bosnia, the troops should be deployed on the timeline of the United States. Additionally, Albright promoted a more aggressive approach to force the Serbs into agreement or consequently the United States would follow through with their threats. After Srebrenica and in the absence of intervention from the international community, there was the strong desire to train Bosnian Muslims to protect themselves against the Serbs. All of these proposals were presented to the president against the long-standing policy of inaction.

The Pentagon and the Joint Chiefs disagreed with the proposals by Albright and Lake. They believed the Serb military should be accepted as a presence in Bosnia and because of this a cease-fire should be established. Luckily, Clinton diverged from this fallacious perspective. According to Albright's memoir, when Clinton was presented with all the differing proposals, he paused and responded, "I agree with Tony and Madeleine. We need to bust our ass to get a settlement in the next few months . . . if we can't get that at the bargaining table, we must help the Bosnian Muslims on the battlefield." Since the government could not reasonably negotiate with the dictator, the American military began to assist the Bosnian victims.

As identified by Albright, three factors ended the Bosnian War: overreaching on the part of the Serbs, changes in the military situation, and "Bill Clinton's willingness to lead" (or changes in U.S. policy). Milošević strategically counted on the hollow threats of the West to sustain his genocide. Since the West did not hold the Serbs accountable but continued to enforce futile economic sanctions, the Serbs continued their campaign of ethnic cleansing and expanded their power unchecked by the global community. After Srebrenica, Croatia retaliated against the Serb violence by using military force to reclaim lost territory. After this counterattack succeeded, much like the Roman Empire, the Serbs were forced to acknowledge that overextending eventually weakened the government. The war was far from over, but Clinton's change in policy helped begin the healing process. Lake's vision for Bosnia focused on, in Albright's words, the "kind of post-conflict Bosnia we [the U.S.] would like to see." Unfortunately, the potential that was present in Lake's requested end-game papers proved pliable to global politics.

After Srebrenica, the United States and the global community took military action and the Bosnian War quickly changed. On August 30, 1995, NATO forces began bombing Sarajevo, the largest airstrike in NATO history. In the next week, the prime ministers of Bosnia, Croatia, and Yugoslavia agreed to recognize Bosnia as a single state. Soon after, the United States also agreed to recognize Herzegovina as a single state. By October 5, 1995, a countrywide cease-fire, which had felt out of reach just a few months earlier, was settled. This shift in policy was the beginning of holding the Serbs and Milošević accountable for the genocidal actions.

In November 1995, members of the international community gathered in Dayton, Ohio, for diplomatic negotiations and to finalize an agreement. As in prior months, Milošević requested the sanctions against Belgrade be suspended during the negotiations and lifted when a settlement was reached. Seeing this as a bargaining tool, the United States refused to lift the sanctions until the implementation stage had been completed. There was concern from U.S. officials that if they pushed Milošević too far he would refuse to show, but this was not the case. The Dayton Accords ended on November 21; having obtained the agreements of multiple countries to compromise, the war in Bosnia was over—or so the administration believed.

The Dayton Accords taught the world that Milošević was still the leader of the Balkans, NATO air strikes were an effective use of power, and the Clinton administration was capable of being a global leader. The president emerged from The Dayton Accords with a new image: the inexperienced commander in chief who prompted military blunders was now a trusted leader who ended genocide. However, Milošević's reign of terror was not over and within a few years the administration would once again have to construct new policies to stop Serbian violence.

The multiple genocides of the 1990s created foreign policy decisions that were complex and multilateral as well as less linear and more multifaceted. Policy concerns in Europe were typically given priority by American leaders because of the traditionally closer ties of that region to the economic and security interests of the United States. The already established domestic and foreign policies of the emerging Clinton administration heavily influenced the policy decisions regarding Rwanda. Additionally, African countries were laden with stereotypes from the days of slavery and colonialism; the assumption was that the region would always be violent and no foreign policy would be able to fix it. This ignorant perspective resulted in inaction and apathy regarding the genocide that would unfold.

One of the greatest of horrors of the twentieth century occurred in Rwanda when over eight hundred thousand people were systematically murdered in only one hundred days. Rwanda is the size of Vermont and before the violence the population was approximately eight million. The murder spree was the largest, swiftest, and most effectual slaughter of the last century: it killed more people quicker (three times the rate) than Hitler did during the Holocaust and was the most efficient extermination since the U.S. atomic bombing of Hiroshima and Nagasaki. On April 6, 1994, Rwandan President Juvénal Habyarimana, Burundian President Cyprien Ntaryamira, and their entourages were killed when their plane was shot down. The attack on the plane and the president was the ruse the Hutu needed to commence the systematic killings. Within hours, the government had collapsed, Hutus were murdering Tutsis, and the genocide in Rwanda was underway.

Before World War I, Rwanda was a German colony known as Rwanda-Urundi. When the war ended, the colony was turned over to the Belgian colonists. Throughout Africa, each of the colonies contributed a different set of assets to the colonizers; unlike the Congo, which had capital sources of uranium, Rwanda-Urundi did not have any wealth organic to the land. In 1962, independence from the Belgians divided the colony into the two new countries of Rwanda and Burundi. The colonists had created a hierarchy of ethnic differences between the two tribes, the Tutsi and Hutu. Even though the Tutsi were only 15 percent of the population, they were granted privileged positions in government and in society. Tutsi were identified by their lighter skin, taller stature, and smaller noses, which resembled Caucasian features. Two years before the Belgians pulled out, the position of the tribes shifted and Hutus gained political and social power, which continued for more than thirty years. Under Hutu power, the Tutsi were second-class citizens, discriminated against legally and socially, and at times were subject to smaller killing sprees. Although divisive colonialism had left the country, the animosity between the two ethnic groups proved irrepressible.

In response to the ethnic antagonism, the Rwandan Patriotic Front (RPF) formed near the Ugandan boarder. This military rebel force was comprised of Tutsi who fled or were exiled when the Hutu assumed power. In an attempt to regain control, the RPF invaded Rwanda in 1990; this later led many to conflate the genocide of the Tutsi with the previous civil war actions. In 1993, Habyarimana, the Hutu president, responded to the RPF by looking for ways to create a government of shared power and ultimately agreed to a peace settlement. This resulted in the Arusha Accords (also known as the Arusha Peace Agreement); however, this compromise was symbolic and brought neither peace nor agreement to Rwanda. In the years after the Arusha Accords, the Hutu began "practice massacres" against the Tutsi and the politically moderate Hutu. In *The Rwanda Crisis: History of a Genocide*, Gérard Prunier explained that many citizens of Rwanda wore badges or hats with symbols or colors to express their political affiliation. The victims could be identified and easily targeted by the perpetrators because of the visibility of identity in Rwanda before the genocide. Between 1990 and March 1993, more than ten thousand Tutsi were detained and two thousand murdered. This violence was symptomatic of what was to come. In the years before the genocide, the global community, the United States, and the United Nations ignored the red flags that foretold genocidal violence. A mass importation of weapons occurred before the Arusha Accords. According to Power, in 1992, 85 tons of munitions had been gathered, as well as 581,000 machetes, which equaled one machete for every third adult Hutu male. The Belgians and the Polish were aware of the surge in weapons and aided the increase of weaponry, which arrived by the planeload. As cited by Power, a 1993 CIA study found "some 4 million tons of small arms had been transferred from Poland to Rwanda, via Belgium."

The escalating violence captured the attention of the United Nations. In late 1993, the United Nations organized twenty-five hundred troops led by Major General Romeo Dallaire. A small peacekeeping mission was sent to facilitate the implementation of the new government changes, known as the United National Assistance Mission In Rwanda (UNAMIR). The United Nations classified the mission as a "Chapter VI deployment," which allowed for only a cease-fire agreement and enforcement of the peace agreement. Dallaire saw the predicted violence quickly come to fruition and requested an additional five thousand troops to aid him in keeping peace in Rwanda. When the United Nations denied his first request, he relentlessly requested at least twenty-five hundred more troops. On October 5, 1993, the UN Security Council apprehensively approved the appeal and agreed to send troops only to Kigali, the capital city. The troops were there to observe and facilitate the situation, not to seize weapons or take action. The limitation of this approval was a result of internationally related political and military events. Two days before the UN Security Council sent the peacekeepers, the U.S. military was attacked in Black Hawk Down.

The events in Somalia continued to influence the other decisions of the United States. Dallaire appealed to the United Nations and countries around the globe to provide additional aid; in tandem, the Hutu created lists of the citizens they planned to execute. The CIA was aware of all of these details. In January 1994, it predicted the deaths of a half-million people in Rwanda. Much like in the Bosnian crisis, the United State knew of the potential for genocide and decided on a policy of inaction. As did Milošević, the Hutu militia strategized around the ignorance and inaction of the Western powers, specifically the United Nations. The UN retreat created a space for the Hutu to commit murder without any repercussions. Additionally, Power explained, the Hutu paid close attention to the previous decisions to withdraw after increased violence. Because the United States had withdrawn troops in Somalia after the death of eighteen U.S. soldiers, the mutilation and murder of ten Belgian peacekeepers was a strategic attack by Hutu to force the Belgians to pull out.

Although there had been previous civil wars between the tribes, this was not the case in the spring of 1994; the violence was systematic and genocidal. Much like ethnic relations in the former Yugoslavia, the Hutu and Tutsi had intermarried and lived peaceably. Many adults were now faced with the challenge of staying with their families or saving their own lives. Much like in the "one-drop rule" in America before 1967 where one "drop" of black blood made a person black, children in Rwanda were not granted a choice; if one parent was Tutsi, then they were considered Tutsi. For politically moderate Hutu, their political affiliation was considered a death sentence. The situations in Bosnia and Rwanda were not mutually exclusive. The decisions of the United States and the United Nations to approach both genocides as diplomatic issues in need of further negotiations or cease-fire agreements further fueled the imbalance in power in the countries. When applying this flawed approach to Rwanda, policy officials advocated for the Arusha Accords, a peace settlement, to be revisited as a solution to the mass killing sprees.

Within the first twenty-four hours of the genocide, eight thousand people were murdered, the government had fully collapsed into chaos, and the smell of the dead bodies in mass graves was unavoidable. Unlike Bosnia, in Rwanda the United States and the United Nations did not have a clear authority figure in charge of the violence, and in Rwanda the Hutu rebels were not a governing body. The United States pulled out of Rwanda on April 7, 1994 because it feared for the safety of its citizens. The Clinton administration's approach to foreign policy in Rwanda was to distance itself from the issues; or in the words of Senate Minority Leader Bob Dole, "I don't think we have any national interest there." The Clinton administration supported the genocide through the only action it took—the removal of UN peacekeeping troops without the deployment of further reinforcements during the apex of the violence. When the Belgians requested troops be pulled out, Christopher agreed to withdraw completely, as the Belgians cited "insufficient justification" to continue a UN presence. Albright and some African nations at the United Nations pushed for a compromise and argued for at least a skeletal force, if nothing else, to be left in Rwanda. Albright's request was once again the minority voice and the troops were withdrawn. As the Belgians intended, the Europeans countries sent one thousand French, Belgian, and Italian soldiers to Rwanda on April 9, 1994 to airlift the expatriates home.

The removal of the UN peacekeepers was a signal to the Hutu that they would not be held accountable for an increase in the violence. Power described the bloodbath that resulted: "when the peacekeepers had departed through one gate, Hutu militiamen entered through another, firing machine guns and throwing grenades." The majority of the two thousand Rwandans who sought protection were murdered. Within three days, approximately four thousand foreigners withdrew from Rwanda; more than thirty-two thousand people were murdered in four days. The support needed to stop the genocide had boarded the planes and left Rwanda.

In less than two weeks, the death toll reached one hundred thousand and the human rights group Human Rights Watch called on the UN Security Council to appropriately label the systematic murders "genocide." During the week of April 21, 1994, the United States and the United Nations voted to remove 90 percent of the peacekeepers, regardless of firsthand reports of the brutality. Throughout the withdrawal process, and with only a few hundred men, Dalliare attempted to provide protection to twenty-five thousand Rwandans, but the genocidal actions of the Hutu prevailed. Power explained that with the vote to withdraw, the UN Security Council "sealed the Tutsi's fate and signaled to the Hutu militia" that they would have free reign over the region. Within the same week as the vote, responding to pressure from Human Rights Watch, the White House released a statement urging the military leaders of Rwanda to "end the violence." However, actions speak louder than words; the vote at the United Nations and the early withdrawal of American troops nullified the press statement. Sadly, this was the most forceful response to the genocide the United States could muster.

The violence could not be monitored through an embargo. Although there were many misunderstandings about the power dynamic between the Hutu and the Tutsi, members of the Clinton administration and officials at the United Nations did understand that the Hutu were not using traditional weapons. People were reportedly murdered with everyday objects such as bike handles and screwdrivers. As described by Prunier, Tutsi were usually murdered with a machete and their deaths were protracted and painful. The brutal method left the people that did survive with extreme mutilations. Equally "hands off" to U.S. policymakers was radio jamming or destroying antennas to prevent military orders and hate speech from spreading. Although in the case of Rwanda radio jamming or counterbroadcasting was at least considered, it would not have helped to stop the Hutu. The Pentagon had rejected this tactic after a request from a desperate Dalliare. By the time the United States contemplated using these tactics, the death toll was over 112,000.

Eventually, the world community paid attention to the reports from Rwanda and grappled with the term "genocide." On April 27, 1994, Pope

John Paul II addressed the atrocity as genocide, and on the same day, Czech-oslovakia and Argentina introduced to the UN Security Council a draft of a new resolution that would include the word "genocide." During a press conference the following day, State Department spokeswoman Christine Shelly resisted the progress made in calling genocide by its right name and skirted around the term, ultimately embarrassing herself and the Clinton administration. When a member of the press asked her if the situation in Rwanda was in fact genocide, she responded, "the term 'genocide' has a very precise legal meaning." She struggled to clarify any difference between ethnic cleansing, genocide, and the killings in Rwanda. She concluded the government would "have to undertake a very careful study before we can make a final kind of determination." Also, Shelly defended the inaction of the State Department by stating that there was not an "absolute requirement . . . to intervene directly." She told reporters that she was not in a position to make judgments about American opinions or policies.

This embarrassment repeated itself a few months later. In June 1994, the State Department agreed, with Christopher's permission, to use the term "act of genocide" in referring to the killings in Rwanda. In front of report-ers, sounding like a broken record, Shelly did not answer questions regarding the difference between "genocide" and "acts of genocide" and defended her position that it was a legal difference. When pushed by the reporter to answer the query "how many acts of genocide it would take to make a genocide?" Shelly responded, "That's just not a question I am in a position to answer." To understand the worldwide trepidation around the word "genocide," one has only to look at the genocide that was happening in tandem in Bosnia. To address the issue in Rwanda would impact the obligations of the United States in recognizing and responding to the Bosnian genocide, and vice versa.

The United Nations declared that the events in Rwanda fitted the 1948 definition of the term "genocide" by the United Nations Convention on the Prevention and Punishment of the Crime of Genocide (CPPCG). However, the United States rejected this claim on the basis that terming the killings "genocide" would require action from the global community. In the first draft of a response, the Security Council addressed and appropriately labeled the genocide; the final draft released omitted the term "genocide" and instead focused on the term "humanitarian law." The Clinton administration

did not intend to actively participate in the fight to stop the Rwandan genocide. This decision was revealed in a May 1, 1994 Department of Defense
discussion paper, which warned its readers, "Be careful. Legal at State was
worried about this yesterday—Genocide finding could commit [the United
States] to actually 'do something.'" Whether this disinterested position can
be attributed to the fear of another Somalia and the lack of economic profit,
or whether there were underlying racial issues behind the unwillingness to
provide aid to Africa, the Clinton administration chose not to take action to
end the violence. This decision was additionally unsettling because on the
same day as the rejection of the term "genocide," the U.S. Department of
State, Bureau of Intelligence and Research, presented evidence that "no end
to the unprecedented bloodshed is yet in sight."

On May 3, 1994, the United States released "Presidential Decision
Directive 25," which officially proclaimed the distance of the United States
from the situation in Rwanda. The new peacekeeping doctrine stated that the
United States was limited to participating in UN missions; it would support
other nations as they carried out UN missions only if it was in the "national
interest" of America. After the directive on the new approach to peacekeeping was issued, the Pentagon rejected a proposal from Dallaire requesting
the use of radio jamming technology. As Powers reported, the Pentagon
argued this method was "ineffective and expensive." The cost for radio jamming was "approximately $8,500 per flight hour." The Pentagon claimed "it
would be wiser to use air to assist in the [food] relief effort." However, this
relief and aid for refugees never came. As the Pentagon ignored the requests
for aid, UN officials were forced to listen to the murders over a two-way
radio. As in Bosnia, without orders from the United Nations or Washington,
the peacekeepers were helpless to do anything and had to sit back and allow
the genocide.

As the violence in Rwanda escalated, it was apparent to the global community that the violence would not recede. The UN Security Council moved
the deployment in Rwanda from a Chapter VI mission (cease-fire and peace
enforcement) to a Chapter VII mission (hostile environment); the largest
difference being the requirement of resources. As laid out by Power, the
UN Security Council was faced with two proposals. The first from Dallaire advocated for an "inside-out approach." He believed it would be in the

best interest of the global community to deploy an additional five thousand armed soldiers to create safe havens for the refugees (the lesson from Srebrenica had yet to be learned). The second proposal was presented by Gore, Lake, and Richard Clarke and labeled the "outside-in" approach, modeled after Operation Provide Comfort in the Gulf War. In 1991, the original mission provided aid to the millions of Kurds who had fled to the Turkish border. The horrific difference between the Gulf War and the situation in Rwanda was that the majority of Tutsi would be murdered before they could make it to the Tanzanian boarder. Power noted that Dallaire's proposal meant that troops would have to find the Tutsi in hiding and provide them protection and escorted access to the safe zones.

A contrary proposal, supported by Washington, required the victims to find their own way to the safe zones, thereby forcing them to walk into a death trap. Meanwhile, Albright was given strict orders to respond to the situation by arguing that the United States was not in a position to deploy troops to Kigali. The U.S. government, the UN Security Council, and the UN Department of Peacekeeping Operations spent the first two weeks in May negotiating the role of the global community in Rwanda. As the conversations developed, the genocide had already taken almost three hundred thousand lives in less than forty days.

After weeks of negotiations, on May 6, 1994, the Security Council voted on Resolution 918 and for the deployment of 5,500 troops to Rwanda. However, Power explained, bureaucratic bickering between the Pentagon and the United Nations over the cost and transportation of the Armoured Personnel Carriers (APCs) prevented the resolution from being implemented. It was another month before the APCs arrived in Rwanda, and the death toll had already reached nearly eight hundred thousand. In the week after the negotiations with the United Nations, President Clinton restated his foreign policy agenda publicly. This was the first public exposition of the Clinton Doctrine and it did not appear dissimilar than previous administrations. Clinton declared, "whether we get involved in any of the world's ethnic conflicts in the end must depend on the cumulative weight of the American interests at stake." Once again, the United States would not participate in any humanitarian action that was not in America's best national (economic) interests.

Another month passed and the United Nations had still not deployed additional troops to Rwanda. Finally, the Security Council authorized France to unilaterally intervene in the southwest corner of Rwanda. As Power explained, based on France's warm relationship with the genocidal Hutu regime, this was possibly the least appropriate country selected to intervene. When the French forces arrived in Rwanda they created "a safe territory"; however, the Hutu controlled these safe areas. Much like Srebrenica, the Tutsi were murdered in the so-called safe areas. The United Nations stated that it was taking action, but the violence was not subsiding. On July 17, 1994, the Tutsi RPF rebels captured Kigali and forced 1.7 million Hutu government officials and citizens to flee to Zaire and Tanzania. The French quickly ended their mission in Rwanda and the United Nations replaced the French troops with Ethiopian UN troops. However, the additional troops that the United Nations promised to Dallaire were never deployed. In light of the absence of the Hutu leaders, the RPF constructed an interim government. When the RPF gained momentum, Clinton closed the U.S. embassy. Although the killing sprees ended, the refugees continued to die from disease and other complications in the camps. At last the systematic killing of Tutsi had ceased after one hundred days and the loss of eight hundred thousand lives.

After the genocide was over, the president announced that the United States would not tolerate genocide abroad. The Hutu who participated in the genocide or who had fled out of fear of a new government were dying, mostly in Zaire, in refugee camps. Clinton responded to the two thousand Hutu deaths a day by allocating $320 million in emergency relief and requested that four thousand troops provide assistance in the Hutu refugee camps. This occurred weeks after the Clinton administration stated that there was no money or troops available to protect the Tutsi victims of genocide. The Senate approved $170 million contingent on the removal of troops before October 1, 1994. The hypocrisy of this decision, as pointed out by Power, was especially frustrating because the administration had spent one hundred days arguing that it did not have the resources to stop the Tutsi genocide, provide peacekeeping forces, or offer humanitarian relief. The United States spent $237 million on relief for the Hutu refugees, but had refused to budget the $30 million needed in the weeks before to save some of the eight hundred thousand lives.

The United States had several options for foreign policy decisions. Much as in Bosnia and other countries in conflict, the United States typically invoked the Powell Doctrine. Such was the multifaceted nature of foreign policy that labeling mass killing a genocide in one country would impact the approach the United States could take to mass killings in other countries. The United States could have provided aide and assistance to victims of genocide without draining the resources of the U.S. military. The administration continuously cited Somalia as the reason for inaction, but the difference in official responses toward the Tutsi and Hutu refugees demonstrated that the United States did not help the victims of genocide, only the perpetrators. Late in 1994, an attempt was made to hold the Hutu accountable through a war crimes tribunal. In the month after the tribunal, Clinton visited Rwanda and apologized for American inaction. This apology came too little too late, and genocide in the 1990s was not over.

At the end of the decade, Kosovo, the 55-mile-long plateau south of Serbia bordering Albania and Macedonia, proved to be the place and the moment in history when the United States decided to stop Milošević. The intervention was predictable. When Christopher was in office, he made it clear that Kosovo was different from Bosnia. If Kosovo were to be under attack it would impact Albania, Greece, and Turkey, creating waves throughout Europe that would inevitably impact the United States. In 1999, after nearly a decade of failed policies and after allowing a genocidal leader to continue terrorizing, Americans decided they had stakes in the struggle of victimized populations.

The tension between the Serbs and Albanians in Kosovo were entrenched in the struggle for power. The Albanian population had grown to comprise nearly 90 percent of the population in Kosovo. Fighting for jobs, political positions, housing, and a better quality of life, the Kosovo Serbs felt victimized by the disproportionately large minority population. The genocide expert Daniel Jonah Goldhagen theorized that genocidal acts are guided by fear; the opportunity for mass violence occurs when the oppressor's desire for power outweighs the victim's desire to live. This was precisely what unfolded in Kosovo. As in Bosnia, Milošević appealed to the fears of the Kosovo Serbs, tapped into anti-Albanian sentiment, and promised a "better" life for the Serbs. In late 1980, the Serbs diminished the Albanians by legally and culturally stripping them of the autonomy granted them by Tito. A new era began of a heavy police presence and the systematic oppression of Albanians in the public and private spheres.

During the Dayton Peace Accords, the Albanians were eager to be included in the negotiations between the United States and Milošević. However, the settlement was agreed on without autonomy or power restored to the people of Kosovo; in fact, the restoration of autonomy was not discussed at all. Power attributed the rise of the Kosovo Liberation Army (KLA) to the resentment of this exclusionary process and loss of sovereignty. Scholars have speculated that the animosity between the KLA and the Serbs was initiated by a comment from the U.S. diplomat Robert Gelbard, who called the KLA "without any question a terrorist group." Milošević believed this statement to be a declaration of support for violence against the Albanians. Before the end of the year three thousand Albanians were murdered and another three hundred thousand displaced.

The Serbs commonly killed Albanians in groups, specifically by family. When a group of KLA members gunned down a Serbian policemen, Milošević responded by torching villages and murdering over fifty-eight relatives of the KLA member Adem Jashari. Albright, an advocate for intervention since the beginning of Milošević's reign of terror, announced that the United States would not "stand by and watch the Serbian authorities do in Kosovo what they can no longer get away with doing in Bosnia." In March 1998, the United Nations ruled that Milošević's violence in Kosovo would not be tolerated the way it had been in Bosnia. UN Security Council Resolution 1160 condemned Yugoslavia's excessive use of force and imposed economic sanctions and banned arm sales to Serbia. However, as with Bosnia, the extreme violence did not cease. The lack of desire for peace was apparent in a national referendum, which showed 95 percent of Serbs rejected the involvement of foreign mediation to solve the unraveling situation. Despite the torching of villages and the mass murder of Albanian citizens, the United States continued diplomatic negotiations with Milošević and the KLA into 1999.

The United Nations was the first to take action throughout the negotiation process. Months into the violence, the UN Security Council approved Resolution 1199, which demanded a cease-fire, Serb withdrawal, and allowance for refugees to return. In a matter of days, the Serbs violated the resolution. In September 1998, NATO defense ministers took the first steps to launch airstrikes against the Serbs when they permitted an activation warning (ACTWARN) to be issued by the NATO's Supreme Commander. The same week, Albright, who supported airstrikes, pushed the strategy at a meeting on Capitol Hill. However, as with the Bosnian genocide, Albright was a lone voice. The administration agreed to continue negotiations with Milošević, but arranged for no troop deployments. However, on October 12, 1998, NATO approved an "activation order" that began preparations for a "limited" bombing campaign. The approval was ineffectual, as the order was suspended to give Serbs time to comply. Milošević manipulated NATO into extending the deadline to benefit him politically.

The next year saw further policy negotiations with and violence from the Serbs. Albright continued to push for airstrikes and action, but other U.S. policy officials did not support her agenda. In the second week in January, the KLA attacked four Serbian policemen in what became known as the Racak massacre. Serb forces retaliated with extreme force by murdering forty-five Albanians, including women, children under the age of twelve, and elderly men in the town of Racak. U.S. Ambassador William Walker arrived twenty-four hours after the massacre and vocally announced on television that the Serbs had "committed crimes against humanity." Invoking the events of Srebrenica, U.S. policy officials, specifically Madeleine Albright, viewed the massacre as a red flag for genocide. Like the previous mass extermination, Milošević denied the violence and accused the KLA of killing their own people to make the Serbs appear guilty.

At last, in January 1999, the Racak genocide caught the attention of U.S. policymakers. Amidst the trial to impeach the president, the Clinton administration approved Albright's appeal for military action. Some scholars have attributed the change in policy to Clinton's fear of more bad press or further loss of credibility. In February, twenty-five thousand peacekeeping troops were deployed to Kosovo, contingent on the ultimatum that if Serbs refused, a NATO bombing campaign would ensue. As Power noted, this was the first time in world history that the global community came together to stop genocide. The Serbian resistance to a compromise confounded the peace agreement process, especially because the KLA was reportedly ready to negotiate. The decade of Serb violence was wearing on everyone: the victims who managed to survive, the Washington politicians who were unable to achieve change, and the surrounding countries who did not have the resources to harbor any more refugees. In March, the United States made a last-ditch appeal to Milošević to avoid the deployment of airstrikes, but the meeting between legendary American diplomat Richard Holbrooke and the Serb leader ended with no progress or change. Two days later, the airstrikes began.

In retaliation, the day after the airstrikes the Serbs began an operation to systematically eliminate the remaining Albanians, executing much of the population. Serb forces escalated the cycle of violence as a message to the international community. Milošević continued the executions as the United States and European allies worked to intervene and stop the genocide. According to Power, one Albanian reported that the Serbs told victims before shooting sprees, "Now NATO can save you." Needless to say, NATO jets did not deter the Serbs. As the policy strategies evolved over the next two months, the genocide raged on. On the U.S. front, regardless of Clinton's rhetoric, which invoked the Holocaust and compared Milošević to Hitler, he still refused to deploy troops to Kosovo. On May 24, 1999, for the first time in history, the International War Crimes Tribunal announced that Milošević would be charged for crimes against humanity. This declaration made the United States and UN troops fear an escalation of violence.

After a decade of terror and genocide, Milošević surrendered on June 3, 1999. At the conclusion of seventy-eight days of bombing, on June 9, an agreement was signed by the Serbs to remove all Serb forces from Kosovo and fifty thousand NATO peacekeepers mediated the transition to an Albanian-led government. At last, Albanian refugees were permitted to return to Kosovo. Within three weeks six hundred thousand refugees returned to their homeland, the most rapid return of refugees in world history. In tandem, over two hundred thousand Serbs began migrating out of region. When the Serb forces withdrew completely from Kosovo and NATO Secretary General Solana (1995–1999) officially ended NATO's bombing campaign, Clinton visited Kosovo. Clinton was previously criticized for taking action in Kosovo only because the violence would impact the European economy and because after his impeachment the order to act would not affect his political career.

Regardless of the complicated history of the Clinton administration in the Balkans, the president achieved celebrity status among the survivors.

Foreign policy in the 1990s was defined both by inactive policies against genocide and the establishment of America in a post–Cold War world. During the Bush and Clinton years, America was forced to adjust to a new world system of globalization. The apprehension of the Bush and Clinton administrations gave way to the George W. Bush agenda (2001–2009) and a full implementation of the Powell Doctrine in the Middle East. After the terrorist attack on the World Trade Center on September 11, 2001, the foreign policy agenda of the United States became the antithesis of the Vietnam Syndrome. Soon after the turn of the century, the U.S. military began a war over a decade long against Iraq and Afghanistan.

Recommended Reading

For the history of genocide in the twentieth century: the Pulitzer Prize winner Samantha Power, *A Problem from Hell: America and the Age of Genocide* (New York: Basic Books, 2013). For more of a military overview of the decade: the Pulitzer Prize-winning journalist David Halberstam, *War in Time of Peace: Bush, Clinton, and the Generals* (New York: Scribner's, 2002), provides a comprehensive look into the Bush and Clinton administrations. Personal insights are available in Madeleine Albright, *Madame Secretary: A Memoir* (New York: Miramax, 2003); and Colin Powell, *My American Journey* (New York: Ballantine Books, 2003).

5

Prosperity and Poverty in an
Age of Global Capitalism

IN 1848, Karl Marx predicted that the global community would become
a "universal interdependence of nations." This prediction came to fruition during his lifetime with the first industrial revolution and accelerated
throughout the twentieth century as multinational corporations and technology created a deeply integrated world. The new global financial structure
of the post–Cold War era was specifically dependent on the American financial system. This codependence ultimately resulted in the world financial crisis of the early 2000s when the "bubble burst." The story of the 1990s in the
previous chapter began after the collapse of the Berlin Wall and ended with
the terrorist attacks on September 11, 2001; the economic boom and bust
of the 1990s followed the same trajectory. Whereas the 1980s is recognized
for Reaganomics, trickle-down economic policies, and increasing class stratification, the legacy of the 1990s is one of financial gains for stock market
investors and corporations before the second major stock market crash and
economic meltdown that followed on the heels of the first in 1987.

In the 1990s, Wall Street made billions of dollars. The stock and bond
successes of Wall Street and the Silicon Valley technology boom were conta-
gious and seductive. People wanted to share in the prosperity that the newly
wealthy flaunted. Johnson explained in *The Best of Times* that the story of
the boom and bust occurred in two parts. The first was the abundant wealth
of the 1980s that resulted from technological innovations by young entrepreneurs. The second, in the 1990s, concerned "young computer 'geeks'

101

and 'nerds' enjoying the most luxuriant lifestyles after capitalizing beyond wildest dreams from overnight start-up ventures and initial public offerings that left them, still in their twenties, richer than any American before them, richer than their Gatsbyesque counterparts in the Roaring Twenties, richer than those favored few of the Gilded Age in the 1880s." The number of young "technotimes" tycoons increased daily; according to studies cited by Haynes, sixty-four new millionaires were created daily in Silicon Valley. The wealth and success spread to Wall Street and investors. The U.S. economic booms were greater than those of the Gilded Age or any other era in American history. After a decade of waiting for the trickle-down effect, a new and exclusive generation of Americans lucratively capitalized on the American Dream, the technological revolution, and globalization.

The American markets of the 1990s aggressively redefined the global economy in the post–Cold War era. Under the Reagan and Bush administrations, Americans were becoming poorer as the lower classes waited for economic prosperity to trickle down and the country slid into a series of recessions. As Americans grew tired of Washington's focus on foreign policy, Clinton seized the opportunity and redirected voters to domestic fiscal issues by campaigning on the famous phrase "It's the economy, stupid." The Nobel Prize-winning economist Joseph Stiglitz explained in *The Roaring Nineties: A New History of the World's Most Prosperous Decade* that during the election process and the first years of his presidency, "Clinton invited Americans to use the economy as their presidential scorecard," and they did just that. Americans viewed the boom of the economy following Clinton's election not only as a reflection of post–Cold War markets but, more important, as an indication of the capacity of the executive office. Stiglitz affirmed that the New Economy was a promise of the end of the ups and downs of the economy and business cycles. Owing to new technologies, people believed they had control over their inventories and that they held the power to stay on top of the market.

American investors had the power to mediate the markets in the rest of the world and acquire an abundance of personal wealth. In the 1990s, $1.5 trillion in capital per day was moving through New York's markets. As the stock market continued to grow, so did consumer confidence. The rapidly expanding technology and telecom industries appealed greatly to those investing. Although Clinton was clear in his campaign about many economic issues, deficit reduction was not included in his platform; however, when he assumed office, economic reform, specifically deficit reduction, became one of his primary goals. Both the administration and the international community were still formulating economic and political policies to meet the post–Cold War reality. Within a short time, Clinton's agenda targeted deficit reduction and control. Clinton's policy agenda also focused on the deregulation of Wall Street investment firms. According to Stiglitz, "[investors] wanted the appearance of a fair market, not the reality—and for them there was thus the risk that government regulators would go too far." The economic recovery was generous to a specific class of Americans, particularly investors and politicians.

The unparalleled economic growth of the 1990s resulted in an even greater bust when the bubble popped. The bigger the growth, the bigger the collapse, and this time international markets were integral to one another because of globalization. The bust was devastating not only to the United States but to the world as well. Stiglitz noted that the leadership role assumed by the United States after the Cold War encouraged the belief that Clinton could fix the recession and lead America and the world into a new era of prosperity. Although the United States has experienced eras of great wealth, the nineties was the "high-water mark" for the financial sector.

Before the bust, the new wealth and growth of the economy was due in part to the number of available employment opportunities. One of the greatest legacies of the Clinton administration was the fulfillment of the campaign promise to create new jobs in America. Clinton vowed to return Americans to work after the recession and did so for the duration of the decade. Jobs grew at a rate unparalleled in U.S. history. Between 1993 and 1997 in Clinton's first term in office, ten million jobs were created, and in his second term, an additional eight million jobs were created. The rise of jobs meant the decline of unemployment numbers and in 1994, for the first time in two presidential administrations, unemployment dropped below 6 percent. The trend was set for the rest of the decade as joblessness continued to decline. Setting an all-time low for the first time in three decades, in April 2000 unemployment dropped to under 4 percent. In the last year of the Clinton presidency, not only did job growth show miraculous robustness but the stock market also peaked. In the words of Stiglitz, it was as if the stock market was giving Clinton a final salute.

Many economists argued that although the inevitable bust came at the turn of the twenty-first century, the "boom" of the 1990s lasted significantly longer than the booms of previous decades. Internationally, more people invested in American markets. Foreign investments and interest in the growing economy grew exponentially as the market did. The seemingly overnight wealth earned by investors, specifically in "dot-com" investments, was seductive. Globally, people invested in both the American markets and the market structure being adopted by other countries at the urging of the United States. This ephemeral wealth via rising stock values proved detrimental in the new millennium.

The North American Free Trade Agreement (NAFTA) was created after the fall of the Soviet Union when trade agreements internationally began taking new forms. In the post–Cold War context, countries were free to trade with fewer barriers. Under NAFTA, the new laws allowed businesses from Mexico, Canada, and the United States to invest and import with greater ease. In theory, NAFTA should have equally benefited all of its participants; however, Mexico was slighted compared with the profits of the United States and Canada. According to the *New York Times*, between 1992 and 2007, Mexico's economy grew only 1.6 percent per capita on average, whereas America's continued to grow at an accelerated rate. The original legislation was a project of the Bush administration but was implemented under Clinton. NAFTA was a contentious issue during the 1992 election between the candidate Ross Perot and the incumbent administration. Whereas Clinton largely supported NAFTA as it was proposed, Perot famously claimed during a 1992 presidential debate that NAFTA would create a "giant sucking sound" as it drained jobs from the U.S. economy "south" to Mexico. However, as president, Clinton continued to support the bill and negotiated two side agreements, the North American Agreement on Labor Cooperation (NAALC) and the North American Agreement of Environmental Cooperation (NAAEC), to change the bill in an effort to accommodate the concerns of (union) labor and environmental groups.

Beginning January 1, 1994, the agreement removed most of the tariffs as well as the trade and investment barriers between the United States,

Canada, and Mexico. The elimination of tariffs spurred economic growth in the United States. Conducting operations abroad now appeared far more attractive because of the cheap labor and operating costs, and perhaps too appealing, as corporations and companies began exporting labor. NAFTA supporters contended that the removal of taxes between North American countries would help employees as a result of changes in trade; however, this policy change hurt workers because American companies sent jobs abroad and significantly eliminated domestic jobs, especially factory work.

Some of the preexisting trade provisions were incorporated into NAFTA; for example, the agricultural provisions of the U.S. and Canada Free Trade Agreement. The NAFTA implementation process was given a lengthy timeline. Specifically, all nontariff barriers were eliminated; other tariffs were phased out over the course of five to fifteen years. NAFTA created the largest free-trade market to date globally; according to the Office of the United States Trade Representative, "450 million people producing $17 trillion worth of goods and services" were now linked. Globalization made the world smaller through more interdependent economies, and NAFTA created new interconnectedness in North America.

The argument against NAFTA was that it not only hurt other countries, specifically Mexico, but it also damaged the U.S. economy and its workers. The factory jobs exported abroad impacted every industry, including the manufacture of clothing, cars, electronic software, and parts. Studies since the implementation of NAFTA estimate that jobs lost in the manufacturing sector account for 60.8 percent of all employment lost as a result of the new policy. Supporters of NAFTA have stated that the falling unemployment rate under Clinton in the years after NAFTA was signed was tied to the new trade regulations. There is still debate on whether NAFTA fulfilled its covenant to the United States and other countries. Stiglitz asserted in *The Roaring Nineties* that the promises of NAFTA did not reach Mexico. NAFTA legislation continued to expand despite the arguments against the agreement; in May 2000 the U.S. Congress passed a new extension of NAFTA that included the Caribbean nations. As the international community became smaller because of globalization, the economies of the world became more interreliant. The wealth of the United States was dependent not only on American investors but also on other countries that followed the U.S. economic model, which

enhanced American prosperity. However, the interdependence of the financial markets in the post–Cold War era proved detrimental when the "bubble
burst" after the world financial crisis of the early 2000s.

For the last three years of the 1990s, each year saw the collapse of economies in a multitude of countries. Because of the interdependence of financial
markets, the collapse of one caused a crisis in or the collapse of others. In
1997, the Thai economy began the economic crisis that engulfed the world
in a few short years. This was the first indication that the global economy
and global capitalism were fallible. The crisis that was originally blamed on
the management of the Thai economy quickly proved to be symptomatic of
the fiscal structure of the global economy.

The financial crisis spread like an epidemic. Within a few months the
economies in Malaysia, Indonesia, the Philippines, South Korea, Hong
Kong, and China also collapsed. In a flash, the Asian crisis rattled stock markets around the world. In October 1997, the Dow-Jones industrial average,
an index of the relative price of securities, plummeted 554 points, making
it the largest points lost in the history of the stock market up to that point.
Unfortunately, this would not be the last time in the 1990s that it would
plummet hundreds of points in one drop. To cope with the devastation,
trading on U.S. stocks was suspended. Despite pushback from nationals, in
December South Korea requested a bailout from the International Monetary
Fund (IMF). In the hope of ameliorating some damage of the Asian collapse, the IMF approved a $57 billion bailout package. Although the pack-
age helped repair the crisis, it was only a matter of time before other world
economies collapsed as well. By January, Asia's largest private investment
bank in Hong Kong filed for liquidation and the economies of Russia and
Brazil were close to collapse.

In June 1998 the Russian stock market crashed. Clinton understood
the drastic impact and devastation that the collapse of the Russian economy
would have internationally. In an action that was representative of post–Cold
War changes, Clinton promised to support the faltering country and its president. Criticisms against communism were still fresh in the United States,
but the reality was that Russia was suffering more under global capitalism
than it had under communism. The Russian GDP declined 40 percent and
poverty increased tenfold. In the capitalist world market, Russia was heavily

dependent on taxes and exports, but as the Asian economic crisis quickly spread, the Russian economy became even more subject to rapid change and instability.

In June, Japan announced for the first time in twenty-three years that it was experiencing an economic recession. To protect the American stock market and Wall Street investments, the U.S. Treasury, the Federal Reserve, and the Clinton administration advocated for an intervention to stop the collapse of international markets. In June, the United States invested $6 billion to buy yen in an attempt to strengthen the U.S. economy. With Russia desperately needing assistance as well, a month later President Clinton called on the IMF to support and negotiate emergency loans for Russia. Three days later, the IMF agreed to grant Russia an emergency loan package of $23 billion—only because international lenders utilized an emergency line of credit. Russian stocks rose immediately. Although the Russian economy was smaller than the economy of the Netherlands, the crisis still reverberated around the globe.

In 1999, the economic crises in Asia and Russia spread as the economies of other countries plummeted. Seeing the inevitable trajectory, Brazil began to negotiate an $18 billion loan with the IMF. By January 1999, the country was paralyzed by its financial crisis and the currency was significantly devalued. As the year progressed, the desolation of the world financial markets continued. Largely due to the breakdown of the Brazil and Mexican economies, the market in Argentina fell into a recession. By 2000, the Argentinian recession had not subsided and debt reached 50 percent of the country's GDP. At the end of 2000, Argentina had been approved for an emergency rescue package that included a total of $20 billion ($14 billion in IMF loans and $6 billion from other lenders). As the countries around the globe continued to fall into deep recessions, the boom of the 1990s came to a close.

Starting in 1998, the global stock markets hit all-time lows, which deterred investors from investing because they feared to lose more money. Throughout the collapse of the Asian, Russian, and Latin American economies, the United States felt the effects but remained strong, peaking in the last year of the Clinton presidency. As the new millennium began, the U.S. economy remained at record highs and reflected the prosperity of the decade. Americans spent the 1990s dominating the global economy and obtaining massive wealth. The culture of Wall Street and the profits from Silicon Valley and the tech revolution made many investors feel financially invincible.

The inevitable "bust" as a consequence of the "boom" became even more apparent in 2000 when the peaked U.S. economy quickly ascended. When the stock market plummeted, the value of companies was drastically depleted. According to Stiglitz, in two years, $85 trillion was wiped off the value of the firms in the U.S. stock exchange alone. The prosperity and high employment rate of Americans swiftly spiraled downward. From July 2000 to December 2001, over two million jobs were lost and long-term unemployment more than doubled. Whereas unemployment reached record lows under the Clinton administration, it now rapidly jumped from 3.8 percent to 6 percent. In this short time, the income of 1.3 million Americans fell below the poverty line. This loss of income impacted access to health care and other basic human needs; 1.4 million Americans lost their health insurance within a year. The crash of the economy accelerated as President George W. Bush took office. There has been much scholarly debate over the change in administration and the timeline of the recession. Many economic scholars conclude that it is undeniable that the recession began under Clinton and the policy decisions of the George W. Bush administration added momentum to an already crumbling economy.

It was not long into the new millennium that many of the companies that were fundamental to the technology and financial booms of the 1990s experienced crashing stock values, specifically the dot-com companies. The inflated value of the stocks of the technology sector now quickly plummeted. As explained by Walter LeFeber, stocks previously worth $80 were suddenly worth $5. Most important, the investors who had believed they were millionaires were suddenly unemployed and strapped with a bleak financial portfolio. At the beginning of the century, it was apparent that companies were financially vulnerable; by 2001–2002 the crash of the dot-com companies proved to be detrimental to every sector of the economy.

As the dot-com stocks crashed, unemployment spread rapidly. Within a matter of months, the record-low unemployment rate of the Clinton administration had already increased by 50 percent. This mass loss of jobs changed the narrative of prosperity. The consumer confidence that defined the market for tech growth had vanished, and stocks were plunging. Internet and website-based companies collapsed under their own weight, and so did transnational corporations. AOL Time Warner was forced to take write-offs of $100 billion. As Stiglitz explained in *The Roaring Nineties*, this depreciation of value was especially significant because ten years previously, at the beginning of the 1990s, AOL Time Warner and other companies were not even worth $100 billion, let alone able to handle losing that much in value and still survive financially.

In the 1990s, the story of transnational corporations and the technology sector began with growth at an unparalleled rate, invoking images of Gilded Age America and the first Industrial Revolution. The historically distinct American corporation was modified by changes in globalization. The '90s represented a new era of transnational power wherein the sheer size of the multinational corporations was unprecedented. In *Michael Jordan and the New Global Capitalism*, LaFeber cites statistics from the 1980s showing that of the hundred largest "economic units" in the world, including companies and countries, fifty of them were individual corporations and fifty were nations. Throughout the decade, transnational corporations acquired more power as globalization contributed to their size and wealth.

The first Industrial Revolution and the Gilded Age not only paved the way for advances in technology and machinery but also for business ideologies. The executives running corporations in the 1990s took notes from their predecessors; specifically, Phil Knight, CEO of Nike, looked to the legendary businessman and philanthropist John D. Rockefeller as he built his empire. One of the differences between the corporate revenue of the Gilded Age and the end of the twentieth century was the immense reliance on new post–Cold War open markets. Unlike post–Civil War era corporations that were sustained by transactions within the United States, LaFeber notes that the Nikes, Coca-Colas, and McDonalds of the world needed global consumerism to maintain profits. In the 1980s, all American corporations received 80 percent of their revenue from overseas production. For example, in 1996 four out of every five Coke bottles were sold outside of the United States. Globalization, and an increased acceptance of Western culture, allowed these corporations to extend their reach.

Since World War I, U.S. dominance over global capital was exacerbated by technology and Wall Street investment firms. When the Soviet Union fell, many scholars viewed the collapse of the Berlin Wall and the Communist government as the last restriction to global capitalism. American markets were now free to reign and influence other international markets. An era of unchecked global capitalism began. Stiglitz referred to this decade as "the Roaring Nineties"—the decade of megadeals and megagrowth; economic growth began to reach new levels that had not been experienced in a decade. During the 1990s, a person's ability to attach to a transnational corporation or the U.S. market was the key to financial success, and this came with a price. The '90s was a new decade, a new economy, a new global era, and a new technological world. This new world became synonymous with the dot-com investment sphere, transnational corporations, and unprecedented wealth for transnational entrepreneurs.

The new open markets, combined with innovative opportunities for marketing through technological advances, allowed for transnational corporations to expand in pioneering ways. A prime example of this throughout the 1990s wand since was Nike, Inc. The idea for Nike began when Phil Knight was attending Stanford Business School during the 1970s. For a class assignment, Knight wrote a paper laying out his vision for a future track-shoe company whose aim was to enhance athletic performance. As described by LaFeber, Knight calculated that the weight of the average running shoe inhibited runners; by reducing the weight of the shoe by one ounce, he could free the runner of 550 pounds during a mile-long run. After graduation, Knight took his ambitious dream to the next level and collaborated with Tiger Shoe, a Japanese shoe company. The fledgling entrepreneur returned to the United States and sold the shoes out of his car under the company name Blue Ribbon Sports. Nike became a brand name when an employee dreamed about Nike, the Greek goddess of victory, and pitched the idea to Knight. Since Knight's Stanford days, he intended for his vision to transform into a global transnational empire. Within a few years, Nike sold half of all running shoes in the world and by the mid-1990s Nike was a $9 billion company.

The rapid success of the brand was attributed to its recognizable advertising. The "swoosh" logo originated in the 1970s when Carolyn Davis, a design student at Portland State University, was paid $35 to create a logo. As the shoe company began to sell internationally, the wordless "swoosh" logo crashed language barriers that challenged most advertisers. Then in 1988,

Nike added to its cross-trainer ads the slogan "Just Do It." Two more years and a $60 million campaign later, the three words were internationally recognizable. Nike capitalized on the growth of television audiences and the appeal of television ads. The legendary movie director Spike Lee took Nike advertising in a new direction when he made commercials for Nike featuring the superstar basketball player Michael Jordan. The commercials appealed to the audience by making Jordan's extraordinary talents appear effortless. LaFeber explained that Jordan, much like the "swoosh" logo, was an icon that transcended words. Knight had stated, "It save[d] us a lot of time . . . you can't explain much in 60 seconds, but when you show Michael Jordan, you don't have to. People already know about him. It is that simple." By the early '90s, Nike was a transnational corporation whose successes depended on global revenue and mass marketing.

Jordan's international fame epitomized market globalization; the ad campaigns shaped popular culture of the 1990s and brought revenue to his multinational endorsers: his endorsements had a $10 billion dollar impact on the U.S. economy alone. Approximately 5.2 billion in revenue went directly to Nike. Jordan's talent was unprecedented in NBA history. His image in society and in the media transcended race and appealed to people of all ethnicities and classes. At the beginning of Jordan's career, in addition to $3.5 million in Chicago Bulls salary, the star athlete earned $17 million in endorsements. This figure expanded exponentially throughout his career as he collaborated with many name brands and high-profile companies. By the early '90s, Jordan's earnings increased to $25 million a year, though there was little to no increase in his NBA salary. Multinational corporations continued to invest in the iconic player and by 1997 his earnings exceeded $100 million annually. As LaFeber pointed out, the success of Jordan's image and income was a result of the "products of the post-1970s technology." Cable television advertisements allowed Jordan to become a global celebrity and the media impact on U.S. and international popular culture was profound. Companies like Nike came to rely on Jordan's ads to keep their customers loyal to the brand and their profits high.

Although Nike's advertisements were international and appealed to all races and socioeconomic classes, the cost of the shoes was priced for more affluent consumers at $150 or more. In the United States, when new models of the Air Jordans were released people waited in 25-degree weather to purchase a pair. Additionally, there were reports of teens who were killed or had committed murder for a pair of Air Jordans. Within the first four months of 1990, the Atlanta police dealt with fifty robberies pertaining specifically to sports apparel, including shoes. Crimes related to the desire for Air Jordans across the country ranged from robberies to murders of youths. As in other decades, the shoes and clothing were a symbol and barometer of success and financial affluence. As LeFeber explained, upward of 80 percent of the shoes and apparel sold within the United States were not purchased for their "intended purpose" of playing sports; instead, they were purchased for fashion and status.

The wild consumer consumption of Nike athletic apparel and the lengths to which some people were willing to go to obtain them was symptomatic of deeper social issues. The inequality between classes and races created a sense of social exclusion and dissonance for many poor teens as they were flooded with images of expensive athletic apparel that they could not afford. The sociologist Elijah Anderson was quoted in *Sports Illustrated* in 1990 regarding the link between economic disparity, the wave of crimes, and consumerism. Anderson explained that many inner-city kids were not exposed to the same economic opportunities as their white middle-class peers, but held the same desires for these material goods; they were "bombarded with the same cultural apparatus [as the] white middle class." When many young teens and adults found they could not afford the shoes and clothing, they turned to selling illegal drugs to obtain the money, and drug trafficking was complicated by gang-related activity.

Along with the social cost to America, Nike and other multinational corporations' labor choices exacted a price abroad. In the 1990s, a pair of shoes cost Nike approximately $5.60 to make in Asia using native labor and the resell price was anywhere between $70 and $150. The production capacity of the company was enormous. In the early 1990s, Nike produced four million pairs of shoes a year. Five years later, Nike had expanded to ninety-seven international production lines that produced forty-five million pairs of shoes. The following year in 1996, Nike reached a production number of seventy million pairs of shoes. Nike's ability to engage in such intensive production was a result of cheap labor. As LaFeber explained, Nike workers in

1996 were paid $2.23 a day, making Michael Jordan's $20 million endorsement fee from Nike higher than the combined yearly payrolls of all of the Indonesian plants producing the shoes.

The end of the Cold War impacted U.S. and international markets and changed business plans for corporations seeking to employ workers, specifically those in previously Communist countries. The changes in previously Communist governments and state-run economies influenced business contracts. Specifically, Asian countries opened up to employment opportunities sought by capitalist countries, which prompted a shift in many factory jobs from the United States to China. As transnational corporations shifted jobs from the domestic labor force to cheaper foreign labor, Americans lost their positions in U.S. factories. Nike eliminated 65,000 jobs in America. The transference to foreign labor practices allowed the company to pay Asian workers $0.14 an hour. The shift to foreign labor began slowly in the 1980s with non-Soviet countries and expanded when trade embargos against Vietnam were lifted for the first time since the Vietnam War. The wages paid to workers abroad continues to violate labor standards in many counties, particularly in the United States, where the company headquarters are located. Nike paid Vietnam workers $1.60 a day in a country where it cost at least $2.00 a day to eat three meals. Workers faced the dilemma of starving or working the extra hours to be paid closer to the $2.00. Many workers would faint from exhaustion and malnutrition as a result of the working conditions and lack of food.

In the new age of globalization, a venue was created for cultural imperialism to be spread internationally and for labor relocation outside the United States. The use of the word "sweatshop" has become synonymous with poor working conditions, labor abuses, and illegal low-paying jobs. The massive labor abuses of the Gilded Age continued in the United States with the spread of globalization. Although sweatshops existed for the production of a variety of consumer goods, they began as a result of urbanization in the mid-nineteenth century. The sociologist Robert J. S. Ross writes in *Slaves to Fashion* that when ready-to-wear clothing became increasingly popular, the clothing industry underwent high demand for these products, which in turn required more labor. Factory owners remedied the labor shortage by employing sweatshop workers and have continued to do so in the century and a half since.

There are no universally accepted conditions that define the term "sweat-shop." According to Ross, it is legally defined in the United Stated by the American apparel industry as "a business that regularly violates both wage or child labor and safety or health laws." This definition is dependent on the Fair Labor Standards Act of 1938 (FLSA), which establishes a minimum wage and requires premium pay for work over forty hours in one week. The FLSA term emerged from an investigation on behalf of then Congressmen, now Senator, Charles Schumer of New York to further explore labor abuses.

As global capitalism has expanded, so has American investment in lower-wage countries. Corporations determine where to employ labor for their companies based on "global scanning," a term coined by Raymond Vernon. As Ross explains, multinational corporations "systematically searched the globe for the most propitious sites on which to place their production facilities and to target their sales effort." The strategic exploitation of workers for cheaper labor draws on the greatest flaws of global capitalism and globalization: companies target areas where unions are weakest and labor protections do not exist or are rarely enforced, and it is easy for workers to be repressed and forced to accept low wages. In the 1990s, company investments in Asian factories became popular because of the lack of regulations in working conditions and wages, unlike European factories. In 1998, garment workers in Burma were paid approximately $0.04 an hour because of the country's abysmal work standards, whereas workers in Italy were paid $12.55 for the same job but were protected by labor laws. In the 1990s, after the implementation of NAFTA, in order to increase their profits companies stopped investing in developed countries with stricter labor laws.

In 1998, eleven million people worldwide were employed to make clothes. When textile and footwear workers were added to this number, they totaled over twenty-nine million worldwide. The wages of this labor force, as in the example of Nike, are still below the cost of living. A prime example of the abuse and exploitation of workers in the '90s, and now, is the GAP factories in Saipan, one of fourteen islands located in the Commonwealth of Northern Mariana Islands (CNMI). After World War II, the islands became a U.S. territory and later in 1975 they joined as a commonwealth. This commonwealth status placed the islands under U.S. sovereignty and jurisdiction; thus the clothing manufactured there may be labeled "made in the USA" even though the labor practices violate American laws. The island continues to provide an ideal loophole for manufacturers and corporations because it is exempt from many U.S. labor restrictions.

The loophole in labor regulations did not go unnoticed by contractors and corporations around the world. Ross notes that it allowed U.S. markets to exploit "the duty- and quota-free access to the U.S. market." In the 1980s, Korean and Chinese contractors brought workers, specifically young Chinese females, to the islands to work as "guest workers" in the factories. This labor strategy allowed companies to avoid many of the legal issues surrounding the immigration status of the workers; there was an absence of accountability and regulation regarding the immigration status of the workers and worker wages. The manipulation of the laws continued into the new millennium, and as late as 2007 the minimum wage in Saipan was as low as $3.05. Loopholes in the law allowed American companies to utilize and exploit unregulated sources of labor.

From the 1980s to the 1990s, Ross explains, the demographics of the island changed drastically. In the 1980s, there was no garment sector on the island and there were approximately 110 manufacturing employees. By the late 1990s, the island was dominated by the garment-sector factories and the dormitories in which the low-wage workers were housed. According to Ross, in 1999, over forty-seven thousand workers were employed on the island, and of this number, over thirty-five thousand were non-U.S. citizens. The corporations benefitted greatly from the low-wage labor, but not without criticism from human rights advocates.

Changes in U.S. trade policies in the 1990s increased the appeal of sweatshops abroad, but many companies continued to employ sweatshop workers in the United States despite the labor laws. The United States is commonly ignored for its sweatshop labor practices and other human rights abuses. Ross writes that people are not "willing (or able)" to envision the same abuses heaped on contemporary American sweatshop workers, as was the reality with Gilded Age America. The unfortunate reality is that labor abuses are still present. As of 2000, more than 60 percent of the contractor shops in New York City and Los Angeles overtly engaged in sweatshop practices. The U.S. Bureau of Labor Statistics estimated in 2000 that at least 435,000 recorded workers in the United States were vulnerable to sweatshop working conditions in the garment industry. The unrecorded workers laboring in sweatshops can only be estimated, as there is no way to count them precisely. Scholars project that unrecorded workers make up another 20 percent and are primarily sewing machine operators.

It is important to place the domestic employment of sweatshop labor in a global context. Because of U.S. labor laws it is easy to ignore the impact American workers had on the clothing and textile industry. Ross surmised that "if we go back to 1998 employment levels, using the 1998 sweatshop estimate, the United States is the second largest employer of clothing workers in the world (after China). Its 400,000 sweatshop workers, if they were separated in a national economy would be the world's fourth largest mass of clothing workers . . . the estimate of 255,000 sweatshop workers for the year 2000 would place the United States' victims of labor abuse as the eighth largest mass of clothing workers in the world." The labor abuses of transnational corporations and companies are frequently overlooked, especially when the laws on the books appear to protect the workers.

Nike and other sweatshop-based brands were criticized in the late 1990s when activists drew attention to the labor abuses behind the products. As quickly as Nike became popular, many human rights groups spoke out against the corporation and its labor practices. Phil Knight once said that "Nike [had] become synonymous with sweat shops." In 1995, one of the most famous celebrity clothing lines criticized for labor abuses was that of Kathy Lee Gifford, the actress and TV personality. Her Wal-Mart clothing line production used child labor in Honduras. However, she denied allegations from the National Labor Committee Education Fund and other human rights and media groups. The accounts of the sweatshop abuses included fifteen-hour workdays in buildings with little ventilation and surrounded by barbed wire and armed guards. Three years after Gifford pledged to end labor abuses in her clothing line production, she was under scrutiny for the same abuses in El Salvador. In response to her alleged abuses, and those of many other companies and corporations, the Clinton administration decided to take action.

The creation of the Fair Labor Association (FLA) and its "code" in 1997 was a direct response to the Kathy Lee Gifford controversy from the Clinton administration's secretary of labor, Robert Reich. L. L. Bean, Reebok, Kathy

Lee Gifford, and Nike formed a coalition in collaboration with the Clinton administration to address the issues and created a "code of conduct" for their factories. The negotiations to discuss accountability began on April 14, 1997. The coalition of apparel and footwear companies created the "code" to assuage the concerns of cautious and conscious consumers. Part of the incentive for companies to meet the standards of the "code" was the label the FLA would place on clothing and consumer goods to restore the faith of the buyers. The participants gathered symbolically at the White House to sign into action the recommendation for employers and workers. The final suggestions included limiting the workweek to sixty hours and maintaining wages at the legal minimum wage of the country in which the factory was located. Additionally, to create external and internal accountability, the organizations publicly agreed to allow external monitors to conduct surprise visits to the factories.

The FLA did not require overtime work to be voluntary, but it did require the employers to pay "at least regular rates." As most workers in the garment workers' industry are commonly paid per piece, this created another loophole for employers and failed to protect the employees. As Ross aptly stated, "if they fail to meet a quota for the day to make minimum wage, they may be (legally or illegally) required by the employers to work extra time without additional pay." Activists slammed this proposal because it was weak on labor abuses. It all proved to be a public-relations stunt when investigators found that workers were still being mentally, physically, and sexually abused and nothing was done to protect them. The only change that occurred after the proposal was to introduce a new loophole for the owners of the factories and the transnational corporations. In many countries the legal payment for work was not equitable to the cost of living.

Because of criticism, corporations began to make changes, not for human rights protections but for long-term stability between the corporation and its factory workers. One example was the women's apparel giant Victoria's Secret. As Thomas Friedman explains in *The Lexus and the Olive Tree*, the pressure from high-profile antisweatshop campaigns resulted in less consumption of goods and forced companies to take a stand. As pressure grew to hold companies accountable, Victoria's Secret, like many other corporations, turned to domestic labor. However, in this case, instead of employing factory workers, they were exploiting prison labor. In an attempt to appear as if they were supporting U.S. jobs, many companies changed their labor investments from overseas labor to cheap domestic prison labor.

A vast number of companies not only took advantage of new trade opportunities through NAFTA and cheap labor abroad but also prison labor at home. The journalist Beth Schwartzapfel, reflecting on the subcontracted labor of the 1990s in a 2009 article in the *Nation*, wrote that "prisoners in the past two decades have packaged or assembled everything from Starbucks coffee beans to Shelby Cobra sports cars, Nintendo Game Boys, Microsoft mice and Eddie Bauer clothing. Inmates manning phone banks have taken airline reservations and even made calls on behalf of political candidates." As will be discussed later, the utilization of prison workers has a long history rooted in slavery and convict leasing and is a current reality rooted in the war on drugs. Prison labor in the United States has been utilized by corporations, business owners, and farmers or plantation owners for almost one hundred nonconsecutive years of American history, regardless of the language of the Thirteenth Amendment: "Neither slavery nor involuntary servitude, except as a punishment for crime whereof the party shall have been duly convicted, shall exist within the United States, or any place subject to their jurisdiction."

Corporations have invested in prison labor since 1979 when Congress passed the Prison Industry Enhancement Certification Program (PIE). According to Schwartzapfel, PIE provided private-sector companies with an incentive to utilize prison labor as a source of employment. Additionally, states offered "free or reduced rent and utilities in exchange for the decreased productivity that comes with bringing materials and supplies in and out of a secured facility and hiring employees who must stop working throughout the day to be counted and who are sometimes unavailable because of facility-wide lockdowns." In the 1990s, post–Cold War elimination of global trade barriers, opportunities domestically for prison labor, and loopholes in labor laws for continental U.S.-based sweatshops permitted companies unprecedented access to cheap labor.

Later in the decade, the backlash from activists raised public awareness. Consequently, beginning in 1998, the sneaker-manufacturing sector of the U.S. economy declined. Although the decline was partially attributed to the hard work of grassroots activists, it was also largely due to the crash of the international market. In 1999, labor rights activists sued eighteen apparel retailers and manufacturers for human and labor rights violations against workers in the CNMI. The list of violators included GAP, Dayton-Huston (soon to be Target), J. C. Penney, Sears, May, Limited, Jones Appeal, Liz Claiborne, Phillips Van Heusen, Polo Ralph Lauren, and Warnaco. The majority of retailers eventually settled with the plaintiffs for $8.75 million in damages. The money compensated for some of the human rights violations and loss of labor, but did not fix the larger issues.

The growth of the U.S. economy became the template for global capitalism as the American government and market leaders pressured other countries to develop the same policies and structures. The symbiotic and parasitic relationships of the new interdependent world economy were fostered by the new era of merging global capitalism. The post–Cold War economy was built on the concept of promises. Some of these promises were rooted in NAFTA, and other policies presented the hope of new financial and technological expansion. This was especially appealing for the developing countries that struggled to succeed globally with the superpowers: the United States, China, and Europe. As Stiglitz explains, the promise of the new economy quickly gave way to stiff trade barriers and large subsidies, which denied farmers in the Third World access to American markets.

Access to the market was far from egalitarian. From the beginning, developed Western countries were favored and the American economy was the top priority. Stigltiz also notes that there was a strong disconnect between domestic policies in the United States and those designed for Third World countries; they were based on two different economic philosophies. The American government's foreign policy was to put American interests first. This protectionist position was present during the 1990s and was tied to a long history of U.S.-controlled economic and diplomatic relations. The complicated, dependent, and manipulated relationship between global economies, as Stiglitz explains, dated back to the Opium Wars with China. As economies throughout the world collapsed in the second half of the twentieth century, it became evident how codependent the countries had become. The boom and bust cycle was experienced around the world.

In 1995, the structure of world trade mediation created the need for a new organization, the World Trade Organization (WTO). Replacing the General Agreement on Tariffs and Trade (GATT), which had been created in 1948 after World War II, the organization, according to the WTO, "provides a forum for negotiating agreements aimed at reducing obstacles to international trade and ensuring a level playing field for all, thus contributing to economic growth and development. The WTO also provides a legal and institutional framework for the implementation and monitoring of these agreements, as well as for settling disputes arising from their interpretation and application."

The members of the WTO hold the power to enforce trade-rule sanctions and ensure that countries are held accountable and follow the rules. When officials met in Geneva in 1995 and established the WTO, it replaced the seemingly antiquated GATT designed to reduce tariffs and oversee multilateral trading. The most evident difference between the two international organizations was the range over which they had authority. Whereas GATT focused on the regulation of goods and merchandise, the WTO targeted regulation. The technological revolution, along with the growing wealth of Wall Street and the stock market, influenced every area of regulation. The WTO was granted the authority to cover the same scope of activity as GATT, and additionally to cover telecommunications, banking, and intellectual property rights. Initially, at the end of 1994, the same 128 countries that were signed to GATT signed to the WTO; by 2013, the number of countries increased to 158. With a $158 million budget, the WTO was officially in effect on January 1, 1995.

The WTO quickly became a point of contention between labor rights activists or critics of globalization and free trade activists. As stated by the historian Michael Kazin in a *New York Times* editorial, the prosperity of the 1990s convinced many that free-market ideologies and policies could benefit everyone. In reality, the wage inequalities and the collapse of many global markets demonstrated that the promises of globalization were ephemeral. A BBC article concisely listed the four main criticisms of the WTO. First, the organization is too powerful; in effect it can compel sovereign states to change their laws and regulations by declaring them to be in violation of free-trade rules. Second, the WTO is "run by the rich for the rich" and does not provide egalitarian access to trade opportunities. Additionally, the problems facing developing countries are not legitimized. One continuous example is the opening of markets; the developed countries have strategically kept their markets closed to products from poorer countries. Third, the WTO is indifferent to the impact of free trade on a variety of issues such as workers' rights [labor abuses], child labor, and environment and health issues. Last, the WTO lacks democratic accountability. The organization operates so that all hearings and meetings regarding trade disputes are closed to the public and the media. As an opinion piece in the *New York Times* in December 1999 explained, "When one country challenges another's trade practices, for example, the cases are decided by panels of three trade experts whose deliberations are cloaked in secrecy. This is clearly a process that needs to be opened up to public view." This absence of accountability only increased the power of the WTO.

Arguments for the organization typically include the democratic origins of the organization—it is a coalition organization comprised of member countries. However, the reality is that although the organization has democratic roots, it is not egalitarian and some countries have more power and voice than others; specifically, the power of the developed countries overshadows the developing countries. Another common argument in support of the WTO is the impact that it has had on global trade and living standards. The Clinton administration cultivated support for the creation of the WTO, but in the years since has attempted to appease both advocacy groups and the WTO. In his presidency, Clinton promoted an agenda of free trade that was based on the argument that it had supported the boom of the 1990s. However, Clinton later shifted his position because of pressure from activist groups pushing for the enforcement of labor and environmental protections. This attempt to combat labor violations was much like the FLA effort to hold Nike and other corporations accountable: it was simply a political act to quell the contempt.

The arguments for and against the WTO, as well as the dispute over free trade and fair trade, culminated in a protest in Seattle in 1999. The fight between the police and the demonstrators created media images reminiscent of the anti-Vietnam War protests of the 1960s and 1970s. From November 29, 1999 to December 3, 1999, the leaders of the WTO met in Seattle,

Washington, to discuss the agenda of the organization and future trading policies. More than fifty thousand protesters gathered to object to the policies. By the morning of the first day of meetings, the dissenters flooded the streets to bring attention to free-trade policies and global injustice.

The chaos was exacerbated by the lack of preparation by the city of Seattle for such a large-scale protest. The city compensated for its absence of a plan with police brutality and restrictions on First Amendment rights. Within hours, the police and the National Guard utilized chemical weapons, pepper spray, rubber bullets, and clubs against those in the area, bystanders included. In response to security concerns regarding the arrival of the president and the escalation of the protest rally and police brutality, Seattle Mayor Paul Schell declared a "civil emergency" and a "no protest zone" in the twenty-five-square block surrounding the Convention Center. The constitutionally guaranteed right to freedom of speech was ignored by the city as it encouraged the Seattle Police Department, the Washington State Patrol, and the National Guard to enforce restrictions on public gatherings and speech.

On the second day of the WTO protest, over five hundred demonstrators were arrested, in violation of their First Amendment right. As the WTO meetings came to a close, the protests were muted. This was in part because most of the protestors were arrested, injured, or both. After the protests were over, on December 6, 1999, Seattle Police Chief Norm Stamper took full responsibility for the events and resigned from his position. The story picks up again in 2007 when, after almost a decade, a federal jury found the City of Seattle "liable for the unlawful arrests of about 175 protesters during the World Trade Organization meeting . . . in 1999." The jury concluded that the city violated the rights of the protestors, specifically in regard to "unreasonable search and seizure." However, it also decided the city was not liable for violating the right to free speech.

Throughout the 1990s, as trade and investments crossed borders, so too did cultural exchanges. The international financial market that was created by Wall Street in the 1980s and 1990s had permitted American culture and markets to further penetrate the world. Anti-American sentiments were rooted in both the cultural imperialism and economic collapses of the late 1990s. The impact of the fiscal crisis and the Westernization of many cultures fostered resentment in many countries and tension with allies. As Stiglitz describes the "darker side of globalization" in the post–Cold War world, not only were ideas, goods, and services able to move more easily across boarders but violence and terrorism were also able to penetrate. In 1998, terrorist attacks on U.S. embassies reminded U.S. officials just how easily borders could be transcended.

On August 7, 1998, bombs exploded 4 minutes apart at the U.S. embassies in both Kenya and Tanzania. In Nairobi, seventy-four people were killed, eight of whom were Americans, and an additional sixteen hundred people were injured in the blasts. In Dar es Salaam, seven lives were lost and seventy-two people were injured. These deaths were symptomatic of the terrorism that was to follow. The United States blamed the attacks on the terrorist Osama Bin Laden and his terrorist network Al-Qaeda. To retaliate, the United States targeted missiles at what was assumed to be the supply sources for Al-Qaeda in both Afghanistan and Sudan. On September 11, 2001, the most extreme terrorist attack on U.S. soil in recent years reminded Americans of just how easy it had become for terrorism to cross borders.

Recommended Reading

The most comprehensive book on the economy of the 1990s: the Nobel Prize-winning economist Joseph Stiglitz's *The Roaring Nineties: A New History of the World's Most Prosperous Decade* (New York: W. W. Norton, 2003). William LaFeber, *Michael Jordan and the New Global Capitalism* (New York: W. W. Norton, 2002), is an entertaining and engaging analysis of globalization through Michael Jordan and American culture. A specific look at sweatshop abuses is available in Robert J. S. Ross, *Slaves to Fashion: Poverty and Abuse in the New Sweatshops* (Ann Arbor: University of Michigan Press, 2004).

6

Science and Technology

AFTER THE FALL of the Berlin Wall and the collapse of the Soviet Union, the world appeared to become smaller as new borders were shaped or at times became indefinable. This was in part due to changes in technology and science. In the 1990s, the international community was living the technology revolution. Communication systems were evolving and made available to unprecedented numbers of people, granting them access to an abundance of new information on computers, and the Internet expanded at an unprecedented rate. Globalization, the Internet, and other innovations in technology made all borders and boundaries subject to change and breakdown. The rise of the Internet brought with it new dot-com companies, one of the most iconic being Amazon.com, where people could purchase books and consumer products. The online store seemed to erase all limitations and restrictions on what consumers could access and purchase with a click of the mouse. For example, in *The Lexus and the Olive Tree*, Friedman writes that after World War II, the German government banned Adolf Hitler's *Mein Kampf*. In the summer of 1999, Amazon opened up the online bookstore to Germans and for the first time since the Third Reich Germans were able to access the book. So many copies were sold that it skyrocketed to Amazon's list of top ten best-selling German books. Amazon argued that the English version of *Mein Kampf* was not restricted under the censorship laws of the German government. However, outrage from customers eventually stopped the dot-com company from selling it. The German people were able to transcend laws and restrictive barriers through their computers, and people everywhere were similarly liberated from a sense of limitation and

124

inferiority. Thanks to unparalleled technological and scientific changes the world appeared open and connected.

Throughout the 1990s, the Internet shaped communications. As explained by Haynes Johnson in *The Best of Times*, the Internet promised open communication, prosperity, sex, and community. It allowed unprecedented access to information and to global communities. Previous boundaries dissipated and cultural exchanges became more frequent, especially under the influence of Western culture. In the post–Cold War era, countries sought their place in the world and America assumed the role of global leader. As countries became more financially dependent on one another, they formed new relationships. The United States was at the forefront financially, technologically, and scientifically.

The technology revolution of the 1990s that re-created the world began in the Santa Clara Valley in California. Since the naming of Silicon Valley in 1957, there has been a distinct relation between the boom of Wall Street on the East Coast and the technological innovations of the West Coast. The quiet, fruit-growing Santa Clara Valley became the inspirational epicenter for technology visionaries looking to make their ideas tangible. In the late 1950s, cheap land in Palo Alto enticed the entrepreneurs of the technology revolution to settle and establish a hub for the emerging tech culture. As in the Gold Rush of the early twentieth century, technology pioneers flocked there to be part of the technology boom, emerging markets, and culture. As many as three thousand people a month migrated to the previously less inhabited area during the 1950s. The obsession with innovative tech culture laid the groundwork for the rise of Apple and Microsoft and the domestic and global changes of the 1980s and 1990s. Although Microsoft eventually settled further north in the state of Washington, the West Coast proved to be the heart of the new global industrial and technology revolution.

The digital age of the 1990s and 2000s was a direct result of the technological advancements of the previous decades. During World War II the U.S. Army created the first computer, and it was the size of a warehouse. In 1971 the microprocessor was created. The technology revolution was dominated by Microsoft, led by the iconic William (Bill) Gates, and Apple, led by the legendary Steve Jobs. Although the rivalry between the two computer companies is renowned, they could not have grown without each other. Many believed that one company would have to fail for the other to succeed. However, they supported each other throughout their evolution both financially and with software development.

Gates and his longtime friend Paul Allen founded Microsoft in 1975. As a young teenager, Gates had developed computer technologies. He dropped out of Harvard in 1974 to pursue software development. The following year, Gates and Allen started Microsoft. Only three years later, led by twenty-three-year-old Gates, the company had a $2.5 million gross income. The company's first high-profile achievement occurred in the 1980s with the creation of the software product MS-DOS for IBM. Within one year, the new program generated an income of $16 million for the company. MS-DOS represented a larger shift in the technology revolution toward more personalized computer products; the innovative merchandise was designed to fulfill the emerging needs of computer users.

Following the success of MS-DOS, Microsoft launched the renowned Windows program in 1985. The success was palpable in the number of computer users buying Microsoft products for both business and pleasure and in the fortune earned by the company. Within eight years, twenty-five million users purchased the Windows product and Gates was named the richest man in America (and would continue to be for the next eighteen years). Although there were other computer manufacturers, such as Dell and Hewlett-Packard, Microsoft and Windows products dominated the market and culture. Outpacing its competitors, in 1989 Microsoft created Microsoft Office, which included Microsoft Excel, Microsoft Word, and other office programs in one software product. The intention was to make computers and software more accessible for business and pleasure, and the software also made Microsoft number one in office programs. In 1998, Microsoft found itself involved in a lawsuit when the Federal Trade Commission and U.S. Department of Justice sued the computer company for the monopolization of computer software products. Ultimately, the suit was settled and Microsoft emerged without damage.

The other computer giant, Apple, was the vision and collaboration of Steve Jobs and Steve Wozniak, known as Woz. In 1976, the two college dropouts founded their company in a garage in California. In the first year, the two technology pioneers created the Apple I computer, and the following year they produced the Apple II, which remained in production for over a decade and a half. The company remained largely successful during its first years. At age twenty-one Jobs was worth $1 million and by age twenty-five $100 million. The entrepreneur's original ideas revolved around the complexity of computers; he wanted to produce a computer for a person who was not "a hardware hobbyist" and could not assemble his or her own computer. Apple expanded at a rapid pace and Jobs was in need of managerial help. In 1983, he reached out to John Sculley, president of Pepsi-Cola, to join the Apple team as president and CEO. However, in 1985, a boardroom disagreement with Sculley forced Jobs to resign from his own company and he sold all his shares in the company for a bad price.

In the late 1980s and early 1990s, Jobs coped with the devastation of leaving his company by investing in Pixar, an animation studio. Jobs originally invested $5 million in Pixar and assumed a 70 percent share of the company; the employees held 30 percent. Jobs continued to invest in the company until he eventually owned it; this venture paid off when Pixar created movie history. In 1995, Pixar brought in billions of dollars when it created *Toy Story*, the first full-length animated film in history. Jobs saw the potential in the new movie and its impact on the movie industry. He invested his money where he saw a future, and his foresight paid off once again. In tandem with his work at Pixar, Jobs founded NeXT Computer with investments from the former presidential candidate Ross Perot and many Apple employees. The new company proved to be a disappointment, selling only fifty thousand computers, and Jobs eventually sold it to Apple. However, the small company was integrated into technology history when its software became the core of the Mac OSX.

The technology ventures of the 1990s were focused on creating "everyday" accessibility to new software and the Internet. At Apple, this meant designing new models for the computers. In 1990, Apple placed its first "low-cost" computer on the market. The new model intended computer technology to be more user friendly. The following year, 1991, Apple produced its first laptop, the PowerBook. With this addition to the market, Apple became the leader in all models of portable computers. Although Jobs was no longer running Apple, his vision for technology came to fruition. Apple computers succeeded in making technology accessible to individual

users. During a 1995 interview, Jobs reiterated that the innovations of the
technology revolution were focused on access for the common user. Computer companies were dependent on creating new ideas to assist the user. In
turn, programmers were faced with the challenge of creating software to go
with new computers and the developing Internet. Computer software programs became assimilated into the everyday lives of Americans.

Under the leadership of Sculley, Apple faltered. Apple's technological
and financial devolution caused the company to fall behind its competitors,
which created an opportunity for Microsoft to become the world leader.
Jobs returned to Apple in 1997 when it was close to bankruptcy, and he
quickly turned the company around. With Jobs as the interim CEO, Apple
approached the end of the twentieth century with a new dream of where
technology was headed. It was not only Jobs who helped saved the company, but also an investment from his former business nemesis, Bill Gates.
The rivalry between the two companies had been played up since the early
years, and a partnership was unthinkable to loyal Mac purchasers. Gates
invested $100 million into the almost bankrupt company, was granted non-
voting stock, and agreed to make Microsoft Office available for Mac in
following years.

At the urging of Jobs, Apple produced a computer in 1998 that was a
self-contained computer and monitor. At the time, the design and color of
the smaller computers was revolutionary, and it was also the beginning of
an evolution toward smaller laptops and, eventually, iPads. Jobs had always
envisioned a version of the iPad; additionally, he imagined a computer the
size of a book that would be used for communications as well as editing,
note taking, and a multitude of other functions. In his vision, this small
device would replace bookstores, music stores, and telephones and would
meet all of a person's needs.

In the 1990s Apple focused on its computer designs, and as the new millennium commenced it fixated on expanding beyond a company that manufactured computers. In 2000 Jobs returned full time as CEO of Apple while
continuing as CEO of Pixar. The new direction of the company included
penetration of the music industry with the creation of the music-buying
program iTunes and the listening device iPods. The technological success
and the monetary gains from the iPod infused Apple with new wealth and

power, and the company continued to grow. The rise of the Internet was fundamental to the evolution of the computer. In 1999, the introduction of the "AirPort" on computers made the Internet more accessible to users, but also created a new age of Internet and information saturation. Jobs's impact was extensive. For example, inspired by a college calligraphy class he had taken in the late 1970s, Jobs decided to apply innovative font to the computer programs and eventually the new fonts on both Macs and PCs were born. Apple changed fonts and color graphics on computers.

Computer innovations not only revolutionized the technology industries but also the industries around it. As described by the musical artist Will.I.Am, Apple was in the music industry long before iPods or iTunes was created because its computers had long been in the recording studios of artists. Not only did Apple change the recording and selling process of the music industry, but it also eventually permeated every aspect of all sectors of society. Apple and Jobs together revolutionized the computer, music, motion picture, and telephone industries.

At the end of the 1990s, when the stock market peaked before its crash, Gates' personal fortune from Microsoft exceeded $101 billion. Whereas most entrepreneurs of the technology revolution looked to the tycoons of the Gilded Age for their business plans, Gates also looked to John D. Rockefeller and Andrew Carnegie for their philanthropic efforts. Gates' legacy was secured not only in his contributions to Microsoft and the technology revolution but also in his commitment to charity. In 1994, Gates and his wife, Melinda, created the William H. Gates Foundation with $94 million and a mission for global health and the community needs of the Pacific Northwest. As the foundation grew, in 1997 a sister project was added to the Gateses' charitable agenda: the Gates Library Foundation. The project provides free computer and Internet access in public libraries. This outreach initiative reflected the Gateses' commitment to information access and the beginning of a shift in culture. Information was increasingly placed on the Internet and, as Jobs had anticipated, there was a societal push away from traditional libraries, bookstores, and music stores. The following year, the foundation exhibited its commitment to public health issues when it used $100 million to create a new philanthropic endeavor, the Bill and Melinda Gates Children's Vaccine Program. Before the close of the century, Bill and Melinda

Gates expanded their commitment to public health by funding issues pertaining to globalization, specifically AIDS. In 1999 the foundation created a $750 million grant to "accelerate the delivery of life-saving vaccines to the world's poorest children." Additionally, it presented the International AIDS Vaccine Initiative (IAVI) with a $25 million grant that allowed for development efforts to more than double. This is the largest charitable gift that has been donated to date to combat AIDS. Addressing disparities in education, the couple gifted a $1 billion dollar scholarship fund to the United Negro College Fund with the intention of increasing diversity in higher education and fostering a new generation of leaders. Moving into the next century, the philanthropic organization changed its name to the Bill and Melinda Gates Foundation.

Apple and Microsoft evolved differently, in a manner that no doubt was influenced by the personalities of the founders: Jobs was charismatic or "cool," Gates was "geeky." Apple looked to the future, whereas Microsoft grew in smaller increments, focusing on each step along the way. Jobs succumbed to cancer on October 11, 2011, and although the visionary's life was cut short, the company still produces products across every sector and sphere of society. As Jobs prophesized in 1995, the Internet changed everything because it did not belong to either company and it held unlimited and untapped potential for communication and consumerism. Jobs knew consumerism would be changed by the Internet through direct accessibility and by tailored customer service. Jobs also correctly believed that the technology revolution and the creation of computers was a special moment in human history. The legacies of each company continue to be far from over as the technology revolution continues.

As computer capabilities improved and the Internet became increasingly available, software programs sought to facilitate easier access for users, specifically through Internet search engines. The most influential of these was Google. In 1995 Larry Page, a University of Michigan graduate, visited Stanford and met the graduate student Sergeu Brin. During the school year, the two computer science graduate students collaborated on a new search engine. Subsequently, BackRub launched in February 1996 and operated on the Stanford servers. After a year of success, the two rebranded the company and named it "Google." Based on the mathematical term "googol," they wanted their search engine name to convey the idea of an infinite amount of accessible information. In 1998, the search engine improved when they received a $100,000 check to incorporate the company, becoming Google, Inc. Reminiscent of Apple's founding a few decades earlier, the young entrepreneurs worked out of a garage in Silicon Valley. By the end of the year, Google was recognized as one of the top hundred websites of 1998. As it expanded, again much like Apple, Google moved out of the original garage space to a new office in Palo Alto. In its first year, the company employed eight people. In 1999 Omid Kordestani, the first employee to be hired as a computer engineer, instead focused on sales, marketing strategies, and branding the company.

Google understood that to reach all potential audiences, and to best serve those using the search engine, more languages had to be made available. In the new millennium Google added fifteen languages, including French, German, Italian, Swedish, Finnish, Spanish, Portuguese, Dutch, Norwegian, Danish, Chinese, Japanese, and Korean. By 2000 Google was the world's largest search engine and created the first billion-URL index. Google changed how people browsed the Internet and digested information. By 1998, three million domains were registered on the Internet and it was estimated to be growing by 1.5 million web pages per day. The following year, there were over five million domain names and approximately one hundred million computers were connected to the Internet. The Internet generated its own economy because of online stores and job growth. In 1999, the Internet was responsible for the creation of 2.3 million jobs and over $507 billion in revenue. Given the vast amount of data available by "googling" for information, Google changed the world and provided a new culture of oversaturation.

Cable television also allowed viewers to access vast amounts of information. In the 1950s, only three major news organizations existed in the United States. By the 1990s, hundreds of channels were available and each station reached tens of millions of viewers, creating a world audience of billions. This was an ideal opportunity for advertising and companies that were looking to reach large groups of a specific demographic quickly and efficiently. Information in the uncharted era of transnational corporations and technology allowed for news conglomerates to monopolize mass communications.

The technology revolution of the 1970s transformed every facet of society. Communication mediums evolved not only because of increased access to information but also because of accessible devices. The world went from an analog to digital. Telephone communications changed with the rise of cell phones and the first steps toward the creation of "smart phones." Jobs envisioned a device that would "do everything," and his idea was beginning to have results. In 1999, when the Blackberry phone hit the market, it functioned only as a two-way pager; however, within a few years, it was the leading phone for business professionals with functions including e-mail, text messaging, web browsing, voice communication, and even faxing capabilities. The phone provided stability and organization for workers and included calendars, address books, and even the ability to access programs such as Microsoft Office. The technology for hands-free devices for the phone, such as Bluetooth, began to be developed in the late 1990s as communication applications were becoming increasingly mobile. These advancements would not hit the markets and be placed into phones until the early 2000s, but a new society was already taking shape. Within a decade, phones would become a societal lifeline for communication and interpersonal relationships.

As online research and the collection of scientific information became more accessible, research projects flourished. During the 1990s, many scientists and geneticists focused on the Human Genome Project, which aimed to determine the sequences of the human genome. DNA is comprised of four types of units called nucleotides; combinations of these four types of units make up approximately three billion base pairs, which are located in the twenty-three pairs of chromosomes inside the nucleolus of the cells in the human body. From the beginning, those working on the project understood that they were developing additional tools to understand and combat destructive human diseases, discover new solutions or cures, and uncover preventative measures. The Human Genome Project had important social implications for DNA discoveries and for the issue of biological determinism (biologism), specifically around issues of race.

The idea of mapping human genes began in the mid-1980s. By 1990, the U.S. government had bought into the idea and had launched a $3 billion dollar project with a fifteen-year timeline. The collaboration of the National

Institutes of Health (NIH) and the Department of Energy, along with many other international partners, sought to sequence the three billion letters (or base pairs) in the human genome that create a complete set of DNA. As described by Dorothy Roberts in *Fatal Invention: How Science, Politics, and Big Business Re-create Race in the Twenty-first Century*, "the genome project was cheered as the Holy Grail that would disclose all the secrets of human life. It was supposed to reveal what it meant to be human." The project originated in 1953 when the molecular biologist James Watson, along with the geneticist Francis Crick, discovered and defined the double helix structure of deoxyribonucleic acid (DNA). Watson championed the Human Genome Project from 1990 to 1993, until he unpredictably resigned. President Clinton replaced the world-famous geneticist and Nobel Prize winner with Francis Collins.

Scientific progress on the genome project created international competition to remain on track with the timeline or complete it sooner. By 1994, scientists established the first thousand bases of the human DNA sequence. The struggle to find the complete set of DNA continued throughout the decade and a significant breakthrough occurred in the new millennium. The project came close to completion on June 26, 2000, when a draft version of the genome sequence was presented to President Clinton from Collins and his colleague Craig Venter. The Human Genome Project not only spelled out the complete human genome sequence but also concluded that all humans, regardless of race or gender, are more than 99.9 percent the same. Collins explained that this evidence showed that race had no scientific or genetic basis and was purely a social construct. This information became public and the first draft of the genome sequencing was published in February 2001. Fifty years after Watson and Crick originally described DNA, the quest for the sequencing was declared complete. In 2003, with the help of twenty global institutions, the project was accomplished, under budget and two years ahead of schedule. The new data changed how people viewed the human body, human evolution, and race and sex. Improved Internet access enabled both researchers and the public to access the revolutionary data.

Questions regarding race and biological inferiority had plagued the genome project. In American history, science had often been used to rationalize offensive narratives of race, gender, and class, and thereby create social hierarchies based on false categories. The new information proving the similarities between human beings created an opportunity for new discussions around racial equality. As Dorothy Roberts explained in *Fatal Invention*, the information came after the race riots in Los Angeles and during debates over affirmative action. The completion of the genome sequence thus had a profound impact on science and on social questions of race.

Since the early 1900s, stem cells have been researched and subject to experiments. According to the University of Maryland Medical Center, a stem cell is "a generic cell that can make exact copies of itself indefinitely . . . [and] has the ability to produce specialized cells for various tissues in the body, such as heart muscle, brain tissue, and liver tissue. Stem cells can be saved and used at a later date to produce specialized cells, when needed." During the 1990s, as stem cell research made unprecedented strides forward, cloning became a politically and socially charged issue.

The debate over cloning was heard by the Supreme Court in the 1979 case *Diamond v. Chakrebarty*. The Warren E. Burger Court (1969–1986) in a 5-4 decision concluded that a genetically engineered new bacterium is a patentable material because it is not created or found in nature and is an artificially engineered microorganism. This was approval from the Supreme Court to continue exploring cloning and stem cell research. The idea of cloning humans gained momentum in 1993 when the first human cells were cloned from cells of defective embryos. The following year, the first U.S. clones of calves were engineered from early embryo cells.

Advancements in technology and science, specifically cloning, occurred in tandem internationally. In 1995 in the United Kingdom, Dr. Ian Wilmut and Keith Campbell cloned the first sheep from embryo cells. The following year Dolly was born in Scotland, the first mammal to be cloned with DNA from an adult animal cell. Dolly (named after Dolly Parton) was created in a test tube, and after six days in the tube with normal development, scientists moved the newly development embryonic cells to a surrogate sheep. Ultrasounds confirmed the surrogate's pregnancy was progressing with no complications. On July 5, 1996, Dolly was born and was genetically identical to her mother, but had no father. This was the first nuclear transfer of adult cells, one of the greatest scientific breakthroughs of the twentieth century.

As the information about the cloning became public, ethical debates pertaining to the cloning of both animals and humans became prominent. In 1997, scientists at the Oregon Regional Primate Research Center took DNA from developing monkey embryos and cloned two Rhesus monkeys, Neti and Ditto. Meanwhile, in the United Kingdom, Wilmut's team of scientists genetically engineered another cloned sheep, but inserted human genes into every cell in her body, further perpetuating the debates over the ethics of cloning. The experiments in cloning had the potential to radically change the natural evolution of species as scientists developed clones of clones. In 1998, Ryuzo Yanagimachi of the University of Hawaii and his team of scientists created multiple clones with mice using nuclear transfer. With this new technique, the team generated three generations of mice. The potential for cloning was seemingly limitless. Scientists used nuclear transfer to save an endangered species of cattle in New Zealand by replicating the cattle. Examples such as these perpetuated the debates over the ethics of cloning and the positive and negative potential of the science. Experiments inevitably turned from animals to humans.

The concerns over human cloning were brought to the forefront in 1998 when a group of scientists investigated repair cells and determined that they could expand human life by as much as 40. Researchers were interested in the question of how long cells could be stored for later cloning. Dr. Xiangzhong Yang answered this question when he successfully cloned frozen cells from Japanese bulls. The direction of research was in exploring the potential uses of stem cells of monkeys and humans. In September 1999, Tetra, the first cloned monkey, was "born." Although monkeys were cloned a few years earlier, Tetra was the first clone produced by "embryo splitting"; consequently, the new monkey clone was the closest in genetic cloning to that of a human. This inevitably spurred further debates over the ethics of cloning and related scientific developments. Scientists working on the project were enthusiastic about the ability to split embryonic cells and create a clone because it would give them the opportunity to test medicines and cures on identical beings. There was now great hope for curing diseases. Given the close genetic link between Tetra and humans, researchers were hopeful that embryo splitting could lead to a cure for HIV/AIDS.

The new technique made many believe that human cloning would happen in the near future. The decade ended with no announcement of successful human cloning, but developments in cloning continued and some of its consequences made the headlines. A few years after Dolly's birth, she showed signs of premature aging and was eventually euthanized because of her failing condition. Scientists attempted to modify this genetic flaw. In 2000, a group of cows were cloned and over the course of their development continued to display healthy and youthful cells. All of the cows were cloned with nuclear transfer, and scientists were unable to explain the phenomenon that the cows were demonstrating cells that lived twice as long as normal cells. The new millennium began with both ethical questions and enormous potential for cloning and disease cures.

Changes in science and technology led to scientific breakthroughs in medicine, specifically for HIV/AIDS. AIDS had devastated communities for a decade, especially in New York City, with no cure or hope in sight. In 1990, the FDA approved AZT, the first drug to combat the illness, including doses for children, who were now being diagnosed with AIDS. Along with the approval from the FDA, two high-profile cases brought the AIDS pandemic into the spotlight. Ryan White was diagnosed with AIDS at age thirteen and was recognized nationally when his mother fought for his right to attend school. His death in 1990 brought with it the Ryan White CARE (Comprehensive AIDS Resources Emergency) Act. The program successfully provides assistance and services to those living with the virus who do not have sufficient health care coverage or access to resources.

Historically, individuals living with HIV/AIDS have been subjected to stigmatization, homophobia, and discrimination. When the basketball legend Earvin "Magic" Johnson announced in 1991 that he was infected, he put a new and famous face to the virus and brought attention to AIDS advocacy. The celebrity used his diagnosis to bring light to the HIV/AIDS community and its struggles. Johnson's celebrity status underscored the reality that AIDS was wreaking havoc on all communities across America and the world, irrespective of age, race, sexual orientation, or socioeconomic status. The virus crossed international borders and impacted all demographics, making any progress for better treatment and a cure significant. In the 1990s the United States had much higher rates of infection than other less affluent countries. In 1992, in the United States, AIDS was the number one cause of death in males aged twenty-five to forty-four; by 1994, it was the leading cause of death for all Americans aged twenty-five to forty-four.

Before the development of effective drugs, when an HIV/AIDS diagnosis was made it was considered a death sentence. Clinton took action to prevent the spread of AIDS when he established the White House Office of National AIDS Policy (ONAP) in 1993. By 1997, more than three million people were newly infected with the virus, which proved to be the peak number of those infected with the virus. At the height of the epidemic, the Clinton administration announced that finding an effective vaccine for HIV within ten years would be a national priority. In addition to the work on the Human Genome Project, the National Institutes of Health developed an AIDS vaccine research center. Testing of the vaccine started on humans in 1999. Developments in HIV prevention at the end of the decade also focused on needle exchange programs. The U.S. Department of Health and Human Services supported the effective program, which studies showed did not encourage the use of illegal drugs. However, the Clinton administration remained committed to banning the use of funds for the program.

Policy decisions regarding HIV/AIDS reached the Supreme Court in 1998, when the Rehnquist court examined the Americans with Disabilities Act and ruled to protect citizens living with the early stages of the HIV virus. However, the court ruled against protecting citizens who have advanced AIDS. By 1999, HIV/AIDS was the fourth largest killer of all people globally. Medicine was available, but a cure for the disease was not. Thirty-three million people were coping with the virus, and it was estimated to have taken the lives of over fourteen million people.

As the virus sufferers accessed medication and education campaigns spread, people were able to better protect themselves from contracting HIV and cope with the consequential illness. The entertainment media also brought the illness to light. In 1993, Tom Hanks starred in the movie *Philadelphia*, based on the true story of a lawyer living with AIDS. Tony Kushner's play *Angels in America*, later to become an HBO miniseries, won both a Tony Award and Pulitzer Prize for drama. The most notable death from AIDS was that of the MTV's *Real World* star Pedro Zamora. Whereas Ryan White's death had policy implications, Zamora's death shook pop culture and teen and young adult viewers. The disease was still highly stigmatized, but now social norms began to change and medicine began to offer new opportunities to stay alive.

It is important to note that globalization shaped advancements in medicine at a cost. In the 1980s, in response to requests from the Food and Drug Administration (FDA) to present research and clinical data on new drugs being considered for approval, pharmaceutical companies moved drug studies, including those related to HIV/AIDS, to developing countries because the testing required for FDA endorsement was less rigorous there than in the United States. These evasive practices have existed for decades without much exposure.

The process to find a successful drug to combat HIV/AIDS has a complicated history, and the clinical trials conducted abroad are usually not discussed. In the 1990s, both the NIH and the Centers for Disease Control coordinated nine clinics in developing countries to test HIV-infected women to observe the transmission between mother and child. Although the drug cut transmission by 70 percent, some women were still given the placebo. Much like the ethical concerns regarding cloning, the deliberate withholding of a beneficial drug from HIV-infected women spurred many heated polemics about the ethics of drug testing for profit. The drug studies wreaked havoc on Nigerian communities in 1996. Over fifteen thousand people died in a widespread epidemic of bacterial meningitis. At the time, Pfizer, the world's biggest drug company, was coordinating the largest pharmaceutical study ever conducted in an attempt to obtain evidence for the antibiotic Trvovan. In 2006, the company was found responsible for violating international law when it illegally tested an unapproved drug on children with brain infections.

In the early 1990s both the Clinton administration and Congress had promised to enact measures to curb the rising cost of prescription drugs and end the legislative loopholes for pharmaceutical companies, but the lobbying power of those companies compromised the proposed accountability measures. At the end of the decade, reports revealed that drug companies spent approximately $256 million for lobbying in addition to $100 million in political and advertising contributions. The tactics of Big Pharma of course influenced the U.S. legislative agenda and hampered efforts to lower the cost of generic drugs. Globalization and technology impacted how drugs were tested and where they were purchased. The rise of the Internet also changed how people purchased and consumed pharmaceuticals. Companies on the Internet earned greater profits when buyers purchased online rather than in store pharmacies.

In the 1990s, technological innovations revolutionized not only mass culture and social institutions but also space exploration. In the decades before the 1990s, U.S. space exploration was largely defined by competition with the Soviet Union. The context changed when the United States emerged as the lead superpower of the 1990s. The greatest space development during the 1990s was the Hubble Space Telescope Program, comprised of a coalition of international space agencies including the National Aeronautics and Space Administration (NASA) and the European Space Agency (ESA). The creation of the Hubble Space Telescope (HST) was a decade in the making; on April 25, 1990, the HST was deployed into space.

The HST program was unique for its long-term timeline and its mission to create snapshots of space. The HST orbits the earth at 17,500 miles an hour and takes pictures with three cameras, two spectrographs, and fine-guidance sensors, allowing scientists to explore the solar system through pictures. The technological developments of the second half of the twenty-first century allowed HST cameras to take clear pictures undistorted by the earth's atmosphere. According to NASA, in the first twenty years after deployment, the HST "made more than 930,000 observations and snapped over 570,000 images of 30,000 celestial objects." Space exploration experienced another landmark event in 1997 when NASA's Pathfinder landed on Mars, the first major landing since 1976 and the first time a space rover reached another planet successfully. The rover, named Sojourner, used advances in Artificial Intelligence to navigate around obstacles on the planet. This landing launched the next era of interplanetary exploration.

Virtual life flourished during the 1990s. The digital age created a virtual world through the Internet wherein people received an overabundance of information and felt as though they had the world at their fingertips. The shift from analog to digital was part of a larger shift wherein users conducted their lives on computers and smartphones. Newspapers and other print sources suffered extensive losses in the twenty-first century as information became available online. Copyright issues concerning both information and music now came to the fore. With the ability to search and access almost an infinite amount of information, new copyright infringement laws were developed to accommodate the change in technology. In 1999, the eighteen-year-old college student Shaw Fanning created a computer code called Napster that allowed for file sharing, specifically of music, through a centralized server. Anyone could now download any song for free. The legal response from the music industry shut down the program, but Apple was able to capitalize on the market opportunity and created iTunes for a profit.

The creation of Napster is indicative of a larger cultural shift in the 1990s that resulted from radical innovations in technology and communications. The oversaturation of information and the desire for instantaneous gratification resulted from the quick pace at which the Internet was able to return data to the user, and with peer-to-peer sharing users now exchanged files around the world with the click of a button. The rise of the Internet and globalization revolutionized communications and social life.

Recommended Reading

Dorothy Roberts, *Fatal Invention: How Science, Politics, and Big Business Re-create Race in the Twenty-first Century* (New York: The New Press, 2012), addresses race and science. Haynes Johnson, "Book One—Techno-times," in *The Best of Times: The Boom and Bust Years of America before and after Everything Changed* (Orlando: Mariner Books, 2002), gives a detailed account of the technology revolution of the 1990s.

7

Pop Culture

MAINSTREAM ENTERTAINMENT in the 1990s reflected the changing political climate and the rising economy. Popular culture embodied the progressive changes made as a result of Stonewall, affirmative action, and Geraldine Ferraro's campaign for vice president, and it echoed the social stratification that resulted from Reaganomics. The mainstream acceptance of MTV, grunge music, and hip-hop allowed singers to voice anti-establishment beliefs and rant about police brutality. Pop culture in the 1990s represented an integration of the social issues of marginalized communities into mainstream entertainment.

In the late 1980s and early 1990s, the pop musicians topping the charts included Whitney Houston, Paula Abdul, Michael Bolton, and Janet Jackson. The popularity of boy bands, especially New Kids on the Block, waned as youth began listening to grunge and gangster rap. In the late 1980s and 1990s Seattle, Washington, became the music capitol of the United States and an epicenter for grunge music. The "Seattle Sound" took America by storm and represented a paradigm shift in the evolution of rock music; the new sound forever changed the Billboards, the "go to" music publication for the entertainment industry that provides information on innovations in music and what is popular. With the addition of Nirvana to the music charts, grunge music had taken over the softer sounds of pop. The sound of the group Nirvana was influenced by front man Kurt Cobain's love for the Beatles and the increasingly mainstream rise of bands like R.E.M. Twenty years later, the TV personality Jon Stewart commented that their second album, *Nevermind*, sounded like "the Beatles had swallowed Black Flag [an iconic hardcore punk band].” Grunge music impacted all aspects of pop culture through MTV and the integration of grunge into fashion—both on the New York City runways and in high schools across America. In January 1992, six months after the release of Nirvana's second album, a symbolic and epoch-making event occurred when *Nevermind* reached number one on the Billboard charts in 1991 and replaced Michael Jackson's *Dangerous*. The pioneers of grunge replaced the king of pop and the musical context of the 1990s was formed.

The music created by Nirvana and other artists in the grunge movement was influenced by the financial reality of the early 1990s. The Reagan administration had sold the country on Reaganomics, a new American dream that offered wealth and prosperity to all. The impact of Reaganomics on the working class was felt across the nation and into the Bush administration. Cobain's hometown of Aberdeen, Washington, a logging town, experienced the hardships facing the majority of working-class Americans. As the economy failed under President Bush, the experiences of the young men of Nirvana were shared by the new generation coming into adulthood during the recession of the 1990s. Courtney Love, Cobain's wife and a singer in the band Hole, commented on the rise of grunge music that it was generation specific and “people over the age of thirty-two aren't meant to understand this.” The music of Nirvana and the other grunge bands took their cue from the rock and roll bands before them and used uncensored lyrics to express their frustrations with love, loss, and conservative values. Although Cobain was never comfortable with mainstream acceptance of *Nevermind* and *In Utero*, Nirvana's fan base grew as angst-ridden teens found their anthem.

Nirvana had achieved visibility nationally via its lead role in grunge music and its first album, *Bleach*. *Nevermind* was released with much hype and anticipation from fans. The most iconic song, “Smells Like Teen Spirit,” is recognized as one of the most important pieces of music ever written. The title came from Kathleen Hanna, a singer in the feminist punk band Bikini Kill. After a long night of spray-painting the building of an anti-abortion center and too much drinking, Hanna graffitied the wall of Cobain's rental apartment. When he called her six months later, he asked if he could use the words “Kurt smells like teen spirit,” which she had scrawled on the wall, for a new song he was working on. It was not until after the song was on the charts that Kurt discovered that Teen Spirit was a popular girl's deodorant. The song, as well as the rest of the album, represented a culture shift in America in reaction to the Reagan ideology of the 1980s.

When the idea for a music television station that would play music videos around the clock was first pitched in the 1980s, many believed it was set up to fail. By the middle of the 1990s, MTV (Music Television) had influenced music, television programming, the film industry, fashion, sports, race, teen sexuality, and politics. The wide-ranging impact of the new cable channel began in August 1981, but some of the most defining moments in popular culture in the late twentieth century occurred in the 1990s. Craig Marks and Rob Tennenbaum write in *I Want My MTV: The Uncensored Story of the Music Video Revolution* that the creation of the channel "signified a transition era when the biggest rock stars were bands that transformed public consciousness, to one where technology filled that role." MTV was a cultural ambassador for the youth generation of the 1980s and 1990s.

Previous to the rise of MTV, videos were live performances that had often been recorded at concerts. Any special effects were part of the original performance, and the subsequent videos were not filled with fast-paced depictions of sexuality, violence, or a story narrative. As Andi Zeisler explains in *Feminism and Pop Culture*, preceding the era of music videos, television narratives seemed to take place almost in real time, conversations were slow and even paced, and plots moved sequentially from event to event. Although music videos originated in the 1930s, MTV revolutionized the way in which teens and young adults processed mainstream culture, counterculture, and technology. The unapologetic videos of pop stars reinvented the consumption of music and the marketing industry.

Music videos were the most integral part of the growth of music in the 1980s and 1990s. Steve Isaacs, former MTV VJ, commented in *I Want My MTV* that he felt as though, "my generation had its moment, and MTV was depicting it." Specifically, Nirvana's first video with an iconoclastic theme aired on MTV and set a new precedent for music videos. Samuel Bayer, the musical and video director for "Smells Like Teen Spirit," took on the video as his first project. In *I Want My MTV*, Bayer explained that the video immediately made his career and that high-profile musicians, including Ozzy Osbourne, Johnny Lydon, and The Ramones, requested that their videos be "imitations of Nirvana." The video director Kevin Kerslake reiterated the sentiments of Bayer and asserted, "'Teen Spirit' crossed the Rubicon." Nirvana became the band to emulate in the way that the hair metal band Poison had been in the 1980s. The Nirvana video served as a model for success for other aspiring bands.

The overwhelming number of musician deaths in the Seattle music scene during the 1990s resonated across the country. Chuck Klosterman described Seattle during the 1990s as America's elephant graveyard for rock stars. Many artists died as a result of drug overdoses, specifically heroin use; some are believed by fans to have been murdered. On April 8, 1994, Kurt Loder of MTV News announced that Cobain was dead. Although the autopsy determined that the singer died on April 4, his body was not discovered until four days later when an electrician found him dead, a shotgun wound to the body and heroin beside it, in the greenhouse of his home in Seattle. The initial worldwide responses to the death varied. Some believed his death was a consequence of the rock and roll music lifestyle; others believed that his wife, Courtney Love, arranged for his murder to appear as a suicide. The belief that he was killed produced one of the largest conspiracy theories in the history of popular culture, although it is not known what in fact happened and there is insufficient evidence on either side. Much like the assassinations of John F. Kennedy and Martin Luther King Jr., or the overdose of Elvis, all of the details may never be known. One consequence of Cobain's untimely death and the resulting heightened fame of *Bleach*, *Nevermind*, and *In Utero* is that it immortalized the sound and individuality of Nirvana.

The other legendary grunge band of the 1990s, Pearl Jam, was led by the iconic front man Eddie Vedder. The media pitched the musical group as the nemesis of Nirvana. The band originated from the grunge band Mother Love Bone, which lost its singer, Andrew "Andy" Wood, to a heroin overdose. When Mother Love Bone split up after Andy's death, Chris Cornell, his roommate and best friend, started the legendary alternative band SoundGarden. Other members stayed together and looked for a new singer. The newcomer Eddie Vedder auditioned for the band; his unique voice allowed them to feel as though they were not replacing Andy but starting a new sound. The new Pearl Jam had four artists—Jeff Ament, Stone Gossard, Mike McCready, and Eddie Vedder, and several different drummers over the years. They rapidly attained fame, selling more than fifteen million copies of their first two albums, *Ten* (1991) and *Vs.* (1993). Pearl Jam continued to be one of the prime grunge and alternative bands of the 1990s and still perform today.

The popularity of grunge culture in the 1990s grew quickly but faded from mainstream consciousness by the end of the decade. Nirvana's music video for the song "In Bloom" mocked fan hysteria. Original black-and-white footage of girls screaming for stars from the *Ed Sullivan Show* was selected to showcase the hype around celebrity culture. By the end of the decade, girls would be hysterical for boy bands in a manner that was reminiscent of early Beatles concerts. The popularity of Nirvana ironically pushed the band into the spotlight where it was given the celebrity status it had discounted in its music. Although grunge music defined subsequent genres, by the end of the decade MTV was far removed from the flannel-shirt and long-hair scene and showcased mob scenes of girls crying for boy bands. Before grunge music dropped off the charts and returned to an underground sound, it changed both rock music and mainstream culture.

As mainstream music expanded its former tight boundaries, it began to include females as rock stars and musicians. Using the momentum of the late 1980s, and as a result of the independent music labels built in the 1970s, women were given the opportunity in the punk and mainstream communities to do more than stand on the sidelines. Although famous pop singers such as Madonna and Janet Jackson had paved new paths for women in the entertainment industry, artists who were on the margins of society because of sexual orientation or political beliefs were still fighting for access to the entertainment industry. In *F 'em! Goo Goo, Gaga, and Some Thoughts on Balls*, Jennifer Baumgardner explores the shift in music during the late 1980s and 1990s, when women musicians were not "chicks or eye candy; they seemed to occupy the same serious space as male musicians." In addition to being a genre, womyn's music was a mindset and new level of consciousness.

The womyn's genre also maintained a political connotation and created a safe space for lesbian separatism and lesbian identity. This musical autonomy was expressed through the all-women music festivals Lilith Fair and Michigan's Womyn's Music Festival and eventually intersected with mainstream top hits. Before the 1990s, it was uncommon for women musicians to play their own guitar parts and they were told their only job was to sing. Amy Ray of the Indigo Girls commented on the band's rise to mainstream culture and acknowledged that womyn's genre was built on the premise of women playing their own instruments. The acceptance of musicians such as the Indigo Girls, Tori Amos, Sinead O'Connor, and Tracy Chapman into the more traditional venue of top Billboard hits demonstrated the breadth of the popular music scene in the 1990s. Groundbreaking androgynous queer musicians were continually juxtaposed with the consumable pop stars of MTV, similarly mirroring the dichotomy between the 1980s punk bands and Madonnas of the airwaves.

Building out of the Seattle Sound, and with a philosophy that criticized sexism and promoted feminist activism, the Riot Grrrl movement quickly gained media attention. The movement was a snapshot of the feminists of the 1990s, who drew from the radical feminism of the 1960s and 1970s. Sara Marcus sees the emergence of the new subcultures as "an uncompromising movement of pissed-off girls with no patience for sexism and no intention of keeping quiet." The primary vehicle of the message was the bands leading the change: Bikini Kill, Bratmobile, Heavens to Betsy, and Huggy Bear, among others. Baumgardner eloquently describes the importance of the feminists of the 1990s, their zines and music, and explains that the aim of the Riot Grrrl movement was to discuss rape and sexual abuse, sexual double standards, and queer sexuality. Pop culture was used as a tool for dialogue rather than protests and pamphlets. According to Baumgardner, the three main revolutionary tenets of the Riot Grrrl movement were "demystifying men's activities (playing in bands, being loud) and opening them to women; connecting women and girls who were isolated from each other, via zines and meetings and shows; and a 'pro-girl line' . . . [meaning that girls] had good reason for their anger, sadness, and occasional failure to thrive." Kathleen Hanna and Tobi Vail from the band Bikini Kill used their music to react to the male-dominated punk scenes in DC and Olympia, and incorporated their knowledge of feminist theory and work in a battered women's shelter. The innovative Riot Grrrl movement inspired zine writing and cultivated activist work.

The radical ideals of the Riot Grrrl movement were too extreme for mainstream culture after the conservative backlash of the 1980s. The late

1990s presented a new wave of music that was the consumable version of the anger of the Riot Grrrl movement. In *Feminism and Pop Culture*, Andi Zeisler analyzed the British pop group Spice Girls and explained that the phrase "girl power" and the personas of the singers were tropes of female traits. The Spice Girls were named Sporty, Baby, Scary, Ginger, and Posh, allowing young girls to identify with the different interpretations of glitz, glamour, hot pants, and push-up bras. The Spice Girls were the 1990s version of the British Invasion led by the Beatles. Their chart topper "Wannabe" climbed to number one faster than any other song previously. "Wannabe," which told the listener what girls "really really want," exceeded the Beatles' thirty-two-year record for the highest-ever new entry into the Billboard chart for "I Want to Hold Your Hand" (1964).

The quintet was a packaged version of the Riot Grrrl movement and the music industry's desire to commercialize the idea of "girl power." Within a short time, "girl power" was commodified through socks, nail polish, and T-shirts. The culture of sex was sold through the sex appeal of the singers and generated an over $50 million empire. Capitalizing on the successes of the band, in 1997 the movie *Spice World*, starring the girls, was released in theaters. Regardless of consumer motivation or the debatable theories on "girl power," the Spice Girls enchanted the majority of young Americans. Young girls wanted to become Baby, Sporty, or Posh.

Female sexuality in mainstream music, music videos, and television shows was complicated by the dichotomy of hypersexualized images of Baywatch girls versus the cultural emphasis on keeping American girls virginal, as the Religious Right organized to dominate politics in the twenty-first century. The pop purity princesses of the 1990s redefined sex appeal in the latter half of the decade by appearing both sexy, if not voracious, and virginal at the same time. The dichotomy between blossoming sexuality in young teens and the need to remain pure was embodied by the young and innocent-looking female stars who topped the charts at the end of the decade with their stylish bare-midriff shirts and pop lyrics suggesting explicit sexual acts. The superstars Britney Spears, Christina Aguilera, and Jessica Simpson were all barely teenagers when their music aired on mainstream channels. They maintained their charisma for years and captured the hearts of teenagers in America.

These teen stars were influenced by Madonna. They broke new barriers with their expressive sexuality onstage, but became equally famous as role models for young girls offstage. Representing the same values as the forthcoming legislation supporting abstinence-only education in schools, the singer Jessica Simpson became the spokesperson for pop stars who waited for marriage to have sex. Number one hits and music videos like "Genie in a Bottle" by Christina Aguilera and "Hit Me Baby, One More Time" by Britney Spears were overtly sexual, but the stars were expected to maintain a virginal appearance. American youth adored the Barbie look-alike celebrities and their numerous chart-topping hits. This combination of purity and explicit sexuality was unprecedented in American history.

In the late 1990s, boy bands dominated American pop culture and musical television; they represented physical beauty and the American dream. New Kids on the Block was an iconic group of the 1980s. Many of the new pop stars who came after in the 1990s had been members of the Mickey Mouse Club as children. Free from the constraints of playing instruments and aided by pre-choreographed dance moves, the young singers were the male counterpart of pop princesses of the decade. The boy bands represented a cultural response to the popularity of the early 1990s grunge scene. Representing the turn away from grunge music, hair metal, and hip-hop, top hits like Disney's *The Lion King* soundtrack and the pop sensation Ace of Base's *The Sign* tied for best-selling album with sales of seven million. These pop idols dominated the Billboard charts and represented the financial stability brought to the American people by the Clinton administration. Whereas grunge and hip-hop was a reflection of class stratification and strife, economic improvements supported pacified mainstream music at the end of the decade.

Pop music of the 1990s provided a sense of comfort at the dawn of the age of global uncertainty. As Y2K approached, the Backstreet Boys *Millennium* articulated the mindset of Americans who were either preparing for the apocalypse and collapse of computer programs or wearing the term "2000" on T-shirts. The idea of boy bands appears almost archaic and redundant now because of the number of such groups throughout the twentieth century. N*Sync, Backstreet Boys, and 98° sang about timeless issues of love and romance, but were also at the forefront of pop culture with their chart-topping songs and contemporary style. Loved by teenage girls and marketers alike, boy bands were the epitome of mainstream music.

In the late 1980s, MTV became the embodiment of rapid cultural change and was inclusive of multidimensional identities. By 1990, MTV played rap videos and the underground hip-hop sound moved to the mainstream. The 1990s was a transitional decade in hip-hop culture when the music changed, much like other genres, from its roots in social commentary to the commodification of women's bodies and gang culture. Gangsta rap originated in the economic inequalities resulting from the boom of the 1960s and the bust of the 1970s. The effects of Reaganomics produced increasing social stratification in black communities. The hip-hop genre owed its success to the 1980s not only because of the iconic figures who gained popularity then but also because of the social consequences of the Reagan administration and the impact of drug culture and police brutality. Rap and hip-hop have historically been an extension of the commentary of communities of color on political, economic, and structural problems. Articulating the experience of de facto segregation, classism, and drug wars, hip-hop provided the same outlet that jazz and blues had in previous eras. The assimilation of marginalized street life into music and MTV programming created a space in which life experience was turned into profit. Like all other music genres, rap and hip-hop are not homogeneous. The heterogeneity of hip-hop, rap, gangsta rap, and commercial party rap allowed for many factions of the genre to evolve separately. The shift in the 1980s and 1990s was not only about black culture responding to oppression by the legal culture and classist legislation, but it was also about the marketplace demands of mainstream consumers.

The evolution of rap as a commodity involved the white acceptance of rap and the whitening of the black experience. It paralleled that of jazz and blues and other music in previous decades that originated in the black community. In the 1950, artists like Pat Boone and Elvis Presley performed marginalized music in a "white" way that allowed the songs to dominate the top of the charts. The "whitening" of rap and hip-hop occurred when white music executives took on a media-digestible version of the black experience in America. As white promoters directed rap and hip-hop concerts and musicians, the explosive lyrics expressing centuries of prejudice and discrimination were now produced for mainstream culture.

MTV's acceptance of rap groups like Run DMC in the 1980s began the black musical experience on cable television. In 1984 Run DMC was the first rap video on MTV, and its gold, platinum, and multiplatinum rap albums paved the way for other artists. The visibility of rap artists on the cover of *Rolling Stone* magazine and new endorsements from major consumer companies moved the genre from a previously underground art form to one that was recognized at the 1988 Grammys. The hip-hop scene of the 1990s happened when the country was negotiating volatile race relations and affirmative action, but the dominant cultural narrative was still lily white. When rap and hip-hop infiltrated the suburbs in the 1990s and white upper-middle-class teens began listening to the patois of street life, the older generations responded much in the way that they had to jazz, blaming the beats and lyrics for the degeneration of society. The mainstream version of rap and hip-hop was a sanitized version of the underground sound. The consumer-endorsed version of rap was void of the passion from which the genre originated. The music became overshadowed by the sexualization of women and the commodification of gangsta rap.

In 1988, when *Yo!MTV Raps* began playing rap, the producers at MTV were unconvinced that they would be able to reach a new audience. They were surprised when hip-hop subsequently became the core genre for MTV. *Yo!MTV Raps* premiered with the video "Parents Just Don't Understand" by the Fresh Prince (Will Smith) and DJ Jazzy Jeff. Although the pair rapped the verses of the song, they presented as suburban kids from Philadelphia. Will Smith's persona of a good-looking and charming young black man drew in white suburbanites, but also built a bridge from the suburbs to the cities. As the rap on MTV expanded beyond Run DMC, the rapper Ice-T observed that "people from the hood were rushing to get cable." As the political commentary of the hip-hop and rap scene changed in 1991 because of the pecuniary motivations of (white) record companies, the iconic rap groups were expected to assimilate to the new status quo. Some groups, like Public Enemy, refused to sell out to mainstream and commercial approaches to the previously remonstrative lyrics and music. Desegregation of the media continued in the 1990s, and with the increasing visibility of street life and violence, criticism of hip-hop and rap music emerged from every direction.

Sex-focused lyrics and music videos were specific to the 1990s. Hip-hop, which had initially voiced issues specific to black communities, now commodified women's body parts and celebrated the bling culture endorsed by MTV. Tracey Jordan commented in *I Want My MTV* that the 1990s represented the beginning of "pimp-rap videos." He observed, "rappers were throwing gang signs up, there was gunplay, and women were more like body parts and props." Along with the rise of party and commercial rap, the exploitive labeling of women as "hos" on cable music television stations became the narrative for hip-hop and gangsta rap in the 1990s.

Many scholars have asserted that the hypermasculine and violent qualities of gangsta rap were responsible for the marginalization of female rappers. The success of the female duo Salt 'n' Pepa in the 1980s showed listeners that women could be unapologetic for their sexuality in their albums and videos. However, as the 1990s progressed, women increasingly served as props, not as equal lyricists and artists. The more hip-hop became a commodity in commercial society, the less voice female rappers had. Women went from MCs in the golden age of rap to scantily clad dancers in the 1990s and early 2000s, and the change was representative of the commercialization of rap and hip-hop in order to sell bling culture and silence volatile issues relating to race and class.

During the 1990s, some female artists, such as Lauryn Hill, Da Brat, Lil' Kim, Eve, and Queen Latifah, stepped outside the expectations regarding woman in the rap industry. Their unapologetic lyrics about sexuality were the antithesis of the sexualization of selective body parts. Eve confronted the issues facing women across America in the same relentless manner that Public Enemy had tackled issues of race. With her shaved head and her tough-girl personality, Eve rapped complex lyrics about domestic violence and black incarceration. The ability of Eve and Missy Elliott, among other female artists, to hold their own in the music industry through the 1990s and 2000s was the ability to express female identity independent of masculinity. Throughout her career, Missy Elliott has remained unapologetic about her appearance and her lyrics that do not cater to traditional standards for females. In 1998, Lauryn Hill won five Grammys with her album *The Miseducation of Lauryn Hill*. Queen Latifah broke many barriers for black women in the music industry by creating her own empire and showcasing an array of talents to make her more marketable. As an accomplished singer, actor, writer, and producer she surpassed all expectations of what women could aspire to or achieve. Regardless of the success of a few female rap artists, rap and hip-hip as a whole were constricted by the apparent proviso of the music industry to invest in consumer culture and the male-dominated sexualization of women. Lil' Kim placed her sexuality front and center in her music videos and owned the camera. Lil' Kim and Da Brat flipped the traditional narrative by articulating their wants and desires regarding men. Not exempt from the shift in mainstream music in the 1990s, however, even many of the female artists spit lyrics that glamorized bling culture on par with their male peers.

Each generation has its musical icon who speaks to youth directly and urgently; Tupac was the voice for his generation. Like many other black youth in the early 1990s, the experience of Tupac and his family was rooted in the discrimination of the 1980s and the dissolving of the Black Panther Party. The children of the counterculture revolutionaries of the 1960s and 1970s were growing up in a decade that was defined by the slogan "greed is good" and the latent racism of the crack epidemic and subsequent war on drugs. Rap and hip-hop lyrics of the 1990s were a continued historical narrative from the black communities of the previous decades. The influence of Tupac's mother, a former Black Panther, is apparent not only in the political consciousness of his lyrics but also in his social activism. Tupac's persona was both a thug and an agent of social change.

The iconic rapper Biggie Smalls, also known as the Notorious B.I.G. or Big Poppa, was born in Brooklyn, New York. With the crack epidemic of the 1980s still raging in the urban communities during the 1990s, Biggie dropped out of high school and sold crack as a way to make ends meet. The hustler was musically discovered after he recorded some beats on a tape recorder in a basement in New York City. When the tape made it to the airwaves, Bad Boy Records picked up Biggie and his first track was released in 1991. His talent was instantly recognizable when his first full-length record, *Ready to Die*, was certified platinum in 1994. The next year, Biggie was named MC of the year at the Billboard Music Awards, a category that had only come into existence as rap was intergraded into 1990s music.

Biggie visited the West Coast and won the hearts of listeners across the country. Toward the end of Biggie's career, the recording artist and producer Sean "Puff Daddy" Combs pushed him into more commercial songs, which demonstrated rap's commodification in pop culture. Biggie's song "Mo Money, Mo Problems," released after his death, represented the pros and cons of the commercialization of rap, its catchy lyrics stating, "It's like the more money we come across/The more problems we see." The street wars between the bicoastal record companies demonstrated that although many artists were reaping the benefits of the commercialization of the rap industry, the violence that the rappers were addressing had not dissipated.

There were stylistic differences between East Coast and West Coast rap as well as an adversarial relationship between the two groups of rappers in the 1990s. Tupac and Biggie Smalls were the faces of the East Coast–West Coast feud. The media and the record companies said it was primarily a feud between the two major rappers, but the violence that ensued was above and beyond the beats and rhymes of their unique approaches to music. In 1994, Tupac was robbed and shot five times by an unknown man while Biggie was in California. Tupac, who survived, believed that his East Coast friend knew and was affiliated with the shooter. After B.I.G. returned home, Puff Daddy released a song that Biggie had previously recorded, titled "Who Shot Ya." This song was taken as a direct attack on Tupac and he retaliated with the song "Hit 'Em Up," which attacked Biggie and implied that Tupac was having an affair with Biggie's wife, Faith Evans. In an interview after Tupac's death and shortly before his own, Biggie declared that the media had played into the rivalry, creating more hype and ultimately more animosity. The deaths that resulted from East Coast–West Coast artistic differences went far beyond ordinary music rivalry and brought to light the issue of gun violence in America and gang violence, specifically between the Bloods and the Crips, two Los Angeles-based gangs who were the most well known in the United States because of high-profile media coverage during the 1980s.

Gangsta rap and hip-hop are commonly criticized for glamorizing violence; in the case of Tupac and Biggie, the artists articulated in their lyrics issues they were experiencing firsthand and that ultimately resulted in their deaths. Tupac was shot in his car while waiting at a stop light, and after six days in the hospital he died on September 13, 1996 at the age of twenty-five.

The rumors and conjectures regarding Tupac's death were reminiscent of those that had emerged a few years earlier after the death of Kurt Cobain. Many fans speculated that Tupac faked his own death and was still alive; they turned to a strategy articulated in Machiavelli's *The Prince* to explain the untimely disappearance of the rapper. Machiavelli wrote about a person in power who had faked his death to maintain power, and since Tupac created his last album around the nom de plume Makaveli, many believed that it signified a hidden message. Rather than interpret Tupac's prediction of an early death as a commentary on thug life and gun violence, some believed he was letting fans in on his plan to escape the life he had created for himself in order to preserve his legacy. Tupac, a young man who died unjustly and whose fans could not accept that street violence could take the life of such a popular celebrity, has been referred to as the "black Elvis" or the "black James Dean." Many scholars speculate that his fans were unable to accept his death because it meant accepting the mortality of all people from the streets. Because Tupac was killed in a violent shooting, acknowledging his death meant accepting the reality of gang culture and the fallibility of humanity.

American music suffered another great loss a year later when Biggie Smalls was shot on March 9, 1997 while visiting California. Six months after Tupac's death, the Notorious B.I.G. was gunned down while stopped at a red light; an unidentified male pulled up beside the GMC Suburban and shot into the vehicle. Biggie suffered four bullets to the chest, was rushed to Cedars-Sinai Medical Center, and was pronounced dead there. He was only twenty-four years of age and was an icon across generations and throughout the country. Evidence pointed to the LA Police Department officer David Mack as the hit man for Suge Knight, the owner of the West Coast record label Death Row Record. The same bullets extracted out of Biggie's chest were found next to a shrine for Tupac, and the same model Impala owned by the driver who shot the rapper was found in Mack's garage. The LAPD ignored petitions from Biggie's family to investigate the case further and has been criticized for intentionally disregarding evidence in the case. The FBI eventually took over the case and investigated until 2005 when the case was finally closed. Throughout the case, the FBI had explored leads on gang-affiliated members of the LAPD and Knight's involvement in the rapper's death. At the time of this writing, there have been no arrests for the murder.

Rap music was condemned as it was integrated from the margins to the center of popular culture. Many social groups, regardless of political affiliation, criticized the glamorization of gun culture and the objectification of women, who were represented as jezebels and objects in videos. Rappers were blamed for problems in society. By the early to mid-1990s, many aspects of gangsta rap had already moved toward a commercial version of itself. The more mainstream the top forty rap hits became, the more the concerns around the music genre made their way from the suburbs to the halls of Congress. In 1994, Senator Carol Moseley-Braun and Representative Cardiss Collins brought this issue to the attention of country. The United States Judiciary Hearing focused on the violent lyrics of commercial rap aired on MTV. The vilification of rap artists during the senate hearings reflected both the conservative views of Americans from the 1980s and earlier and the scapegoat mentality of Congress, which avoided holding all facets of American culture accountable for the racial- and gender-based violence.

The conclusion of the congressional hearings resulted in two significant outcomes. After 1994, artists were required to record a "clean" version of the songs considered questionable for radio play. The second resolution increased pressure on television networks to regulate music video programming. These criticisms in 1994 mirrored many previous condemnations from the 1980s that surfaced again in the 2000s. The pressure to clean up the lyrics was reported by newspapers and news stations; however, the commercialization of rap and mainstream acceptance outweighed concerns from anti-rap activists. Although the conversation at the hearings focused on misogyny and violence, the hearings concentrated exclusively on the lyrics produced by black rappers, not misogyny and violence in popular culture as a whole. The "clean" versions of songs were released on the radio for the rest of the decade, but with access to the Internet and imagery on cable television, American teenagers were exposed daily to the expression of sex, violence, and discrimination.

MTV not only revolutionized music on television, but in the beginning of the 1990s it also changed television programming for the twenty-first century. Since its inception, MTV was a lifestyle channel. Teens and young adults looked to the station as a guide to fashion, music, and what was hip. The music videos presented social cues to the young adults watching. With the rise of MTV during the 1980s and the early 1990s, viewers exposed to the cable television station absorbed information through the mixed messages in the variety of music videos. Television was once again revolutionized in 1992 when MTV created a fictional television series. The television station known for music videos was now responsible for new programming that within a decade would consume American culture.

In May 1992, television programming as Americans knew it would once again be revolutionized. MTV originally pitched the idea of a television show, *The Real World*, based on daytime soap operas. The financial cost of a fictional TV show was beyond MTV's budget; it could not afford to write scripts, pay actors, or create sets or costumes. In 1973 PBS had produced the documentary *An American Family*, which chronicled the daily life of an American family. The premise of a documentary allowed financial concerns about costly scripts to be put aside in favor of "real" situations. Building on the idea of "reality TV," MTV News promoted the new show as if it was "better than" a soap opera and enticed viewers with video clips of provocative conversations about race, sexuality, and HIV.

The Real World created modern television programming for the twentieth century with its "reality TV" approach. The show opened with the famous lines: "This is the story of seven strangers picked to live in a house. Find out what happens when people stop being polite and start getting real. *The Real World*." The first season showcased seven cast members: Becky, Andre, Heather, Julie, Norman, Eric, and Kevin. The small but diverse group was placed in a New York City loft and followed by a film crew. The young people selected by the producers were a sample of the youth population and each character brought a different personality trait, predefined demographic, and stereotype to televisions across America.

The first season of *The Real World* was inherently unique. The pop analyst Chuck Klosterman explained that this new show carried no expectations from previous seasons or other mass-produced reality television shows. During the first season, no cast member of *The Real World* was able to intentionally express the kind of stereotype, expectation, or agenda that would be present in subsequent seasons and later reality shows. The personality characteristics of the first season became a litmus test for who would be allowed on the show. Klosterman elaborated on the archetypal personalities displayed in the initial episodes of *The Real World* and notes that every season after the first, the viewer was able to deduce whom a Real Worlder was depicting by the second commercial break of the first episode.

MTV and the first cast of *The Real World* created the opportunity for explicit mainstream conversations about racism, (homo)sexuality, HIV/AIDS, and abortion. The first season examined prejudices rather than relying on stereotypes and was quite different from subsequent reality TV. Jennifer L. Pozner writes in *Reality Bites Back: The Troubling Truth about Guilty Pleasure TV* that in the following seasons, the show reversed its initial curiosity about candid conversation and instead began sensationalizing sexism, racial prejudice, homophobia, sloppy hookups, personal traumas, and drug and alcohol addiction in an effort to pull in viewers.

Reality television pretended to depict the real lives of the participants. According to Klosterman in *Sex, Drugs, and Cocoa Puffs*, each episode of *The Real World* (whether it was "real" or not) was portrayed as "a seamless extension of reality." The confrontations and experiences of the characters were presented to the viewers as dramatic and edited versions of everyday people. Although *The Real World* changed television, it also transformed how many young people moved through the world. For as long as there has been Hollywood and cable television, there have been classic character "types" on television and in film. In *The Breakfast Club* (1985) we see the beautiful one, the deviant one, the smart one, the basket case, the jock (the Princess, the Criminal, the Brain, the Kook, the Jock). *The Real World* placed these stereotypes in one house and converted them into archetypes. Although MTV intentionally wanted to represent diversity in personality, race, and experience, young viewers came to see reality TV stars as peers and role models. The viewer's fascination with reality TV participants allowed everyday people to become celebrities. *The Real World* created the belief that anyone can be a star.

With each of the twenty-nine seasons of *The Real World*, the reality TV show has increasingly supported the belief that young people should strive for success and that it was easily obtainable. Everyday people were the rock stars of MTV. Applying this same mentality to reality TV, anyone in America could now walk the path to fame. Television viewers received the message that any individual could fulfill the American dream and become a self-made person (this message was later fed into the culture around YouTube and its rising stars). As more people accessed the lifestyles of the rich and the famous through their remote controls, and as the economy stabilized under the Clinton administration, Americans became increasingly more obsessed with the bling culture that MTV supported. Sinead O'Connor commented on the link between that culture and reality TV. "I hold MTV entirely responsible for the bling culture. It started when they made that show *Cribs.* Now you have a whole generation of young people who've been brought up to believe that fame and material wealth is what it's all about. You don't have young people saying, 'I really want to be a singer,' they say, 'I really want to be famous.' Then you've created a culture of people who feel they're nothing unless they live in a huge house and have seven cars."

Unlike the appeal of the stock market for the wealthy in previous decades, MTV created a new bling culture that gave hope to those living below the poverty level. It represented a chance for a new start and the hope of providing for one's family. Although the idea of "making it big" and living the American dream is as old as America itself, the 1990s were the first time in American history that people could translate their street experiences into a commodity that led to better housing and salaries.

Ironically, MTV and Reality TV programming allowed the cable station to hire anyone cheaply for its programs. Labor union laws were evaded. In *Reality Bites Back*, Pozner identified this cinematic *Schadenfraude* as existing for one reason: reality television programming created a new cheap programming strategy. On average, it costs 50 to 70 percent less to make a reality television show than it does a scripted program. For example, in 2001 NBC paid only $500,000 per episode for the reality show *The Weakest Link*, whereas the political drama *The West Wing* cost the station $9 million per hour. As we know, in the 1990s the laws for employers often changed regarding equal rights and unionized labor. The lax labor laws for reality television decreased the opportunities for union-represented actors, writers, and other crew members. Pozner writes that the reality programs did not have to provide the same benefits as the scripted programs, such as fair pay and health insurance; still, they could slash their budgets in other ways and create more programming.

During the 1990s, reality programming spread from MTV to other stations and by the early 2000s it dominated the rated shows. In the years since seven strangers shared their stories in a loft in New York City, an entire Emmy category was created for reality TV programming. Much like the concept of a television station that just played music, when the idea for reality shows was pitched, it was new to the American public. However, within a few years nonscripted programming became fundamental to the survival of every cable station.

Reality TV changed television. Nick Rhodes, the keyboardist of legendary '80s band Duran Duran, correctly summed up the impact of *The Real World*: "That's when MTV ended. That's when it became entirely crap." His analogy for this cultural shift is apt. "I saw a newspaper headline that said TOYS 'R' US WANTS TO GET OUT OF THE TOY BUSINESS. That's what happened to MTV. They wanted to get out of the music business." Simon Le Bon, John Lack, and many others identified as players in the golden age of MTV echoed this sentiment. Le Bon remembers watching the first episodes of *The Real World*. "When you saw [it], you knew it [the previous programing and moment in music television] was gone." With that, the era of music television and scripted shows changed.

As television programming shifted, MTV aired *Beavis and Butthead*, a cartoon duo of two teenage heavy-metal music fans who maintained a running commentary on the music videos that were still aired on the music station. The show, featuring "America's favorite cultural critics," was a hit until it left the air in 1997. It commented on the social changes of the 1990s, including the Senate hearings on violence, but ultimately gave way to reality television. While MTV aired fewer and fewer music videos after 1992 and focused on reality TV, the show for watching music videos—*Total Request Live* (TRL)—became the new obsession of teens in 1998.

TRL was a one-hour television show broadcast live on weekday afternoons from Times Square. It was notorious for drawing the biggest and hottest recording artists, actors, and celebrities. Appearing on TRL was for many celebrities a milestone in their career, showing that they had made it. The fans outside would mob musicians and movie stars as they entered the MTV building. A staple of the show was the sight of thousands of people waiting outside with signs for a chance to see the stars in the enormous windows of the second-story studio. The fans were reported to be so loud that businesses across the street were unable to make phone calls. The NYPD was called to shut the crowds down because of the noise. The boy band phenomenon could bring upward of eight thousand people to the Times Square studio to catch a glimpse of the pop stars.

During the programming, teens called "800-DIAL MTV" to request their favorite music video of the day. The majority of the audio and video was often dubbed over with requests and dedications. While the videos played, the focus was on the youth who requested the videos and the celebrity figures in the studio. TRL provided a space to value celebrity culture. Carson Daly, the host, projected a sense of humor and the style of an all-American, clean-cut, preppy young man. He transcended various music categories with his engaging personality as he met with artists across the music spectrum. The singer Brandi, known for the 1998 hit "The Boy Is Mine," noted that Carson's success came from his ability to adapt his personality to each guest that came on the show. Carson himself was a celebrity and the fans adored him.

TRL ended on November 16, 2008. Although its popularity had waned considerably, it's legacy as the last music television show of the music video era was considerable. Carson Daly explained that TRL was additionally about community for youth in a pre-social-networking era. Teens connected across America through the music as well as through popular culture and the social cues of mainstream culture. In the weeks after the 9/11 tragedy, Mayor Rudy Giuliani came on the show to give a message of support to the youth of America. The end of TRL represented a full shift away from the golden era of MTV to a new era of reality show like *Cribs* and eventually the comparable shows *Jersey Shore* and *16 and Pregnant* in the 2000s.

From its inception, MTV was highly criticized by many right-wing religious groups. Religious and conservative critics believed the "sex, drugs, and rock and roll" culture of the music videos and rock stars was detrimental to the youth of America. Condemnation also came from academic circles and cultural critics regarding the lack of intellectual substance for the young generation. Although the station changed drastically over the years, MTV left a number of cultural legacies. The station has continuously provided a lifestyle channel for adults and teens alike. In step with the latest technology, MTV spawned the new television hit series *American Idol* and contributed to the Internet sensation YouTube. MTV created a visual world through which people consumed media programming. However, by the end of the 1990s, the popularity of reality television took over and the golden age of MTV ended.

Family-oriented television sitcoms were broadcast on the major cable stations in the 1990s. Many of the shows, like *Married with Children* and *Roseanne*, began in the late 1980s and carried over into the 1990s. The tribulations of working-class families dominated many plots, both comic and dramatic. In the early and mid-1990s, *The Simpsons*, *Grace under Fire*, *Thea*, and *704 Hauser* (a spin-off of the 1970s show *All in the Family*) explored the family dynamics of middle-class American parents and children. *Roseanne* was a powerful interpretation of family life in the late 1980s and 1990s because of the genuine portrayal of family. Roseanne Connor, played by Roseanne Barr, owned the screen as an unapologetic, strong-willed, overweight, middle-aged mother of three. The show defied the conventional depictions of motherhood; Roseanne was a blue-collar factory worker and in later seasons had more pink-collar jobs as a beauty shop assistant and waitress. *Roseanne* provided a real interpretation of a working-class family and its daily challenges that was the polar opposite of previous television mothers like June Cleaver and Claire Huxtable. Roseanne was a particularly innovative show because it was not afraid to feature issues of race, intimate partner violence, and sexual orientation. The post-Reagan administration necessity of pinching pennies and utilizing family credit cards for purchases were not overlooked in the sitcom. The show ran almost the entire decade of the 1990s and provided blue-collar Americans with entertainment that did not trivialize the real challenges of American families, and it did so with humor.

Other television families in the 1990s included the Tanner Family of *Full House* (1987–1995), who stole the hearts of multigenerational viewers on ABC. In this untraditional family, three men were raising three young girls, with no matriarchal figure. The widower Danny Tanner had three daughters: D. J., Stephanie, and the toddler Michele. Looking for help, Danny called on his brother-in-law, known as Uncle Jesse, who was loved by women for his Elvis rock star looks and bad boy appeal, and Uncle Joey,

Danny's best friend, a talentless stand-up comic and the Tanner household's third adult. Americans loved the endearing relationships of this nontraditional family, the punchy one-liners, and the celebrities who played the characters. Bob Saget, John Stamos, and Mary-Kate and Ashley Olsen all became household names. *Full House* was rooted in comedic premises and used a soft touch regarding life lessons learned by the girls as they matured.

Racial minorities were presented on TV during the 1990s in a variety of capacities. Many television shows, like *The Real World*, relied on stereotypes to depict people who were not white, heterosexual, or cisgender (someone who identifies as the biological sex they were assigned at birth). For decades, many shows used stereotypes to introduce minority groups to primetime television. Cable programming, whether it was MTV or family sitcoms, was influenced by changes in society. With the rise of the civil rights movement, black characters were introduced into the cable mainstream. In the midst of the push for civil rights, American television programming launched its first all-black character show in 1951, *Amos 'n' Andy*, which aired until 1953. The show moved beyond tokenism and stereotypes and depicted black business people, judges, lawyers, and policemen. This success was historic, but also short lived; as race relations in America became increasingly volatile and controversial, plotlines continued to follow white Americans. The 1970s and 1980s reintroduced varying levels of popular marginalized families back into the mainstream. Americans fell in love with the universal humor and themes of *The Jeffersons* (1975–1985) and *Good Times* (1974–1979). In the late '80s and early '90s, new images of the black American family appeared on *The Cosby Show* (1984–1992) and *Family Matters* (1989–1999), giving audiences access to the normalcy of middle- and upper-middle-class black families. These characters faced the same issues and comedic situations as the characters on *Roseanne* and *Full House*.

Other shows more subtly represented the commodification of gangsta rap and black culture. *The Fresh Prince of Bel-Air* (1990–1996) inimitably bridged the MTV generation and family sitcoms through the rapper Will Smith's fictional depiction of himself and the Banks family. The theme song by Smith rapped the comical interplay of a rich family who lived in a California mansion and a goofy teen from West Philadelphia who left because "I got in one little fight and my mom got scared and said 'you're movin' with your auntie and uncle in Bel-air.'" Smith had already obtained celebrity status from his breakthrough on MTV. The sitcom embraced the timeless theme of generational dissonance between family members living under one roof and showed new ways that teens could drive the paterfamilias crazy. The family-oriented sitcoms of the 1990s portrayed many socioeconomic situations, but whether through comedy or drama, they all focused on the nuclear family (of any variety), the challenges of parenting, and the special qualities of youth coming of age. The shows were a social commentary on the assimilation of multiculturalism to mainstream culture. These shows revealed the pop culture interpretation and the pulse of social stratification and race relations in America.

In the 1990s audiences across America fell in love with new characters, some of whom carried viewers from the era of President Bush into the new millennium. As with the television shows of other decades, the majority of mainstream television shows focused on the lives of high-school students learning to navigate difficult life decisions. Teenagers of the 1990s could now access the pulse of American sexuality and expectations. Both the comedic and dramatic high-school shows struggled with coming-of-age issues and romantic interests.

Freaks and Geeks was a popular 1990s television show that lasted only one season but tackled the big life questions that arise through the teenage years and high school. It launched many major actors of the 2010s such as James Franco, Jason Segel, and Seth Rogan. The television show based on the book *My So-Called Life* (1994), starring Claire Danes as Angela Chase, also lasted only one season; however, this authentic depiction of teenage culture and the high-school experience won a Golden Globe for its first and only season. Chuck Klosterman described *My So-Called Life* as byzantine, unpredictable, and emotionally complex, and argued that it was the well-crafted nuances that allowed Angela to appear as an individual. She captured the hearts of viewers who were enthralled with the grunge and punk culture of the 1990s. Angela Chase did not reflect any archetype, she simply struggled with love, friendship, and family in a manner that reflected the experiences of the viewers. In its short nineteen episodes, Angela, her gay best friend Rickie, and her best female friend Rayanne Graff explored issues of sexual violence, child abuse, homophobia, teenage substance abuse/

alcoholism, homelessness, adultery, and school violence. This was a unique show within the context of many other well-produced but cookie-cutter teenage dramas and sitcoms.

Continuing into the 2000s, melodramas like *Dawson's Creek* and *Felicity* replaced many of the nightly television slots for "teen shows." Packed with classic plot lines and romantic triangles, the shows were both loved and predictable, containing prototypical portrayals of high school and college students navigating the shift to adulthood. These shows were some of the last programming in television history before the irreversible cultural shift to reality television programming. The romantic and coming-of-age plotlines of the 1990s did not confront Reaganomics or the race riots in Los Angeles, but engaged the immutable story lines of young love and coming-of-age challenges. *Saved By the Bell*, *Boy Meets World*, and *Beverly Hills 90210* all focused on high-school students and followed the teens into their young adult years at college, but also overlapped in less obvious ways. All three shows focused on an iconic lead character that was the nice and virtuous high-school boy.

Saved By the Bell (1989–1993) originated on NBC from the show *Good Morning, Miss Bliss* (later syndicated as *Saved By the Bell: The Middle School Years*), which focused on the lives of five middle-school students and their teacher (played by Halley Mills). Four of the cast members survived the transition to *Saved By the Bell*: Zack Morris (Mark Paul Gosselaar), Screech Powers (Dustin Diamond), Lisa Turtle (Lark Voorhies), and Principal Richard Belding (Dennis Haskins). From 1989 to 1993, viewers followed the bright clothes and moral dilemmas of the six high-school students, and later into the spin-off shows *Saved By the Bell: The College Years* (1993–1994) and *Saved By the Bell: The New Class* (1993–2000). Klosterman described the show's main character Zack Morris as a "good-looking blond kid with the ability to talk directly to the camera like Ferris Bueller. [He] possessed a cell phone years before that was common; [he was] something of an Eddie Haskell/James Spader type, but with a heart of gold." The close circle of friends was completed by Zack's longtime love interest Kelly Kapowski, who embodied the girl next door, and Screech Powers, who was a "uber-geeky Zack sycophant." The rest of the cast included A. C. Slater, the good-looking bad boy and rival of Zack; Jessie Spano, a 4.0 GPA overachieving student who believed in feminist ideology and was recognizable by her big, beautiful '80s hair; and Lisa Turtle, a rich girl who was the object of Screech's unrequited love. The character of Zach Morris embodied the archetype of the nice boy who was always making mistakes.

In addition to Zack Morris's nice-boy personality and ability to call time-out to talk to the viewer about plot developments, he also taught life lessons through his constant mistakes. Klosterman explained that, predictably, within the first ten minutes of each episode one of the characters, usually Zack, was placed in a precarious position where he or she would be tempted to do something obviously wrong. The character's peers would caution against whatever was about to occur and the character would still do it. The episode always concluded with a lesson learned and the person who was in the wrong admitting that the others were right all along. The surface development of the comedic show allowed the characters to act predictably and morally. It countered many of the teen dramas of the '90s, providing a specific type of character that audiences were comfortable laughing along with and engaging emotionally with as they encountered challenges.

Zack Morris had more obvious parallels to the *Boy Meets World* character Cory Mathews, played by Ben Savage. Much like *Saved By the Bell*, the characters in this comedy also had an authority figure, their teacher Mr. Feeny, who cared about the well-being of this selective group of students. Both Corey Mathews and Zack Morris were first introduced to viewers as awkward prepubescent adolescents. The viewers followed the young men and their friends into adulthood. Whereas *Saved By the Bell* and *Boy Meets World* were comedies with serious moments, *Beverly Hills 90210* was a soap opera for teens. The show's protagonist, Brandon Walsh, was a more developed version of the high-school nice boy. Beginning in the pilot episode, he was thrown right into the hook-up culture of the '90s and the bigger moral dilemmas of navigating intimate relationships.

The plot of *Beverly Hills 90210* followed the lives of a group of wealthy teenagers who attended West Beverly High School into their college and adult years. Over the decade that the show was on the air, the stories were about love, drama, friendship, and big issues of the 1990s such as South African apartheid and AIDS. Much like the original idea for *The Real World*, which premiered two years later, *90210* was intended to be a primetime teenage

soap opera. From 1990 to 2000, young adults across America were infatu-
ated with the show. The *New York Times* writer Dave Itzkoff captured the
significance of the show for many teens and young adults with a simple question: "What event defines the 1990s for you? Was it the day the Dow Jones
industrial average crossed the 10,000-point mark? Bill Clinton's admission
of an inappropriate relationship with a White House intern? Or was it that
fateful prom night when Brenda Walsh lost her virginity to Dylan McKay?
For millions of television viewers who came of age in that decade of irrational exuberance, it's hard to overstate the impact of *Beverly Hills 90210*." The
show enthralled young viewers as it chronicled the relationships and rivalries
of a clique of telegenic young Southern Californians. During its run from
1990 to 2000, *90210* truly captured the decade's style and music in the love
lives and tribulations of the West Coast teens.

In the pilot episode of *90210*, the viewer is introduced to Brandon
Walsh, played by Jason Priestley in a mullet-inspired haircut, as he reluctantly
attends his new high school with his sister Brenda Walsh, played by Shannen
Doherty. The leggings, big hair, jean jackets, and brown lipstick clearly indicate that the 1980s had only just ended. Shoulder pads and parachute pants
had begun to fade away as crop tops, long-line jackets, baggy jeans/wind-
pants, preppy long-sleeve turtlenecks, and grunge-inspired flannel T-shirts
came into style. The fictitious teenagers of Beverly Hills wore bold, bright,
body-conscious clothing. The affluent lifestyles of the teens was antithetical
to the economically challenged communities from which grunge culture was
growing. Nevertheless, the teens provided many youth with cultural messages about relationships and fashion, and the series addressed serious issues
that were on the minds of high-school students.

The subplots of *90210* addressed social issues such as HIV/AIDS, rape,
domestic violence, gun control, bulimia, steroids, substance abuse, shop-
lifting, and LGBTQ concerns. Although there was some criticism of the
relatively short portrayal and then death of the character Jimmy in the 1996–
1997 season, the show did break barriers by depicting a gay man with AIDS
without the stigma or stereotypes associated with the disease. Viewers tuned
in to the developing dramas of the characters. Teenage girls loved Dylan
McKay, a bad boy with a troubled past, played by Luke Perry. He also won
the hearts of the two female leads, Brenda Walsh and Kelly Taylor, played

by Jennie Garth. Brandon, Dylan's best friend and Brenda's twin brother, was the lead male and the good boy. As the token virtuous and ethical male, Brandon was relentlessly loved and respected by the other characters. The much-loved characters of *90210* entertained youth across America through-out the rise of reality TV; the spin-off *Melrose Place* also ranked as one of the most watched TV shows during the '90s.

Melrose Place, a drama of the personal and professional lives of a group of yuppies in Los Angeles, was on the air from 1992 to 1999. Much like *90210*, the plots centered on interpersonal relationships, love affairs, black-mail, and revenge. It did at times push the limits of plausibility, for example, when a bomb destroyed the apartment complex the characters lived in and they were brought back from the dead. Nevertheless, the show maintained its popularity through every season before coming to an end shortly before the new millennium.

The sexual revolution of the late 1960s changed the attitude to sexuality in entertainment as well as in real life. Both sexuality and sexual orientation were explored more openly on television during the 1990s. Cable television reflected the sexual revolution of the 1960s and the cultural changes of the 1970s and 1980s. The visibility of the lesbian, gay, bisexual, and transgender citizens in the post-Stonewall riots years created a new political and social con-text for LGBT Americans. Although traditional conservative values and the historical puritanism of the United States dominated the narrative regarding sexuality, with the launch of *Playboy* in 1953, Hugh Hefner created an empire that championed a new masculinity and reshaped how Americans experienced sex. In 1960s and 1970s America, the sexual liberation associated with the counterculture revolution changed how people talked about sex. In Vietnam, in addition to opium, U.S. soldiers were given access to American *Playboy* magazines. This unprecedented access to nudity and sex-related material in the mass media was supported by the hedonistic and promiscuous Studio 54 culture of the 1970s and created an almost predictable conservative political and social backlash in the 1980s. The relatively liberal popular culture of the 1990s was in tune with the social and political climate of the Clinton adminis-tration, which changed the social conversation regarding sex because of both progressive legislation and the president's interdicted affair with an intern. Sex was everywhere on display and discussed in American culture at this time.

Sexuality on primetime television was influenced by the increase in sexual material in music videos and an increasing acceptance of sexual diversity in American culture. The 1990s version of the sexual revolution, *Baywatch* (1989–2001), centered on a group of lifeguards at a beach resort. David Hasselhoff, as the veteran lifeguard Mitch Buchannon, and Pamela Anderson, as the bombshell lifeguard C. J. Parker, now embodied the term "sexy." Viewers tuned in to their photoshopped-looking bodies clad in swimsuits for the duration of the show. The appeal of the newly discovered actress Pamela Anderson (much like that of actress Anna Nicole Smith) harked back to the sex appeal of Marilyn Monroe. Iconic imagery of the bathing suit babes of *Baywatch* was created and was representative of the cultural attitude to sexuality at this time. When *Baywatch* left the air in 2001, popular culture had begun a return to traditional conservative values. After September 11, 2001, the dominant narrative of female sexuality in popular culture and for women was increasingly expected to emulate Britney Spears' and Jessica Simpson's sexualization of virginity.

The iconic fashion-forward and female-centric *Sex and the City* launched in 1998 and remained on air until 2004. The show depicted nontraditional female sexuality. The pilot episode featured four successful women in New York City who decide to "have sex like men." Although the show followed all four women, Carrie (Sarah Jessica Parker) and her friends Charlotte, Miranda, and Samantha, the focus remained on Carrie, her two love interests, and her enormous shoe collection. Viewers laughed and cried along with the businesswomen, wondering if Carrie would find true love with her notorious on-and-off-again paramour, Big. In previous decades, the explicit sexuality on *Baywatch* and *Sex in the City* would have been shunned or not allowed.

The visibility of lesbian and gay characters on television exposed many heterosexual Americans to what it meant to be gay in America in the 1990s. The national dialogue regarding gays in the military resulted in a heavy backlash against openly gay servicemen and women; the conversation on marriage equality for same-sex couples resulted in the Defense of Marriage Act (1996) and state-by-state legislation to ban or legalize same-sex marriage. The increasing visibility of gay and lesbian characters on television went hand-in-hand with newly gained civil rights for same-sex couples, and the question of which came first is arguable. Although the gay rights movement began in the 1970s, the influence of personable and well-rounded characters on television allowed the LGBT community to be accessible and visible within the American mainstream.

Much like the emergence of black characters on television, there was no linear progression of increasing acceptance of the LGBTQ community; gay characters emerged sporadically on television shows, but never took the screen as the protagonist. Supporting roles were assigned to gay characters with the 1992 creation of the character Matt Fielding on *Melrose Place*, played by Doug Savant. The *90210* spin-off took a holistic approach to his personality and did not rely on stereotypes for plot development or comedy. He was considered by viewers to be likeable, well adjusted in society, and intelligent. This character launched a new age of gay personas that moved slowly away from stereotypes and exposed Americans to more developed characters, although television still struggles with the decision to include LGBTQ characters.

The attention of viewers from all demographics was caught by a new show in 1998 that stepped outside melodrama programming and into sitcoms. When *Will and Grace* aired on NBC, the pop culture reference point became the activities of two gay men. However, the show relied heavily on effeminate stereotypes and catered to the underlying desire of viewers for the gay male, Will, to romantically end up with his best straight female friend, Grace. The show has been criticized for perpetuating stereotypes of effeminate gay men, specifically the character Jack. Much like the inclusion of other minority groups, the show depicted a digestible version of the gay lifestyle for mainstream entertainment. As an extremely successful lawyer with a best female friend, Will presented a new image of homosexuality in New York City apart from the rioters at Stonewall and the Village People. The difference between Will and previous gay characters, real or fictitious, on television, was that he was able to connect with the audience through his humor and appear as another successful white male American with good friends, a good heart, and a fun-filled life. The show's reinvention of the mainstream gay male was not that different from the reinvention of girl power through the *Spice Girls* or black culture though the *Fresh Prince of Bel-Air*.

Other classic American sitcoms like *Friends* (1994–2004), *Seinfeld* (1990–1998), and *Frasier* (1993–2004), a spin-off of the TV show *Cheers*, embraced the timeless story lines of life and love in America's big cities. These shows did not represent the counterculture movements that were being integrated into the mainstream, as some of the other television shows did. The record-setting thirty-seven Emmys won by *Frasier* spoke to the comedic value of a show with a simple, smart, and funny plot line that was heartwarming to fans. Style cues were taken from actors and actresses. Jennifer Aniston, who played Rachel on *Friends*, cut her hair into the iconic 1990s choppy layers that became known as "the Rachel." These comedies provided a break from reality for viewers and helped transition audiences into the new millennium and the post–9/11 world.

Over the first decade of the new millennium, reality shows took over cable television stations. Celebrity culture in the decades after the emergence of *The Real World* was fabricated from the popularity of reality television stars. In 2010, Mike "the Situation" Sorrentino from MTV's *Jersey Shore* earned more money than President Barack Obama. The legacy of pop culture of the 1990s provided mainstream listeners and viewers of the twenty-first century with consumable versions of previously underground or radical movements. The commodification of gangsta rap and the mass production of hypersexualized and scripted shows created a new culture for the new millennium that aimed to provide entertainment to a young generation already fixated on immortality and sexuality. Pop culture in the 1990s had featured class, race, sexism, and sexuality reinterpreted through the beats and scripts of the entertainment industry.

Recommended Reading

The most comprehensive oral history of the MTV generation is Craig Marks and Rob Tennenbaum, *I Want My MTV: The Uncensored Story of the Music Video Revolution* (New York: Plume, 2012). For an oral history of the grunge movement, see Mark Yarm, *Everybody Loves Our Town: An Oral History of Grunge* (New York: Three Rivers Press, 2012). Michael Eric Dyson is the premier scholar on hip-hop and black culture in America. His books include *The Michael Eric Dyson Reader* (New York: Basic Civitas Books, 2004); *Know What I Mean?: Reflections on Hip-Hop* (New York: Basic Civitas Books, 2007); *Between God and Gangsta Rap: Bearing Witness to Black Culture* (Oxford: Oxford University Press, 1996); and *Holler If You Hear*

Me (New York: Basic Civitas Books, 2001). For an examination of feminism and pop culture, see Jennifer Baumgardner, *F 'em!: Goo Goo, Gaga, and Some Thoughts on Balls* (Berkeley, CA: Seal Press, 2011); and Andi Zeisler, *Feminism and Pop Culture* (Berkeley, CA: Seal Press, 2008). For an engaging read about the emergence of reality television, see Jennifer L. Pozner, *Reality Bites Back: The Troubling Truth about Guilty Pleasure TV* (Berkeley, CA: Seal Press, 2010).

Race Relations

DURING THE LATE 1800s, Americans were tasked with rebuilding the country to accommodate the changes that accompanied the loss of lives in the Civil War, the assassination of President Lincoln, and new civil rights laws. The same need to restructure was repeated a century later after the passage of the Civil Rights Act of 1964, the assassination of President Kennedy, the Watergate scandal, and the rapid U.S. military escalation and withdrawal from the Vietnam War. These events produced a transitional period during the 1980s and 1990s in America that the historian Manning Marable called the "Second Reconstruction"—it was a shift away from the "liberal reforms" of the 1960s and 1970s on race-related issues, which created an "increasingly uncertain and unequal racial future." The policies of the 1990s were a social and legislative backlash to the progress of the civil rights era. The reform policies of the Reagan, Bush, and Clinton administrations compromised the civil rights advances of the post–*Brown v. Board of Education* era.

Just as Reconstruction came after the Civil War, legal and social changes occurred in the years after Vietnam and the movements for equality. America fought a second civil war during the 1960s and 1970s; however, this time the "battle" was fought on the social, cultural, and political front. At times the battlefront was literal; for example, the student uprisings at Kent State University and Columbia University resulted in militia assaults on protesters and student deaths. The black liberation movement in America was a new interpretation of the Emancipation Proclamation for the twentieth century: the Civil Rights Act of 1964. The 1980s saw legislative backlash against newly won civil rights for marginalized groups, such as the right to legal abortion advocated

172

for by feminists, progress in legal protection and employment opportunities for marginalized groups, and the legacy of the Great Society, which initiated the war on poverty. In previous decades policies were created to make it safer for the formerly disenfranchised, specifically black Americans, to go to the polls. With the progressive attainment of voting safeguards, the 1990s saw the benefits of the Voting Rights Act fully implemented. The social, cultural, and political "wars" in America did not have a definitive beginning and end, as with the Civil War. For the purposes of this book, the "Second American Civil War" concludes with the end of the Vietnam War in the wake of Watergate and the decline of the counterculture movement. The 1980s and 1990s subsequently became the "Second Reconstruction" in America.

Social policy changes of the 1980s were highly influenced by the Cold War and America's new geopolitical position. Cold War policies, which lasted until the fall of the Berlin Wall, resulted in newly acquired civil rights for black Americans. The Second Reconstruction began with the conservative shift in American politics to Reaganomics. However, the conservative legislative agenda was limited by Cold War policies. Heeding the lesson learned from World War II, American policymakers knew they could not advocate for democratic human rights abroad while repealing civil rights at home. With the fall of the Berlin Wall, the new post–Cold War decade offered America a chance for a new agenda at home and globally. Perestroika (the policy or practice of restructuring or reforming the economic and political system after the collapse of the former Soviet Union) allowed both the Bush and Clinton administrations to create new policies on all domestic and foreign issues. The Second Reconstruction began with the Reagan administration and continued through the Bush and Clinton presidencies.

The black and minority experience in America has not been a monolithic one. The new policies of the Second Reconstruction profoundly impacted all areas of fundamental liberties for communities of color. Welfare-reform policies disproportionately impacted single women of color and the exploding rate of mass incarceration from the war on drugs targeted young black men. As the historians Maurice Isserman and Michael Kazin explain in *America Divided: The Civil War of the 1960s*, the agenda of the Clintons was perceived by conservatives to be the antithesis of the Reagan legacy and Bush policies. However, as president, Clinton demonstrated how deeply entrenched the policies of the Second Reconstruction were in the 1990s by advocating social policies that were previously pushed by conservatives, including "a balanced budget and the end of guaranteed welfare payments to single mothers with small children." The new restrictions placed on welfare disproportionately targeted minority communities.

Appallingly, violence against the black community has been interwoven throughout U.S. history since the colonial period. In Los Angeles, Police Chief William Parker intentionally recruited white southern police officers with racial biases during his tenure (1950–1966) in an endeavor to further the racial, political, social, and class divide between whites and people of color. The animosity between the Los Angeles Police Department (LAPD) and black communities resulted in decades of unrelenting violence. In the spring of 1991, the habitual viciousness of the LAPD against blacks was caught on videotape and, for a brief moment, changed the conversation of race relations in America. Footage from a home-video camera recorded the excessive beating of a black citizen by the LAPD and presented the world with authentic and tangible evidence regarding long-standing police brutality against black and Latino communities.

Rodney King inadvertently became the face for race relations in America after his attack by the police. LAPD police were chasing King on the Foothills freeway one night in March 1991. He knew there would be repercussions for running from the police, especially for a parolee and a black man, but could not have predicted the brutality that would result and the effect it would have on the country. When King stopped his car, he was ordered to lie face down on the ground by a group of all-white police officers: Sargent Stacey Koon and officers Laurence Powell, Ted Briseno, and Timothy Wind. Within minutes, and despite the other twenty-three officers on standby, King was shocked twice with a taser gun and received fifty-six baton blows. The beating left him with nine skull fractures, a shattered eye socket, a broken leg, and nerve damage that paralyzed part of his face. The violence against King on March 3, 1991 was not atypical, but rather represented the countless testimonials of marginalized citizens who experienced police brutality. George Holiday, a bystander, captured the beating on tape. After Channel 5 News obtained the tape, the footage was quickly broadcast internationally.

Consequently, the public was newly informed and discussions around the events became the predominant focus of the media.

Waiting for the trial to begin, Americans, specifically blacks in Los Angeles, felt both tension and hope. Four days after the assault, the L.A. district attorney dropped all charges against King and within the week the L.A. County Grand Jury indicted the four officers for the beating of King. Sergeant Koon and officers Powell, Wind, and Briseno were charged with felony assault; however, all four were released on bail for the duration of the pending trial. Police Chief Daryl Gates was placed on leave, but was quickly reinstated. The Grand Jury refused to indict the bystander officers. A third-party analysis of the events by the Christopher Commission Report documented excessive force and racial harassment by the LAPD, and called for Gates to resign and structural reform of the LAPD.

In November 1991, after arguments from the defense about prejudicial pretrial publicity, Superior Court Judge Stanley Weisberg moved the trial to the East Ventura County Courthouse. This area was disproportionally white and more politically conservative than Simi Valley. Some believed the move represented the police officers' constitutional right to due process, and for others it was a sign of dominant-culture bias. When the trial commenced, the white jury selection reflected the demographics of Simi Valley. On April 29, 1992, the jury found all four officers not guilty of crimes against King; specifically, they found no use of excessive force and no misfiling of reports. When the jury was hung on the count against Powell, the judge declared a mistrial. Within the hour, Los Angeles erupted in protest and was engulfed in flames that burned so severely that an orbiting satellite observed them as a "thermal anomaly." When the verdict was announced, all hope that the LAPD would be held accountable was lost. People were devastated by the blatant racial discrimination and disregard of evidence. King's experience of police brutality was not uncommon and the case symbolized decades of tension between the urban poor and the LAPD. Visual evidence coupled with the acquittal of the officers exposed the new face of racism in America.

The acquittals were the spark that ignited the riots in Los Angeles. The riots began immediately at the courthouse upon the announcement of the jury's decision. By 5 pm on April 29, the violence, looting, and fires engulfed

southern Los Angeles, and at 8:45 pm Mayor Tom Bradley declared a local
state of emergency. This was not the first time the residents of Los Angeles
burned the city in protest against the racial biases and discriminatory practices of the legal system and government of California; their explosion this
day was the result of years of discriminatory legal decisions on the local,
state, and federal level. The L.A. riots in the spring of 1992 were the first
episode of urban unrest in Los Angeles since 1968. These acts of rebellion
caused the most deaths since the New York City Draft Riots in 1863. The
previous L.A. riots of the '60s were in response to California's new legislation to circumvent the 1964 Civil Rights Act. California had responded
to the groundbreaking legislation with Proposition 14, which specifically
targeted the fair housing component of the bill. The riot in the summer
of 1965 lasted six days, left thirty-four dead, approximately one thousand
injured, and resulted in almost four thousand arrests and $40 million in
damages. Both riots were rooted in decades of systematic discrimination by
the legislative and judicial branches of the government. Although the riots
were a quarter of a century apart and apparently different, at the core they
were both a response to unjust legislative and judicial decisions.

The post-verdict chaos in Los Angeles affirmed 1980s and 1990s hip-hop
lyrics. Some have argued that the music "predicted" the riots, but it was not
so much prophetic as inevitable because of the rising animosity between the
police and black citizens. The verdict of the Rodney King case was the iconic
breaking point of this enmity. The financial hardships caused by the economic
recession and Reaganomics only exacerbated an already tense situation.

The experience of black communities in America is not monolithic and
the L.A. riots were no exception. The violence occurred at the intersection
of Florence and Normandie in South Central Los Angeles. When the police
evacuated the area, chaos ensued. A flashpoint in the riots occurred when
Reginald Oliver Denny, a white truck driver, drove through the intersection
and was pulled from his truck by a group of four rioters, referred to as the
"L.A. Four." The hatred unfolded on live television as the men beat Denny
to near death. Four local citizens watched Denny struggle for his life on
national television and took him to the hospital. Denny survived the attack,
but not without permanent nerve damage, impaired vision, and a constant

ringing in his ears. In the aftermath of the beating, Denny received over twenty-seven thousand get-well cards from supporters.

Visuals were integral to the manner in which the American people interpreted the Los Angeles events. The media used the violence against Denny to stereotype inner-city residents. Denny's beating was a turning point in the riots because outsiders felt entitled to justify the oppression and beatings by the LAPD. The riots erupted as a voice for the people of Los Angeles, who were struggling in the '90s without access to grocery stores and steady jobs. The media focus on Denny allowed the riots to be attributed to black racism against whites instead of structural inequalities in housing and employment that put black residents at a disadvantage in Los Angeles. In a 2002 interview with NBC, Denny reiterated the need to address structural inequalities and explained that he understood that the riots were an extension of these inequalities and a voice for the marginalized community. Henry Watson, one of the L.A. Four, rationalized Denny's beating as a sacrifice that had to be made for the revolution that was consuming Los Angeles; this perspective of course is based on the premise that the riots created revolution.

Many pointed to the brutality against Denny as the bookend to the King beating. The media played a different narrative based on the race of the attackers and victims. Some tried to rationalize the violence against Denny as the "boomerang effect" of racism against blacks and the retaliation against any non-black citizen of Los Angeles. In addition to Denny, Fidel Lopez, a Guatemalan immigrant, and Choi Sai-Choi, an immigrant from Hong Kong, were also pulled from their cars and beaten near the same location as Denny. The media did not attach themselves to these acts of violence, even though the beatings were caught on camera.

As Los Angeles burned with no response from the fire department, the rioting continued. On May 1, 1992, Rodney King appeared on national television and pleaded tearfully to the rioters: "Can we all get along? Can we stop making it horrible for the old people and the kids?" King's plea for peace was taken as an insult by many of the rioters. What began as a redemptive call to justice for Rodney King by the third day became lawlessness. When the police retreated from the Florence and Normandie area, the city became a free-for-all for vandalism. The chaos of South Central Los Angeles quickly spiraled to the mass looting of abandoned stores and setting build-ings on fire.

In "April 29, 1992 (Miami)," the popular California band Sublime por-trayed the looting as a reflection of poverty and the needs of the people in the region. The lyrics describe a mother, accompanied by her children, buy-ing diapers at a store. The singer also addressed the desire for luxury items, indulgences, and destruction as looters rob a liquor store: "I finally got all that alcohol I can't afford. . . . And then we turned that liquor store into a structure fire." The on-the-street amateur footage exposed people discussing looting as a way of obtaining luxuries that the poverty-stricken of the area could only have dreamed of before that.

Many looters intended to resell the loot to make money, which was an indication of the severity of the poverty of the area. Not all of the looting was for essentials, such as food; footage showed citizens leaving stores with household luxury items, taken from music and electronic stores. The loot-ing of the record stores and grocery stores confronted the problem of racist commentary by the media, which would similarly become an issue during the news coverage of Hurricane Katrina in New Orleans in 2005. The chaos that consumed Los Angeles for six days in 1992 originated from feelings of disenfranchisement and grew into pandemonium and mayhem. Revolution-ary attitudes were distorted by rage and confusion as the protests became more about personal vindication than structural poverty and racism.

The riots changed the long-standing antagonism between the black and Korean communities in Los Angeles. Just two weeks after the beating of Rodney King, in the year before the riots, the death of a fifteen-year-old high-school student increased the tension between the black and Korean com-munities. Latasha Harlins was shot and killed by Soon Ja Du, a Korean Ameri-can grocer in South Central Los Angeles. The young girl entered the store to purchase a bottle of orange juice. She placed the juice in her backpack and approached the counter, money in hand, to pay for it. This prompted Du to grab the teenager and accuse her of stealing. Feeling threatened, Harlins struck the shopkeeper and Du retaliated by shooting her. Du's family shared the footage from the security camera in the hope of exculpating the young girl.

When the police department turned the footage over to the media, some members of the public were outraged; others speculated that the LAPD was attempting to distract the public from the controversy around King's beating. The footage did not bring retribution. On November 15, 1991, a jury convicted Du of voluntary manslaughter and the judge sentenced her to five years probation, no jail time, four hundred hours of community service, and a $550 dollar fine for killing the teenage girl. The outrage at the Rodney King verdict was exacerbated by feelings of injustice for now two victims. As the riots erupted in the hours after the Rodney King verdict, the name "Latasha" was spray painted on Korean stores across Los Angeles. Along with over 1,800 other Korean-owned shops, Du's store was burned during the riots. The total damage accrued during the riots cost the city of Los Angeles over $1 billion, with over $3 million in damages specifically to Korean-owned businesses. News footage of the growing animosity between Koreans and blacks began to resemble guerilla warfare footage after gun stores were looted and the violence was taken to the streets.

In the post-riot aftermath, some of the tensions between the two communities were released through music. Ice Cube's "Black Korea" spoke specifically to the escalated hatred. The lyrics of "Black Korea" were racist, discriminatory, and above all a barometer for the sentiments of many in southern Los Angeles regarding interminority racism. Tupac reflected on the death of Latasha in the song "Thugz Mansion," giving resolution to her story as he rapped, "Lil' Latasha sure grown/Tell[ing] the lady in the liquor store that she's forgiven." Throughout the next few years of his career, Tupac also mentioned her in "Something 2 Die 4," "I Wonder If Heaven's Got a Ghetto," "White Man's World," and dedicated the song "Keep Ya Head Up" to her. During the riots, many members of the black and Korean community alike felt they needed to protect themselves against the racial violence.

Music played an integral role in the riots as an outlet for frustration about disenfranchisement. When the violence erupted, many of the participants found an anthem in NWA's 1988 song "F—— the Police," which was heard playing from cars and boom boxes throughout South Central Los Angeles. After the riots, music became an outlet for rappers to process the events of the spring. In the song "The Day the —— Took Over," Dr. Dre mixed audio clips from handheld cameras and news footage and created a new narrative for the riots that commented on media representation, looting, the burning of buildings, and the decision of the Bloods and the Crips to unite over the riots. Sentiments of injustice regarding the verdict and the desire for retribution were loud and clear in the lyrics of Ice Cube's song "We Had to Tear This Mother—— Up." The rapper articulated the need for marginalized communities to have their voice heard: "To get some respect we had to tear this mother—— up." Although gangsta rap became more traditionally mainstream, the black response to the riots was heard on a level that would not have been possible before its commodification.

In addition to the West Coast hip-hop response to the riots, bands who watched the riots from the periphery, for example, Tom Petty and the Heartbreakers and Tori Amos, contributed their own musical interpretations of the events. Music was the voice of the people before the riots and many of the recordings during the trial incorporated the events of the spring. *The Chronic* by Dr. Dre and *Doggy Style* by Snoop Dogg both integrated the anger and frustration of the riots into albums that were increasingly popular because of exposure through mainstream music.

The United States government responded to the chaos in the inner city on the third day by declaring it a federal disaster area. In an attempt to quell the riots, President Bush deployed twenty thousand federal troops and the National Guard to Los Angeles. This deployment was also a political move for the upcoming election. The White House, much like the rest of America, anticipated public outrage in response to the building tensions and violence in Los Angeles. The riots impacted the Republican Party and how President Bush campaigned for reelection. Although the president disagreed with the initial verdict of the Rodney King case, after the riots began he spoke out against the protesters and blamed the violence on mob mentality. As the historian John Robert Greene analyzed in *The Presidency of George Bush*, the president's reelection campaign began with a slow start, and the effort to respond to the riots and obtain additional California votes fell flat. The president's delayed respond to the chaos and violence was unsettling to Californians.

The president finally acknowledged the street violence in an address to the nation on the third day of the rioting and laid out his plan for deploying troops. He "guaranteed" the American people that "this violence will end." But the response was too little, too late. Greene's interview with David Demarest disclosed that Bush's director of communications blamed

Sam Skinner, the chief of staff, for his indecisiveness over drafts of speeches for three days, which seemed like an eternity to the media. The president's apparent apathy and disengagement was exacerbated by the five-day delay before he made the trip to Los Angeles to address the riots. Bush stood abashed before potential voters as the media lambasted his seeming unwillingness to act decisively.

The president was not the only member of his administration who expressed an opinion about the events in Los Angeles. The White House had to do damage control in the month after the riot on comments from members of the president's cabinet. During the riots, Press Secretary Marlin Fitzwater openly blamed the riots on Lyndon Johnson's Great Society programs. As pointed out by Greene, in the weeks after the riots, Vice President Dan Quayle also created a press calamity when he publicly blamed the riots on "a poverty of values." The infamous conservative sound bites added to the complications the White House was having with the Bush-Quayle ticket for the 1992 campaign. Bush decidedly distanced himself from the comments of the vice president, but not without losing valuable percentage points in the polls for the way he handled the unrest. Additionally, Clinton, as a challenger to the incumbent president, capitalized on the riots and Bush's mishap. The presidential hopeful knew his comments regarding the riots could influence the polls. However, the commentary provided by both of the presidential contenders yielded to other political priorities by the election.

After six days, forty-two deaths, seven hundred buildings gutted by fire, over five thousand people arrested, and damages that exceeded $1 billion, the riots ceased. The riots were not forgotten as the city rebuilt and recovered from the extensive damage to homes and businesses. On August 4, 1992, the previously acquitted officers were indicted by a federal grand jury. The following April, more than two years after the beating of Rodney King and a year after the riots, Koon and Powell were both convicted for violating King's civil rights. U.S. District Court Judge John Davies later sentenced them to thirty months each in a federal correctional camp. Once again, officers Wind and Briseno were acquitted. The response to this verdict passed quietly and unnoticed.

The six days of unrest in April and May 1992 were evidence of frustration and the desire for justice, but did not cause a social revolution. The next year saw the lowest crime statistics since 1984. Over the week, as the riots spilled into other parts of Los Angeles, the voices of those who had suffered police brutality and discrimination in the criminal justice system were temporarily heard, and for a brief moment in history, the news focused on the other Los Angeles beyond the beautiful Hollywood community of the rich and famous. The legacy of the riots included some advancement for racial minorities; for example, Willie L. Williams, the first black police commissioner of both the LAPD and the Philadelphia Police Department, was appointed police chief after Gates resigned. However, many of the appointments were simply political. Although the riots are regarded as one of the most violent moments of the 1990s, it led to a lasting truce and cease-fire between the Bloods and Crips.

Social revolutions by definition overthrow the government or oppressor. The riots showed the power of disgruntled citizens, but police brutality and injustices of the court system did not end with the King case and continued full strength into the next century. In February 1999, on the East Coast, the New York City Police Department (NYPD) came under scrutiny when four plainclothes police officers shot Amadou Diallo, a citizen, forty-one times as he reached for his wallet to produce identification. The following year, the officers were acquitted. Thousands took to the streets of New York City to protest. Much like the riots in the early 1990s, the protest brought national attention to the issue of discrimination and police violence against people of color, but did not fundamentally change the sociopolitical structure of race in America.

Diallo's death and the protests resulted in an adverse response from the NYPD in the following years. According to the historian Manning Marable, after the protests, studies headed by the Attorney General of New York concluded that the NYPD increased the number of its pedestrian stops and stop-and-frisk procedures, disproportionately targeting men of color. Although the protesters wanted protections for men like Diallo, data showed that in the following years only 8 percent of those stopped by the NYPD were white. Despite the rhetoric that attempted to rationalize the searches as a form of gun control, only 0.15 percent of the stops resulted in a weapon found on the person being searched. The chaos in the spring of 1992 was a wake-up call to white authority in America, but sadly, police brutality has continued in the decades since.

The startling reality is that "there are more blacks under correctional control today, in prison or in jail, on probation or parole, than were enslaved in 1850, a decade before the Civil War began," Michelle Alexander explained in an interview. The history of labor, imprisonment, and the racial caste system in America has been long, complex, and enduring. The 1990s witnessed the socioeconomic phenomenon of mass incarceration of blacks. The fact of social and physical racial segregation has been told in slave stories and the history of Jim Crow, and is also part of the contemporary narrative. The all-too-common belief that America has moved into a post-racial society is not only wrong, but it also ignores a large portion of the disenfranchised population that has grown since the 1980s. A defining element of the 1990s was the mass incarceration of people of color as a result of the drug laws of the 1980s and 1990s. As defined by Michelle Alexander, the new Jim Crow shapes the experience of Americans through the literal imprisonment of citizens and the virtual restrictions that create second-class citizens. Additionally, Bush and Clinton perpetuated the existing social and legal discrimination against poor people of color through "law and order" and alarming welfare and housing reforms.

The prison-industrial complex and the concept of "convict labor" in America, which defined the experience of many citizens in the 1990s, was a consequence of slavery. After the end of slavery and before the "birth of Jim Crow," the laws in America continued to confine black citizens much like plantations and slavery had. Mississippi created the first convict labor camp disguised under the name Parchman Farm. In *The New Jim Crow*, Michelle Alexander discusses the historian David Oshinsky's analysis of Parchman Farm; in the years following Reconstruction and the Civil War, the convict population grew at ten times the rate of the general population. As increasing numbers of citizens were sentenced to the farm, the demographic of the convicted citizens was primarily black young men. Although Reconstruction was a century removed from the policies of the 1990s, the masked racism in the prison-industrial complex has remained constant in American history and demonstrates resilience against the civil rights movements.

The racial hierarchy in America throughout the last few centuries has been both malleable and consistent. The views of blacks as "less than" has created "adaptable racism," which has been unfaltering because the laws have accommodated discriminatory beliefs. The cyclical pattern of racial oppression and progressive legislation creates predictable decades of progress followed by backlash and the reconstruction of social norms and laws. The virtual and physical constraints of the war on drugs and mass incarceration created an entire generation of second-class citizens without rights. All of this, combined with the reforms of the 1980s, propagated the New Jim Crow in America.

The 1990s began with the highest incarceration rate in United States history. In 1989, there were over one million people imprisoned in the United States and over half of this demographic were black males. By the end of the decade, the prison population was eight times higher than in the previous three decades. In 2001, the prison population exceeded two million incarcerated citizens and more than 70 percent were people of color. In New York State alone, by the end of the 1990s, black and Latino inmates made up 83 percent of all state prisoners. Of the prisoners incarcerated for drug offenses, 94 percent were people of color. The prison system expanded at an unprecedented rate during the 1990s due to federal funding and recently added sites of incarceration. Between 1981 and 2001, New York State added thirty-eight new prisons to the system, more than the number of prisons built between 1817 and 1981 in total. California also added twenty-one new prisons to its system. These drastic changes were made possible by the support of the Clinton administration.

During the Clinton administration, the president and Congress reallocated funds and shifted monies from public housing to construction for correctional facilities. As Alexander points out in *The New Jim Crow*, the Clinton administration escalated the war on drugs beyond what the conservatives had imagined; in the 1990s, the money "devoted to the management of the urban poor" was "radically altered." The money previously reserved for Aid to Families with Dependent Children (AFDC), or food stamps, was shifted to the penal budget. In 1996, funding for public housing decreased while funding for prison construction increased. The public housing budget was reduced by 61 percent, which translated to $17 billion, whereas the budget to construct prisons in America was increased by 171 percent, or $19 billion. The prison population continued to boom as new laws were enacted regarding arrest, parole, and incarceration. The high recidivism rate of the 1990s was not a reflection of new people committing new crimes; rather, statistics proved that by 2000 the number of people who returned to prison for parole violations was equivalent to the number of those in prison for any reason in 1980. Two-thirds of the inmates who returned to prison were there for parole-related violations.

All three branches of the U.S. government had a formative influence on the construction of the war on drugs and mass incarceration. President Reagan launched the war on drugs in October 1982 and his drug policy expanded through the Bush and Clinton administrations. During this time, the Supreme Court upheld laws that supported racial discrimination in police departments and in the court process. Throughout the 1990s, the Supreme Court enacted laws pertaining to how police departments conducted searches and arrests. Unlike other legislative items, all three presidents had the support of Congress on law and order issues and successfully passed related laws. The legislative branch restructured the drug laws in America in the 1980s using language that reflected the racially charged policies of the Reagan administration and the accompanying media campaigns against crack in the black communities. Even though the Reagan administration constructed the war on drugs, the policies were enacted and sustained through Congress, the Supreme Court, and the presidencies in the years that followed.

From the inception of the war on drugs, the discriminatory laws disproportionately targeted black communities. The Antidrug Abuse Act of 1986 revised the mandatory penalties for crack and powder cocaine. The 100:1 ratio for crack and cocaine was implemented. In the language of the American Civil Liberties Union (ACLU), now under federal law, "the amount of crack versus powder cocaine necessary to trigger mandatory minimum prison sentences" had changed, meaning that "possession of 5 grams of crack cocaine would mandate the same minimum sentence as 500 grams of powder cocaine." A person found with cocaine would have to be in possession of one hundred times more cocaine than crack for the same prison term. The implementation of the Antidrug Abuse Act disregards the Drug Enforcement Administration (DEA)'s conclusion that crack rocks are 75–90 percent cocaine. The racial associations for crack and cocaine were clear; crack use was rampant in black neighborhoods, whereas cocaine was just as prolific in affluent white circles. When the act was reassessed in 1988, the language was changed to include stricter penalties and to impact access to housing. The 1988 revision supported the eviction of any tenant who "allows any form of drug-related criminal activity to occur on or near public housing premises and eliminated many federal benefits, including students loans, for anyone convicted of a drug offense." Additionally, sentencing changed under the new provisions. Previous to the 1988 act, the longest a person could be imprisoned for any drug offense was one year. In the 1990s drug sentences increased at an astonishing rate and the prison population grew at unprecedented percentages in American history.

The new drug laws in the 1980s were indicative of the changes that would come to all three branches of government in the 1990s. One of the political cues President Bush adopted from his predecessor was the policy direction for the war on drugs. Bush believed drugs were the most pressing problem facing the nation in the late '80s and early '90s. By appearing tough on "law and order" and using rhetoric that marginalized poor communities, Bush capitalized on the support from some voters to advance his political position. The language of the 1992 election, as well as 1988 and 1996, was shaped by the acute awareness that Bush and Clinton had of the social dynamic of race in America during the backlash against the civil rights movement.

When a Democrat took office for the first time in twelve years, the "Second Reconstruction" did not slow down; in fact, federal policies became even more extreme. The Clinton administration followed in the footsteps of the two previous presidencies and expanded the war on drugs, welfare reform, and housing restrictions for convicted Americans; these in turn increased the homelessness rate during the 1990s. According to Alexander, Clinton's "tough on crime" election platform was originally a "three strikes and you are out" policy but evolved into a "one strike and you are out" policy. During the 1994 State of the Union address, Clinton "challenge[d] local housing authorities and tenant associations: Criminal gang members and drug dealers are destroying the lives of decent tenants. From now on, the rule for residents who commit crime and peddle drugs should be one strike and you're out." The racially loaded implications of this policy were tied to the racial profiling associated with the disproportionate arrests and incarcerations of the war on drugs.

The Supreme Court protected and extended the right of police to discriminate based on race and to conduct searches and seizures under the Fourth Amendment, which states: "The right of the people to be secure in their persons, houses, papers, and effects, against unreasonable searches and seizures, shall not be violated, and no warrants shall issue, but upon probable cause, supported by oath or affirmation, and particularly describing the place to be searched, and the persons or things to be seized." Between 1982 and 1991, the Supreme Court ruled on over thirty cases related to the rise of prosecutions for narcotics arrests. The dominant narrative remained the same for all these cases. As Alexander explained, all except for three of the cases upheld the right of the police to search and seizure under the Fourth Amendment.

In the late 1980s, a case that appeared to be about the death penalty inadvertently set a new precedent for minorities bringing lawsuits to court. In 1987, the Supreme Court declared in *McCleskey v. Kemp* that racial bias could not be asserted under the Fourteenth Amendment, which is the right to due process and equal protection under the law. Although on the surface this decision was a ruling about the death penalty, the deeper commentary was about the protections, or lack thereof, of the Fourteenth Amendment. Racial minorities could no longer claim discrimination under the Fourteenth Amendment. Although most cases regarding racial discrimination in the Second Reconstruction were brought to trial under the Fourteenth Amendment, the *McCleskey* ruling was also about the Eighth Amendment, which prohibits cruel and unusual punishment. The impact of the case on the war on drugs was apparent in the extreme number of racially charged cases that proceeded through the courts in the following decade. Much like racial discrimination in the Antidrug Acts of 1986 and 1988, punishments for blacks and whites have statistically been unequal; the Supreme Court has continued to uphold laws that support racial discrimination.

Although the war on drugs originated in the executive office and expanded through the legislative branch, the Supreme Court perpetuated the expansive guidelines and set new precedents. In 1990, *California v.*

Acevedo allowed the court to question whether police should be permitted to conduct a warrantless search of cars. The Supreme Court ruled under the Fourth Amendment that "police [may] conduct a warrantless search of a container with an automobile if they have probable cause to believe the container has evidence." In this 6-3 decision, the "automobile exception" modified how police conducted searches of vehicles when suspected persons who were minorities were stopped. As discussed in *The New Jim Crow*, after the *Acevedo* ruling, police could justify car searches without providing proof of evidence. A new dynamic was put into play between the police and those they stopped. Without the restriction of a warrant and with the blessing of "probable cause," the police were essentially given free rein to search vehicles.

Six years later, the court revisited the issue of car searches. Plainclothes police officers were working undercover in a community that was considered to be drug dominated. During the investigation, they watched a vehicle that was stationed near an intersection for a "long period of time." When the vehicle finally moved, the police pulled the truck over for failure to use a turn signal. The warrantless search of the vehicle resulted in an arrest for possession of crack cocaine. When the case of *Whren v. United States* reached the Supreme Court, *Acevedo* had already set a precedent for the question of constitutional legitimacy of police searches: Should police be free to "use minor traffic violations as an excuse to stop motorists for drug investigations—even when there is no evidence whatsoever that the motorist has engaged in drug crime"? The court unanimously decided— yes.

An essential component of the *Whren* ruling was the conclusion that racial bias in court cases could not be argued under the Fourth Amendment. In the *Whren* case, writes Alexander, "the Court barred any victim of race discrimination by the police from even alleging a claim of racial bias." The court allowed a caveat that permitted citizens to claim discrimination under the Fourteenth Amendment, but because of the *McCleskey* precedent this is nearly impossible for anyone to prove. The uninhibited searches now protected under the Fourth Amendment created a new context for the stop-and-frisk tactics of the police in the war on drugs. Arbitrary searches of young men of color would become an anticipated process for those living in urban areas—with or without a car.

Additionally, during the 1990s the courts created new precedent in the jury selection process. During jury selection, judges of the lower-level courts were permitted to exercise their own racial prejudice and many other forms of discrimination. As discussed by Alexander, in 1995 the issue of prejudice in jury selection came to the Supreme Court in the case of *Purkett v. Elem*, which created a new precedent. To the dismay of the anti-racism advocates, the Rehnquist Court decided that any race-neutral reason that is presented, regardless of how irrational or unfounded the rationale, is enough to justify the exclusion of an individual from a jury. The examples during the oral argument included haircuts, mustaches, and beards as acceptable race-neutral explanations. Consequently, this absurdity disproportionately impacted people of color throughout the jury selection process.

Simultaneously with the New Jim Crow, the American legal, educational, and employment systems of the 1990s responded to beliefs that America had become a post-racial society through affirmative action. The Cold War had protected affirmative action in the years after the original affirmative action case, *Regents of the University of California v. Bakke*. During the 1990s, violence and discrimination against blacks in American society transcended into the political sphere and created the impetus for new legislation. The narrative against affirmative action in America was rooted in the notion of "reversed racism" against whites that was believed by persons, mainly whites, who were convinced they were living in a post-racist America. As opposed to the 1970s when the civil rights movement was still fresh in the minds of Americans, the apparent success of affirmative action in the 1990s rationalized the backlash against the civil rights movement.

Affirmative action has been a contentious topic since it was first introduced to the courts in 1978. Allan Bakke applied to the University of California Medical School at Davis twice, and was rejected both times. The nation turned its attention to the case as Bakke and his attorneys argued from California courts to the Supreme Court that his rejection was based solely on his race. The Supreme Court was forced to answer if the University of California was violating the Fourteenth Amendment and the Civil Rights Act of 1964 by practicing affirmative action. The nine justices could not reach a concise decision on the question of affirmative action. They ultimately decided that a race quota system violated the Civil Rights Act; however, race could be used as one of several criteria for admissions. In other words, affirmative action is permissible. This ruling influenced how students were admitted to schools, hired for jobs, and treated professionally until the precedent was challenged again in the 1990s.

Although schools were the target of most affirmative action disputes, the Supreme Court reviewed the case of *Adarand Constructors v. Pena* (1995) and the debates around workplace hiring. The case originated in 1990 when Adarand Construction Inc. lost a federal subcontract to Gonzales Construction. The company that chose the minority firm (Gonzales) over the nonminority firm (Adarand) did so because it received a federal monetary incentive to use a minority firm. Upset over the loss of business, Adarand sued. The *Adarand* case questioned whether there is a presumptive disadvantage based on race alone that creates favored treatment or discriminatory practices and did this violate each American's right to due process under the Fifth Amendment? This same year, the Regents of the University of California voted privately to abolish affirmative action in their admissions practices for students and in the hiring process. The Supreme Court ruling and the school's decision were both indicative of a much larger shift that was to come the following year.

In 1996, the focus on affirmative action turned back to the education system. The U.S. Court of Appeals for the Fifth Circuit revisited the topic of affirmative action in *Hopwood v. University of Texas Law School.* Cheryl Hopwood sued when she was denied admission over minorities despite her higher test scores and grades. Unlike the Supreme Court decision in *Bakke*, the Circuit Court decided on a more cohesive opinion on the controversial issue: "The University of Texas School of Law may not use race as a factor in deciding which applicants to admit in order to achieve a diverse student body, to combat the perceived effects of a hostile environment at the law school, to alleviate the law school's poor reputation in the minority community, or to eliminate any present effects of past discrimination by actors other than the law school." Through this ruling affirmative action programming was effectively outlawed in Texas, Louisiana, and Mississippi.

During the 1990s, the courts, Congress, and the executive branch of government all addressed affirmative action. Additionally, the question of affirmative action was posed to some states. In November 1996, it was placed on the California ballot as an amendment to the State Constitution, Proposition 209; 54.6 percent of the voters in California voted yes to "prohibit public institutions from discriminating on the basis of race, sex, or ethnicity." As a result of the decision, students mobilized on college campuses, specifically Berkeley, in a manner that was reminiscent of the antiwar demonstrations of the 1960s. Twenty-three students were arrested when they seized the bell tower in protest. Many scholars view the votes on Proposition 209 to be the catalyst for the dialogue regarding affirmative action going into the twenty-first century.

The national evaluation of affirmative action became inevitable from that point forward; like many other cases, the controversial topic did not stop with the voters. Pro-affirmative action advocates brought the issue back to the courts and the California Supreme Court ruled that Proposition 209 was in fact constitutional. The debate over affirmative action traveled in and out of the California courts, and in 2012 the constitutionality of Proposition 209 was upheld. Before the 2012 decision, the rising tensions around the national debate made another assessment inevitable. It was only a matter of time before the Rehnquist Court ruled for the country on the issue of affirmative action.

The debate never ceased and appeared in various guises, but for the first time in twenty-five years, the Supreme Court explicitly addressed the issue of school admissions and race. In 2003, the court decided on two separate but parallel cases, one concerning law school and the other undergraduate admissions. The case of *Grutter v. Bollinger* conclusively upheld the law school's affirmative action policy in a 5-4 decision, but when deciding on the undergraduate component in *Gratz v. Bollinger*, the justices ruled 6-3 to strike down the policy. In the ruling, Justice Sandra Day O'Connor set the court up to review the issue in another few decades when she stated that affirmative action was still needed in 2003, but "we expect that twenty-five years from now, the use of racial preferences will no longer be necessary to further the interest approved today." Contrary to O'Connor's prediction, subsequent legal decisions have demonstrated that the conversation around affirmative action is far from over.

During the 1900s, dialogues regarding race were not limited to employment and school admissions; the country became obsessed with the celebrity

football player and actor O. J. Simpson when he was placed on trial for murdering his wife, Nicole Brown Simpson. The wealth, celebrity status, and
racial politics surrounding the murder and trial inevitably placed the case in
the media spotlight. America tuned in from the beginning not only because
the two were high-profile celebrities but also because they were an interracial
couple. It was referred to as the "perfect storm" on PBS's *Frontline*; beauty,
perjury, and the latest technology in video and audio tapes added up to one
mesmerizing event that unfolded before American viewers.

The story began with the brutal murder of Nicole and her friend Ron
Goldman in California. Following the discovery of the bodies, the police
informed Simpson he was a suspect. After a time for him to surrender to
the police had been determined, he fled; the cable news stations interrupted
primetime television to follow the police chase of O. J. Simpson in his white
Bronco. The cameras followed the police and Simpson, who had a gun to his
head, for fifty miles as Simpson's friend and football teammate Al "A. C."
Cowlings drove. As described by Haynes Johnson in *The Best of Times*, cars
pulled over to the side of the highway and people cheered on the "Juice"
as the celebrity sped past them. Close to one hundred million Americans
watched the chase; "millions more than voted in the last presidential election in 1992, millions more, even than watched the last super bowl, which
attracts the greatest national TV audience." The chase ended when the
Bronco pulled into Simpson's house and the police apprehended him. The
media obsession was just beginning; soon cable news coverage was all O. J.
Simpson, all the time.

The jury was informed of evidence against Simpson that included blood-
stains matching the victims' blood found in his car and on his bedroom car-
pet, audiotapes of Nicole being abused by Simpson, the murder weapon that
was sold to Simpson five weeks before the murders, and the most famous
piece of evidence, the glove at the crime scene that matched one from his
house with DNA not only from Simpson but also the two victims. Additional evidence was exempt from the trial and many believe that it would
have changed the outcome. Despite the overwhelming evidence against the
celebrity, Americans were in suspense as they watched the trial and anticipated and placed bets on the verdict. Issues of racial identity, sexism, class,

and stereotypes presented themselves in the arguments of the lawyers and the barrage of media coverage.

The not-so-distant L.A. riots cast a shadow on the trial; many believed that if Simpson were found guilty the reaction would be similar to the anger that erupted after the verdict in the Rodney King case. Whereas the L.A. riots were rooted in the arduous relationship between racial minorities and the police, the O. J. Simpson trial was about celebrity culture and violence against women. The Simpson trial did, however, allow racist comments the opportunity to go from subtle to overt. Seemingly antiquated comments about race, the social inferiority of blacks, and the supposed criminal nature of race surfaced in the wake of the trial. Critics articulated racist biological assumptions that blacks were predisposed to being more violent and that black jury members would excuse O. J. because they believed in violence.

The trial was moved to downtown Los Angeles and this decision was viewed as a move to appeal to potential minority jurors (unlike the Rodney King case, which was moved out of Los Angeles to appeal to white jurors). The trial lasted 372 days and the continually building suspense captured the attention of citizens. In an interview with PBS, the anchor Ted Koppel said of the *Nightline* coverage of the trial, "I felt a certain amount of embarrassment about doing it on a regular basis . . . every time we did O. J. the ratings went up 10 percent." The media obsession only fed the appetites of Americans throughout the long duration of the trial.

The fixation on his celebrity status was apparent in the prosecution's first argument against O. J. Simpson. The lawyers aimed to differentiate between the actor and the abuser: "What we've been seeing, ladies and gentlemen, is just a public face, a public persona, a face of the athlete, a face of the actor. It is not the actor who is on trial here today. . . . It is not that public face. . . . He may also have a private side, a private face. And that is the face we will expose to you in this trial, the other side of O. J. Simpson." The prosecution enumerated the abuses committed by Simpson but underestimated the victim-blaming mentality of the jurors and viewers. The American people had preconceived notions about race and sex and were not willing to let those prejudices go; this resulted in the dismissal of some jurors.

The LAPD was once again involved in a high-profile case. The lead detective Mark Fuhrman had a long history of racism and there had been some speculation that he falsified documents. When asked on the witness stand if he had planted evidence in the case, he invoked his Fifth Amendment right against self-incrimination. Many believed Fuhrman planted the evidence during a warrantless search of Simpson's house. Tapes were released that had Fuhrman spouting racial epithets and displaying contempt for black citizens. The growing speculation that Fuhrman had been responsible for planting evidence against Simpson brought the attention back to the credibility of the LAPD. Although there was no denying that the DNA evidence linked O. J., Nicole, and Ron Goldman, the question was whether this was another example of the police "tightening up" a case. The evidence was further distrusted when footage of the glove showing that it did not fit Simpson was released; it appeared that the prosecution had lost the case and Simpson would walk.

When the verdict was broadcast live on October 3, 1995, it proved to be the most watched event in the history of television up to that time, as 150 million American viewers tuned in. When the verdict was revealed, the whole country paused to watch, causing long-distance phone calls and trading on the stock exchange to drop. Crowd control was hired to restrain the reporters outside of the courthouse. The long-anticipated acquittal had become a reality.

Before the trial even began, many whites in America believed that Simpson was guilty. In addition to the tremendous evidence against him, stereotypes of black male perpetrators shadowed Simpson. The case was complicated because it was rooted in race, but O. J. Simpson proved to be an exception to the norm, in part because of a malleable racial identity that came with his celebrity status. The multifaceted approach of the media to black identity created a storyline of heroism and stereotype; the whitening of O. J. was enhanced by his previous corporate endorsements of products from shoes to soda. Although he had integrated into popular culture, when it came to the trial, racism took precedent.

During the O. J. Simpson trial, race was the omnipresent elephant in the room. The image of the athlete fit into a specific normative reference point of black citizens. As pointed out by Michael Eric Dyson, "O. J. was a term that represented every black person that ever got beat up by the criminal justice system." Americans were intrigued by Nicole's murder and the arrest of O. J. because the brutal murder and the dramatic trial spoke to the heart of the discriminatory beliefs that were present in many of the new policies of the 1980s and 1990s. O. J. the athlete represented skill in professional football and the malleable qualities of black identity—a "colorless image" of the black man. Dyson elaborated on this paradox: "Americans [became] addicted to the Simpson case for more than its grotesque exaggeration of our secret racial fears. From its very beginning the case was overloaded with huge social meaning we claim to not be able to understand under normal circumstances." In an era when the war on drugs was ravaging poor communities of color, the loaded rhetoric that targeted Simpson as a black man, and not as a batterer, made the case about all black males, not just one.

Black identity in the 1990s was complicated because of the social mobility granted to those able to transcend the oppressive boundaries of the Second Reconstruction. The trial was deeply embedded in the schemas of "all black men as perpetrators" and "O. J., the athlete who embodied black exceptionalism." The controversial racist remarks that emerged during the year of the trial were a reflection of the Second Reconstruction. O. J. Simpson was extremely popular with all demographics of Americans, regardless of their race or ethnicity and despite his record of domestic violence. The racially loaded tone of the case proved that America was indeed experiencing a backlash against the civil rights movement and a regression away from progressive state and federal policies. The allegiance of many former fans and many black men, simply because of race, created a narrative around the case that will be analyzed indefinitely.

The 1990s demonstrated an unparalleled restriction on opportunities for minorities that did not label the policies "segregational," but tough on "law and order." The racially loaded rhetoric of the presidential campaigns and the welfare reforms created and rationalized policies that disproportionately impacted communities of color. The unspoken racism of the Supreme Court decisions masked the discrimination of the 1990s. Moving forward into the twentieth century, many believed that with the election of Barack Obama in 2008, the country moved forward into a post-racial society. The mass incarceration of black men that continues to expand daily amply demonstrates that America is not living in a post-racial society, but simply that the Second Reconstruction created a new context for race relations in America.

Recommended Reading

Michelle Alexander, *The New Jim Crow: Mass Incarceration in the Age of Colorblindness* (New York: The New Press, 2012), examines mass incarceration. Doris Marie Provine, *Unequal under Law: Race in the War on Drugs* (Chicago: University of Chicago Press, 2007), examines the war on drugs. Manning Marable, *Race, Reform, and Rebellion: The Second Reconstruction and Beyond in Black America, 1945–2006*, 3rd ed. (Jackson: University Press of Mississippi, 2007), provides a comprehensive look at the 1990s.

9

LGBT and Women's Rights

IN 1991, Susan Faludi published *Backlash: The Undeclared War against American Women*. Fifteen years later, in the 2007 edition of the iconic book, reflecting on the 1990s and early 2000s, she acknowledged the paradox of progress that felt uneasy, and noted that women's liberation continued to be an abstract idea for many Americans.

> In the early '90s, after the long despond of the Reagan years, American women shook off their torpor and began again to fight. The televised sexist spectacle of the Senate Judiciary Committee members mocking Anita Hill's allegations of sexual harassment against the Supreme Court. . . . After all this time, indignant women told each other across the nation, these men still "don't get it." Indignation led to anger, which led to mobilization, which by the spring of 1992 led to a massive pro-choice demonstration in Washington (one of the largest protest rallies of any kind in the nation's capital), the birth of dramatically effective feminist PACs like Emily's List, and a record number of progressive women running for national office. But women's political awakening provoked instant political reprisal.

She noted the apparent progress made in the "year of the woman," but "the year proved short" when right-wing policies took effect. In the 1990s, the need for protections for women facing sexual harassment, for members of the gay community, and for those seeking abortion services were brought to light across all government and private sectors, but the cases that came to trial did not inspire hope that progress could be made through the courts.

The legal decisions concerning gay and lesbian rights in America in the 1990s represented the struggle between the movements for and against litigation supporting LGBTQ equality, and resulted in a conservative backlash. By the end of the decade, there was an unprecedented federal law denying marriage equality to same-sex couples and "Don't Ask, Don't Tell" (DADT) was fully implemented. Whereas other minority groups achieved further social equality through protections guaranteed by the Fourteenth Amendment, the LGBTQ community still sought safety and equal opportunity from all three branches of government.

The case of *Bowers v. Hardwick* (1986) brought the legal debate of gay rights to the forefront. Georgia law declared homosexuality illegal by making all acts of sodomy illegal, and a sentence of up to twenty years if convicted. When the police invaded the home of Michael Hardwick, he allegedly said to the officer, "what are you doing in my bedroom?" When the case was brought to the Supreme Court, Hardwick sought protection under the Fourteenth Amendment. In June 1986, the court ruled that under the Fourteenth Amendment the right to privacy did not extend to "private consensual homosexual sodomy" on the grounds that "old law is good law." The 5-4 ruling specified: "(1) Homosexual sodomy is not a fundamental right. (2) A state legislature need only show a rational basis for criminalizing homosexual sodomy. (3) The promotion of public morality is a sufficient rational basis for justifying the criminalization of homosexual sodomy." Many scholars viewed the ruling in *Bowers* as the "second death of substantive due process." This ruling set a precedent for legal restrictions on the social agency of gays and lesbians in the 1990s.

During the 1990s, the struggle for equal rights was fought on both the federal and state level. Most notably, in Colorado there was a push for an amendment to the Colorado constitution. According to Lambda Legal, Amendment 2 "was a statewide antigay initiative prohibiting all branches of state government in Colorado from passing legislation or adopting policies prohibiting discrimination against lesbians, gay men or bisexuals based on their sexual orientation." On behalf of the plaintiff, Richard Evans, the American Civil Liberties Union (ACLU), the Colorado Legal Initiatives Project, and Lambda Legal worked as a coalition in *Romer v. Evans* and won a preliminary court ruling that placed a hold on the new amendment until the court case was resolved. The case was appealed to the Supreme Court and in 1996 *Romer* was decided 6-3 for the plaintiff. The justices ruled that Amendment 2 singled out homosexual and bisexual persons, imposing on them a broad disability by denying them the right to seek and receive specific legal protection from discrimination.

Justice Kennedy argued that the law under the equal protection clause could still disadvantage a specific group, so long as it could be shown to "advance a legitimate government interest." As described by the political scientist A. J. Richards in *The Case for Gay Rights*, Kennedy also argued that the case lacked any rational relationship to legitimate state interests and reflected unconstitutional prejudice. By depriving persons of equal protection under the law because of their sexual orientation, Amendment 2 failed to advance such a legitimate interest. Justice Kennedy concluded: "If the constitutional conception of 'equal protection of the laws' means anything, it must at the very least mean that a bare desire to harm a politically unpopular group cannot constitute a legitimate governmental interest." Kennedy's argument in *Romer* did not explicitly show that *Bowers* could have been overturned through the justices' language, but it certainly moved closer to viewing equal protection for gay, lesbian, and bisexual citizens as a basic human right. *Romer* set a precedent that the Colorado State Amendment 2 "singled out homosexual and bisexual persons, imposing on them a broad disability by denying them the right to seek and receive specific legal protection from discrimination," and that they were in fact protected under the Equal Protection Clause of the United States Constitution.

Bowers set an important precedent and context for the 1990s. It brought attention to the fight for equal rights and to multidimensional issues such as military and marriage equality. *Romer* represented an unprecedented victory; the LGBTQ community now had the right to seek the same protections as other minority communities. The ruling turned lesbian, gay, and bisexual Americans into a protected class. Although *Romer* changed American law, the lesbian and gay community was not thereafter free from discrimination. During the 1990s, many states in America still considered sodomy a criminal act, and rationalized the firing of lesbian, gay, and bisexual employees and withholding certain civil rights on the grounds that because of sexual orientation, these citizens were criminals. The ruling on

Colorado Amendment 2 was groundbreaking and many understood it was a first step to recognizing full civil rights for all Americans. *Romer* was essential to moving gay rights in America forward; however, it did not guarantee future rulings that would protect the rights of gay, lesbian, and bisexual Americans. In the 1990s, legal rulings on privacy and government invasions of homes did not protect LGBT citizens. Although a significant legal victory was just around the corner in 2003, in the 1990s the personal was the political and also the prosecutable.

After being discharged from the army for being gay, "outed" U.S. Army Captain Jonathan Hopkins spoke out about his firing. In a *New York Times* article, Hopkins wrote that being in the military under DADT forced him to spend "every hour at work trying, like all my peers, to be the perfect Army officer, taking care of and leading our soldiers. I also spent every day being paranoid, worrying about who suspected I was gay, and what they might do about it." This was not an uncommon experience for gays in the military during the 1990s, when progressive legislation ultimately created further oppression, rather than progress, for the gay, lesbian, and bisexual community.

In the 1990s, the laws on lesbian and gay rights (which typically did not include gender identity) were primarily focused on marriage equality and exclusion from the military and were rooted in the progress made during the late 1970s, after the Stonewall riots, and in the 1980s. LGBTQ individuals were classified "second-class citizens" and restricted from many benefits and rights because of marriage restrictions. All three branches of government were creating new laws that kept the LGBTQ community in a minority status. Although many have argued that DADT was originally designed to help protect lesbian, gay, and bisexual servicemen and women, it created the predicament that those in the military could serve, but not openly. The policy created by the Clinton administration in the 1990s was designed to allow Americans the opportunity to engage in military service as long as they did not disclose their sexual orientation. The law was protective if gay servicemembers were silent about their sexual orientation and served with discretion. The flaw in the law was that it rationalized the firing of military personnel for their sexual orientation. Over the years, the law intended to protect lesbians and gays in the military became a liability for those in service.

Throughout U.S. history, the American military has been forced to deal with the challenge of integrating blacks, women, and gays into a traditionally white, heterosexual, cisgender military service. This challenge resulted in the creation of many different policies that aimed to both include and exclude minority groups. In 1982, President Reagan proposed a defense directive that stated, "homosexuality [was] incompatible with military service" and homosexual acts were grounds for discharge. When Bill Clinton was campaigning for office, he promised the American people to overturn the long history of banning gays in the military. Although decades later DADT appears to be a conservative approach to the challenge of integrating the military, in a historical context it was considered an innovative proposal.

Within the first week after Clinton's inauguration, the promise he made attracted national attention from opposition groups within the Pentagon, on Capitol Hill, and in the private sector. Clinton responded by ordering the secretary of defense to draft a policy that would end discrimination based on sexual orientation. The political strategy of the proposal was to create an interim period that would address the resistance to and logistics of the shift to an integrated military. When DADT was presented, there was a visceral response from both Congress and conservative groups in the private sector.

The bipartisan legislature decided on the wording "Don't Ask, Don't Tell, Don't Pursue" as a compromise. According to the *Washington Post*, members of Congress inserted language into the bill that required the military to continue the regulations put into place by Reagan in the 1980s. When Clinton signed the bill into law, the government was now restricted from "ask[ing]" recruits to disclose their sexual orientation, as long as they did not "tell" if they were gay, lesbian, or bisexual: "A service member may be investigated and administratively discharged if he or she: (1) states that he or she is lesbian, gay, or bisexual; (2) engages in physical contact with someone of the same sex for the purpose of sexual gratification; or (3) marries, or attempts to marry, someone of the same sex." When the bill was signed, it was criticized on the grounds that it was forcing gays in the military to live a lie every day and was forcing further oppression through silence, though some viewed DADT as an improvement over the previous ban that prohibited gays from serving under any circumstances.

DADT was intended to protect lesbian, gay, and bisexual military personnel, but the number of discharges under DADT increased from the previous years under the Reagan protocol. The Servicemembers Legal Defense Network (SLDN) (now known as OutServe, SLDN) compared data from 1996 and 1997, which demonstrated the increase in violations of DADT and discharges each year in the 1990s. The study showed that there was a 39 percent increase in "Don't Ask" violations between 1996 and 1997, the majority of which were from the U.S. Navy. The "Don't Pursue" part of DADT showed the most violations. There was a 23 percent increase from the previous year, but unlike the "Don't Ask" violations, almost half of those reported came from the Air Force. Across all branches of the military, anti-gay harassment increased under DADT. The study showed that between 1996 and 1997 there was a 38 percent increase in harassment, including physical assaults and deaths. In the eighteen years DADT was in place, more than 14,500 service members were fired legally.

DADT did not provide protection to the servicemen and women it was designed to serve. The number of discharges continued to rise for six of the seven years of the Clinton presidency after the enactment of DADT. In the 1990s alone, thousands of people were discharged; there was a high of 1,301 discharges in one year before the start of the Afghanistan War, and women were disproportionately discharged during this time. The *New York Times* reported that although women were a smaller demographic in the military, close to 15 percent, they accounted for nearly 50 percent of the discharges. In 2001, when the number of discharges declined, it was due to the United States preparing for war after September 11. Historically, discharges of gay and lesbian service members have consistently declined during wartime. Clinton stood by his decision for many years, arguing that it was the only achievable progress at the time. DADT remained in effect until the Obama administration repealed it in December 2010.

During its first ten years, DADT cost almost $200 million. The cost to investigate a service person, remove the person from the military, and find and train a new replacement was estimated at approximately $52,800 per person. By the time the law was repealed, the cost of DADT from 1993 to 2010 was reported to be over $363 million. Those who were "outed" or came out while DADT was in effect were commonly threatened with criminal charges, confinement, nonjudicial punishment, and public disclosure during the investigation process. The logistical implementation of the law on the ground was found to contribute to the rising number of discharges. Even as late as 1997, the majority of leaders in the military had not read or received a copy of regulations and guidelines on investigating cases under DADT.

The policy intended for positive social change instead trapped enlisted gay, lesbian, and bisexual service members into an oppressive position of silence out of fear of termination. The hope that had risen in the LGBTQ community after the promise of the Clinton campaign was now dashed. Although DADT had been implemented, discrimination was still present and discharges increased. In 2010 during an interview with Katie Couric, Clinton said he wished he had not pushed DADT because it was not the policy he had wanted. He also blamed the discrepancy between what was proposed and what came about on Colin Powell. Clinton told CBS, "[Powell] sold me on 'don't ask, don't tell.' Here's what he said it would be: gay service members would never get in trouble for going to gay bars, marching in gay rights parades, as long as they weren't in uniform, that's a very different 'don't ask, don't tell' than we got." DADT is now viewed as a political blunder.

Three years after DADT, a new policy prohibiting same-sex marriage was introduced into Congress; this legislation was a negative response to pressure from the judicial system for marriage equality and was part of an extreme backlash against the LGBTQ community prompted by the 1993 case *Baehr v. Lewin*. The Defense of Marriage Act (DOMA) was the work of anti-gay activists to create anti-marriage equality laws on the state level, with the goal of including a federal restriction on same-sex marriage. These discriminatory laws gained momentum quickly; beginning with Utah in March 1995, some states passed legislation against legalizing same-sex unions. A. J. Richards reviewed the scholarship by William Eskridge and Mark Strasser, who argued that the denial of same-sex marriage is unconstitutional on the grounds of abridging the basic human right to intimate life, of which the right to marriage is an important institutional expression. Richards expanded on this argument to support the legality of equal rights for lesbian and gay citizens. He examined the rights granted by the Thirteenth and Fourteenth Amendments and the scope of basic rights that slavery violated (conscience, speech, intimate life, and work). By arguing

that discrimination is moral slavery, Richards reasonably asserts the constitutional right of equality for all LGBTQ citizens.

Baehr v. Lewin sparked a national debate on marriage equality. Although
the case was volatile and ultimately created one of the largest backlashes
against same-sex marriage, it also started a dialogue regarding equal rights
and mobilization for the LGBTQ community. The grassroots activism on
both ends of the political spectrum created new legal and social contexts for
same-sex marriage or marriage equality. *Baehr* reached the highest court
in Hawaii in 1993. The court ruling was the first in American history to
declare that banning same-sex couples from marrying was discriminatory
and illegal. This epoch-making decision was challenged and sent back to
trial court to determine if the state could justify its conclusion. *Baehr v.
Lewin* began in 1993; in 1996 a new state defendant appeared and *Baehr v.
Miike* began trial. Nevertheless, the trial judge rejected the state's position
and concluded that it was unjustifiable to deny marriage licenses to same-
sex couples.

The national focus turned away from DOMA and to Hawaii when a
state constitutional amendment prohibiting same-sex marriage moved to the
ballot. Anti-gay groups from across the country spent millions of dollars to
support the amendment and to raise voter and political awareness. In 1998,
Hawaii residents voted "no" to marriage equality, which set a new precedent
for the constitutional right of states to deny same-sex couples their civil right
to marry. Additionally, it placed restrictions on the definition of the term
"marriage," which it said could only exist between a man and a woman. In
1999, the Supreme Court of Hawaii decided in favor of this constitutional
amendment. According to Lambda Legal, the court's decision overrode a
lower court's ruling to grant marriage licenses to same-sex couples. That
same year the Hawaii Supreme Court's final decision on *Baehr v. Miike* was
that under the constitution of Hawaii there were no longer protections for
gay and lesbian citizens regarding their civil right to marriage.

Congress has stated that the passage of DOMA "was motivated by the
Hawaiian lawsuit" (*Baehr v. Lewin*) to recognize same-sex marriage. In
response to the ruling in Hawaii, DOMA was passed by the 104th Congress
and signed into law by President Clinton. Section 2 stated:

"No State, territory, or possession of the United States, or Indian tribe, shall be required to give effect to any public act, record, or judicial proceeding of any other State, territory, possession, or tribe respecting a relationship between persons of the same sex that is treated as a marriage under the laws of such other State, territory, possession, or tribe, or a right or claim arising from such relationship." Under federal law, same-sex marriages were not legally binding outside of the particular state that had granted the marriage license. Section 3 went on to define the terms "marriage" and "spouse" to exclude same-sex couples: "the word 'marriage' means only a legal union between one man and one woman as husband and wife, and the word 'spouse' refers only to a person of the opposite sex who is a husband or a wife."

There was a long history of discriminatory laws targeting gays, and the explicit language of the same-sex marriage bans was a part of the conservative backlash to the progress made in the courts for equal rights for the LGBTQ community. DOMA was especially powerful because from 1996 to 2013 it overruled state laws and protections and granted states the right to refuse to recognize same-sex marriages in other states.

The conservative backlash against *Baehr* resulted in thirty states passing same-sex marriage bans, and some states also passed constitutional amendments that defined the term "marriage" as existing between a man and a woman exclusively. After Utah became the first state to implement DOMA in 1996, thirteen states passed legislation banning same-sex marriage: Arizona, Delaware, Georgia, Idaho, Illinois, Kansas, Michigan, Missouri (according to the National Gay and Lesbian Taskforce, Missouri's 1996 anti-marriage law was overturned by its state supreme court, but another law passed in 2001), North Carolina, Oklahoma, Pennsylvania, South Carolina, South Dakota, and Tennessee. With the momentum gained from DOMA, nine more states passed anti-marriage legislation in 1997: Arkansas, Indiana, Maine, Minnesota, North Dakota, Mississippi, Virginia, and Texas. Virginia, Texas, and Utah passed legislation that allowed for both a narrow and broad statutory ban on same-sex marriage as well as a constitutional amendment. Also in 1997, some states took steps to further broaden prohibitions against lesbian and gay relationships. The laws passed in Arkansas, Florida, and Montana allowed the states to ban all forms of same-sex partner recognition: marriage, domestic partnerships, and civil unions. For some states, as with sodomy laws, these legislative changes impacted the rights of unmarried heterosexual couples. Alaska was the fifth state in 1998 to pass legislation and adopt a constitutional amendment that banned same-sex marriage. At the end of the decade, Louisiana also passed legislation and Nevada joined the anti-gay legislative push in 2000 with a state amendment. The states' responses to the "invitation" from Congress through DOMA to pass laws banning same-sex marriage swept the country in just a few short years.

DOMA served a political purpose and like DADT was introduced around election time. The *New York Times* noted that "[DOMA] was enacted in 1996 as an election-year wedge issue, signed by President Bill Clinton in one of his worst policy moments." In an interview, Representative Barnett "Barney" Frank stated that DOMA "was used by Congress in part to put President Clinton in a tough political spot ahead of his re-election race against Bob Dole." Many political analysts have recognized that the issue of marriage equality and the passage of DOMA were used to manipulate elections and that Clinton signed the bill into law as a political tactic out of fear that he would not achieve reelection. The president specifically drew criticism from LGBT rights groups who believed he could have recovered politically after vetoing the bill. Paul Yandura, who worked in the White House gay and lesbian liaison's office at the time, expressed his frustration: "[Clinton] could have said, 'Look, I'm just going to veto this.' If you look at the polling around that time, he was way ahead in the polls. And so, could he have taken a five-point dip? Sure. Were we worth it? I guess they decided that we weren't."

Clinton's stance on gay and lesbian equality during his presidency was complicated and wavering. The president commented on the bill publicly three months before it came to his desk to sign. Although he was not able to articulate the bill accurately when he first spoke about it, his press secretary confirmed that he would sign it. Clinton's campaign platform included equal access to military service for gay, lesbian, and bisexual Americans, but his domestic blunders in his first term in office ultimately created a weak agenda.

The initial ruling of *Baehr v. Lewin* provided LGBTQ couples in Hawaii with new rights, but after it passed in 1998 more extreme laws to exclude lesbian and gay couples were created. Those advocating for and against equal rights now strongly positioned themselves to organize and advocate. In 1999, three same-sex couples filed suit in Vermont on the grounds that the statute disallowing same-sex marriage was unconstitutional under state law. Their suit, *Baker v. State*, reviewed the constitutionality of discrimination against same-sex couples for marriage benefits. The December 1999 ruling stated that the state was required to extend marriage benefits and protections under Vermont law to couples of the same sex. But following the trend in many other states to ban same-sex marriage, in January 2000 the Republican Vermont state senator Julius Canns introduced legislation to amend the Vermont constitution to define the term "marriage" as between a man and a woman. It was designed to support the recent ballot measure in Hawaii. After months of legal battles, the Vermont legislature passed a bill that created "a legal coupling for gay and lesbian couples who [could not] legally marry." Signed into law in April 2000, the bill legalized civil unions for same-sex couples of Vermont.

Baker showed how fragile the movement for marriage equality was, but it also showed that the movement to secure full civil rights for the LGBTQ community at the end of the decade was determined. Still, it did not gain the same traction as the anti-gay movement until almost a decade later. The first challenge to DOMA did not reach the courts until 2003. The historic case of *Goodridge v. Department of Health* granted the right of marriage to citizens of Massachusetts.

In the 1990s the courts had the opportunity to rule on the right to reproductive choice. In 1992, *Planned Parenthood of Southern Pennsylvania v. Casey* was taken to the Supreme Court, and asked the question, as articulated by Oyez, "Can a state require women who want an abortion to obtain informed consent, wait 24 hours, and, if minors, obtain parental consent, without violating their right to abortions as guaranteed by *Roe v. Wade?*" The mass movements and major court rulings of the 1980s and 1990s rejected the progressive gains in civil rights of the 1960s and 1970s, and the growing strength of the anti-choice movement continued to erode the rights that *Roe* had granted. Three decades after *Roe*, the question of legal abortion was again up for review by some of the same members who had set the precedent for legalizing abortion in 1973. The Supreme Court reviewed the legality of a Pennsylvania law that issued five provisions to the Pennsylvania Abortion Control Act of 1982, which included: certain information requirements, a parental consent requirement, a judicial bypass procedure for parental consent, a husband notification requirement, notification exceptions, a definition of the term "medical emergency," and reporting requirements for abortion providers. The court's strong commitment to the doctrine of *stare decisis* had been present in other Fourteenth Amendment cases, and now the justices ruled again to "stand by decided matters." Although *Casey* did not overturn *Roe*, it upheld most of the Pennsylvania restrictions on access to abortion and represented a legal and societal trend to control and set limits on reproductive rights law. In *Casey*, the Supreme Court granted the state the right to decide how a woman could access abortion services within the state as long as it did not impose an "undue burden" on women who, prior to viability of the fetus, sought to have an abortion. Moving forward in the new millennium, this decision would craft the new political strategy of anti-choice advocates as they undertook, state by state, the creation of abortion restrictions.

Casey was a backlash to *Roe v. Wade* and to protections under American law for women to end a pregnancy. Although *Casey* did not overturn *Roe*, and reproductive-rights activists were grateful, the changes that were made to abortion access were alarming and confirmed the opinion of the justices that there was still a significant government bias against reproductive rights for women. The opinion by Justice O'Connor, Justice Kennedy, and Justice Souter stated: "nineteen years after our holding that the Constitution protects a women's right to terminate her pregnancy in its early stages, *Roe v. Wade*, that definition of liberty, is still questioned. Joining the respondents as amicus curiae, the United States, as it has done in five other cases in the last decade, again asks us to overrule *Roe*." And yet although the justices upheld the right to obtain an abortion, they severely limited access to lower-income women. *Planned Parenthood v. Casey* allowed states more leeway in their reproductive rights laws. The general perception is that O'Connor's swing vote kept abortion from becoming illegal in America and that the court has continued to uphold the right of women to terminate a pregnancy. However, the conditions placed on some social groups, specifically minors and women of color, for access to abortion are severe.

Casey is important not only because of the precedent it set for judicial activism, but also because it clarified how court decisions are made. Both *Roe* and *Casey* have been viewed as activist decisions because of the drastic changes they made to society and because they embody judicial independence and the conservative agenda of the late twentieth and early twenty-first centuries. The political scientist Thomas Keck has argued that legal decisions such as *Casey* and *Lawrence v. Texas* (which struck down state sodomy laws as they applied to gays and lesbians) were simply examples of liberal swing-vote moments in a conservative court during the 1990s and 2000s. Keck attributes the *Casey* ruling to Justice Sandra Day O'Connor's loyalty to *stare decisis* and substantive due process under the Fifth and Fourteenth Amendments that require all governmental intrusions into fundamental rights and liberties to be fair and reasonable. The abortion cases heard by the Rehnquist court polarized the bench between the liberals and conservatives and left Justice O'Connor and Justice Kennedy as the swing positions on the court. The court took a surprisingly broad interpretation of the Constitution and affirmed *Roe* (citing *stare decisis*) in a 5-4 ruling. Rehnquist, along with Justices Scalia and White, did not sway from their previous opinions in *Roe* to abide by a strict textual interpretation of the constitution. Although Rehnquist's fight to overturn *Roe* was overruled, *Casey* did impose the most extreme Supreme Court restrictions on abortion since 1973.

Casey specifically revealed the myth of rights for minority women and women living in poverty. The *Journal of the American Medical Association* (JAMA) reviewed the case and saw that the weakened legal protections disproportionably affected young, poor, minority, and rural women. These women would be hard hit by new obstacles to abortion that included mandatory waiting periods, biased counseling, and parental notification requirements. JAMA predicted that the restrictions would also exacerbate the shortage of physicians providing abortion services by making the procedure more costly and the providers' jobs more dangerous. Abortion was still legal in America, but the *Casey* ruling was made knowing that it excluded many populations from accessing the legal service. The women who did not have financial resources were challenged and defeated by the waiting periods and victims of domestic violence had to accommodate the new standard for multiple visits per termination and spousal notification. Because of poverty and racism, many women of color had significantly fewer options and depended on government funds, which did not support abortion procedures. Financial and race-related limitations also impacted women beyond the black and Latino communities: non-English-speaking women, women who were dependent on service jobs, and immigrants. As pointed out by the historian Dorothy Roberts, in the *Casey* ruling, Justices O'Connor, Kennedy, and Souter crafted their argument to underscore the importance of equal access to abortion by all communities. Legal rights and the ability to choose are integral to a woman's identity and social status.

Race has played an important role in reproductive laws. Roberts has noted that the ability of the law to impact reproductive rights for specific groups of people is tremendous. Whereas most pro-choice white women have spent their time fighting for the right to access safe and legal abortions, many women of color have spent their time avoiding sterilization and eugenics laws. The first major assault on *Roe* came with the Hyde Amendment in 1977, which banned Medicaid coverage for the termination of a pregnancy, but not prenatal care. These attacks on "teenagers and low-income women" have exploited racism and the stigma against single pregnant women by both denying them welfare rights and restricting their access to abortion.

Paradoxically, although it was a Supreme Court case that decriminalized abortion for women in America and granted them the right to choose, for minors in many states their decision to abort is still contingent on decisions made in a courtroom. After *Roe*, the courts began applying the criteria of age to the right to a legal abortion. The decision to abort is time sensitive; however, the restrictions against minors do not recognize this fact. Teens are able to abort their pregnancies, but not without first meeting several challenges imposed by the law. Those under the age of eighteen are able to use "bypass procedures" through the courts to evade the parental consent requirement. However, the law reveals that the right to choose is a myth because it extensively discriminates against women who are victims of incest, who are of lower socioeconomic standing, and women who live in rural areas.

Helena Silverstein analyzed the discrimination inherent in the law in *Girls on the Stand*. She argues that many pro-choice activists have "fallen victim" to the ideology of the myth of rights under the law, which has ultimately created "a naïve faith in the impartiality and functionality of the judiciary." This misplaced faith is not due to an inability to understand the discriminatory law per se, but stems more from the belief that the courts when deciding these cases will protect the young women. Although there have been moments in American history where the legal system has ruled in favor of protecting women, this has decidedly not been a universal judicial standard. Silverstein argues that "in the context of parental involvement laws, the myth of rights fosters an idealized view of the bypass process . . . those lured by the myth of rights presume that courts will be prepared to handle bypass requests, that minors will have access to those courts, and that, by and large, judges will treat requests neutrally."

There are apparent legal protections for minors who seek abortions, but they have proven to work as an additional barrier. For example, minors have the right to sue the court if they believe the law has been misapplied in their case. However, if a minor is even able to appeal to the court to take her case seriously and time is of the essence because of trimester considerations, not only would it not be in her best interest to sue the court, but the chance of a young girl taking legal action against the state is "almost unimaginable." As if seeking an abortion were not challenging enough for young females, they are required to go through the long process of appealing to the courts at the very moment they require the abortion—clearly an unreasonable requirement. Even communicating to a stranger who has the authority to determine the rest of one's life can be devastating and deterring. These social and psychological factors are a part of the protection of the myth of rights and make the laws that are supposed to protect women oppressive and ineffective.

Activists have different opinions regarding the flaws in the bypass laws; some call for the eradication of the laws, whereas others want reform. Silverstein argues that the gap between legal rights on the books and those that are in fact applied is enormous. A judge's personal religious beliefs make the myth of rights even more apparent. The assumption that if a law has been passed it is enforced and is not influenced by social factors is idealistic, but not realistic. Abortion is one of the most controversial and contested issues in the law and in society, and because of this there is the feeling that it is not a personal decision or right. One sees frequently the belief that a male judge knows what is best for a young girl. In the law, these discriminatory practices are rationalized to give the illusion, through the process of appeal and bypass laws, that the right to choose as a whole is still protected. Silverstein notes that "while *Casey* does not explicitly apply the undue burden test to Pennsylvania's parental consent mandate, neither does it limit application of the test to those regulations of abortion that affect adult women." So although *Casey* did not impact minors' rights explicitly and Silverstein argues that the new law did not unduly burden minors, the law still impacted youth and supported previous rulings that restricted minors' access to reproductive decisions.

As was aforementioned, Keck pointed out that rulings such as *Casey*, and other cases dealing with sexuality, do not reflect an overarching liberal agenda, but are moments in American history that show liberal swing votes within a conservative Supreme Court. The access that women have today under *Casey* is without a doubt different from the previous criminalization they experienced before *Roe*. Nevertheless, the restrictions from the 1992 decision have failed women in those areas where discrimination already existed. It is challenging to accept that although activists have worked exceptionally hard for progress, the law still does not in fact impart the protection that it is required to provide.

The movement against sexual harassment had gained significant momentum in the decades before the 1990s. The term "sexual harassment" was not used until the 1970s. Like many other acts of violence against women, there had previously been no term for the violations women were subject to in the public and private sectors. The innovative changes in state, federal, and workplace policies in previous decades made women believe that for the first time in history they would have legal protections. Many women in the 1990s came forward with accusations against harassers. They spoke up, only to be let down by the law. The Senate hearings on Anita Hill's testimony against Clarence Thomas, the end of the first class-action lawsuit on sexual harassment in the workplace, and the attention given to military-related incidents created a new era for the fight against sexual harassment, but ultimately left victims without support and resolution.

In 1986, *Meritor Savings Bank v. Vinson* ruling granted women access to the legal system for sexual harassment suits. *Meritor* is arguably the most important sexual harassment case in legal history, and was the first such case to reach the Supreme Court. The ruling gave a clearer definition of the terms "hostile environment" and "quid pro quo," in which "submission to or rejection of [unwelcome sexual] conduct by an individual is used as the basis for employment decisions affecting such individual." Once the legal definition of sexual harassment was established in *Meritor*, women could file lawsuits under the new precedent. Although *Meritor* was essential to advancements in sexual harassment law, women continued to be let down by judges and juries across America. The case broke down barriers, but did not provide a universal solution. Judges have consistently defined the term "sexual harassment" inconsistently and have used women's personal histories against them. Although the legal process often appears anarchic and victims often find that they are not protected, the cases have resulted in legal statutes that ostensibly protect victims of harassment.

The media attention given to sexual harassment in the 1990s was unparalleled in American history, but did not facilitate the deep social reforms that many had expected. In *The Women's Movement against Sexual Harassment*, Carrie Baker concluded that the courts pushed the sexual harassment law in a progressive direction during the 1990s. She attributes this push to the number of high-profile scandals that occurred during the decade across social spheres—including all three branches of government, the military, and the private sector. Although the high-profile nature of the scandals is undeniable, the progress made is debatable. There was significant improvement in creating a term to define the action of "sexual harassment" and subsequent improvements in the law. In the 1990s, the term "sexual harassment" was still new in American society. Of all the court cases on sexual harassment and the rights of women in the workplace, the story of Anita Hill has become the most widely discussed. In subsequent public scandals, Hill and Clarence Thomas were commonly referenced and quoted; they remain the high-profile faces of an age-old issue now discussed openly.

Anita Hill brought the problem of sexual harassment to the forefront of public awareness and discussion. Hill was a Yale graduate who had been employed as an assistant to Clarence Thomas, a friend of her law firm and a young black man who would assume the top civil rights position in the

Department of Education. As Jane Mayer and Jill Abramson wrote in *Strange Justice: The Selling of Clarence Thomas*, this exciting career opportunity to "be [Thomas's] single special assistant seemed like the break she had been waiting for her whole life." The story of the events that unfolded in the next three to five months were familiar to many women across America who were employed in the male-dominated professions and industries. Thomas began asking his assistant Hill out socially in June 1981 and would demand that she justify her reasons for turning him down. When she would not go out with him, Thomas began discussing sex in front of her: he boasted about his sexual history, the pornography he watched, his sexual preferences, the size of his penis, and oral sex. According to Mayer and Abramson, Hill felt vulnerable, uncomfortable, and did not feel that "he was genuinely interested in [me]—only in coercing me." As the harassment from Thomas worsened, like many other women in similar situations, Hill became increasing worried about losing her job and not being able to find other suitable employment. The final straw for Hill came after Thomas made sexual references to her clothing and body, and the infamous pubic hair on the coke can incident. Hill explained in her own words at the Senate hearings, in response to a series of questions from the chairman (and future vice president) Senator Joseph Biden (D-Delaware), that when they were working at the United States Equal Employment Opportunity Commission (EEOC) office, Thomas had stood up from his worktable and looked down at a can of soda on his desk and asked, "who put pubic hair on my Coke?" Hill writes in her memoir, *Speaking Truth to Power*, that, disgusted and shocked, she left the office as he laughed behind her. And she had to relive each humiliating incident that occurred with Thomas when she testified before Congress.

The struggle for protection against sexual harassment had been ongoing for decades, and in 1992 it was presented live on televisions across the country. When Bush had first nominated Thomas, it was expected that he would win the confirmation for the associate justice seat. The Senate vote to confirm Thomas was postponed by Hill's accusations and the hearings that were held to address the scandal. Chairman Biden began the hearings on October 11, 1999 by stating: "This is a hearing convened for a specific purpose: to air specific allegations against one specific individual, allegations which may or may not be true." The Senate hearings were important to how the issue of sexual violence against women was handled by the American government and also spoke to the bipartisan issues in Washington during the early 1990s. Rosemarie Skaine argued in *Power and Gender* that the open seat on the Supreme Court represented a fight between Congress and the White House for control over the government. During an election year, the Senate hearings were not only about a woman bringing charges of sexual harassment against her employer, but also about the sides that the Democrats and Republicans felt they must take to attack the opposition, the Democratic Congress, the Republican president, and upcoming vacant seats in the electoral arena. Taking all issues of gender-based discrimination and harassment out of the equation, the Republicans knew that by supporting the confirmation of Thomas, they would not be allowing the Democrats to further limit the powers of President Bush. The political complexity of the issue explains some of the politics and victim blaming permeated the Senate Judiciary Hearings on the Thomas-Hill case.

Although many improvements in the laws to protect women from discrimination and harassment were made on the state and federal level in the 1970s and 1980s, the 52-48 appointment of Thomas to the Supreme Court signified the indifference of Americans and the government to hold employers and politicians accountable for inappropriate behavior with vulnerable employees. When Hill worked for Thomas, he had threatened that if she ever came forward about his behavior, she would be ruining his career. The dismissal of women's allegations of sexual harassment in the workplace, including complaints by government employees, was apparent in the response of all branches of government to support the appointment of Thomas and by the media response to Anita Hill.

In the decades since the hearings, Hill has been highly stigmatized publicly. The conservative writer David Brock attacked Hill in a lengthy article that examined her allegations and the Senate Judiciary Hearings. Brock posed the question, "So Hill may be a bit nutty, and a bit slutty, but is she an outright liar?" As Debran Rowland points out in *Boundaries of Her Body*, Brock has since recanted his character assassination of Hill, but his catchy dig at the young woman has been used in the years since to blame women victims of sexual harassment and to dismiss their allegations and question their character. This pattern of belittling women by using their (perceived) sexuality to destroy reputations and credibility dates back to the biblical era and has been continuous. The blaming of Anita Hill and the other women who came out as victims of sexual harassment during the 1990s ran rampant in the newspapers and on television; the media narratives attempted to destroy the women who came forward as victims of a crime to seek protection under the law.

In the movie *North Country* (2005), which interpreted the court case *Jenson v. Eveleth Mines*, Woody Harrelson's lawyer character reiterates the sentiments of David Brock during the Anita Hill scandal. He tells Charlize Theron's character Josey Aimes (a victim of sexual assault, based on the real-life Lois Jenson) that the courtroom will not fix the problem of sexual harassment in the workplace, particularly not in the male-dominated mining industry. He explicitly warns her, "Look at Anita Hill, because she's you. You think you're outgunned at the mine, wait till you get to a courtroom. It's called the 'nuts and sluts defense.' You're either nuts and you imagined it, or a slut and you asked for it. Either way, it's not pleasant." When Lois Jenson discussed the trauma of having to testify about the abuses she endured, she mentioned that she and other women looked to primetime television to the Senate hearings and Hill's allegations against Clarence Thomas. Along with thirty million other Americans, Jenson watched the media take a story that so many women were familiar with and play it out with fourteen white male senators as judges. Jenson would soon make her own history when United States District Court Judge James Rosenbaum allowed *Jenson* to proceed as the first class-action lawsuit for sexual harassment. Lois Jenson, her colleagues, and lawyers soon learned, however, that the trial would turn into an almost decade-long proceeding, during which the legal system would consistently provide protection to the defendant with the most money.

After a six-month trial, U.S. District Judge Richard Kyle decided liability in *Jenson*. In May 1993, Kyle ruled that he did not believe that Eveleth Mines was liable for preventing sexual harassment in their workplace. However, he decided that it was responsible for the development of programs that would educate all Eveleth employees on sexual harassment. That summer, the retired federal magistrate Patrick McNulty was assigned to oversee the trial and determine the monetary compensation for the women's traumas. McNulty used the centuries-old tactic of investigating the victim's personal history to discredit their character. The women's medical records, from their births to the present, were released and made fair game in the trial. The medical records allowed Eveleth's attorneys to interrogate the women about previous relationships and experiences. McNulty allowed the record of Jenson's high-school rape, which produced her first child, to be used as evidence against her, despite the fact that the case concerned current sexual harassment in the workplace. The inclusion into evidence of previous sexual encounters and the testimonies of former boyfriends and husbands permitted the women to be judged solely on their perceived sexuality and not on the circumstances of workplace harassment.

The trial for damages continued, with breaks, from summer 1993 to March 1996, after which McNulty wrote a 416-page report that labeled the women "histrionic" and publicized the details of their personal and sexual histories. After a nearly three-year trial and the public shaming of the plaintiffs, McNulty ruled that the women be compensated on average for only $10,000 in damages. In December 1997, the Eight Circuit Court of Appeals reversed McNulty's opinion and ruled that a new jury be assigned to re-try the case against Eveleth.

On the night before the new jury would have reviewed the case, the women who filed the first class-action lawsuit against their employer for sexual harassment were forced, after seven years of court battles with Eveleth Mines, to settle outside of court and receive $3.5 million in damages. After years of litigation, the women ultimately won monetary compensation when they settled the case. Although not an ideal ending to a long story, the visibility that the case brought to the women's movement against sexual harassment, and the growing activism, was essential to future successes in court to protect workers.

Even American football was not exempt from sexual harassment of women. In 1990, the *Boston Herald* sports reporter Lisa Olson sued the New England Patriots for sexual harassment that occurred during her interview with some team members in the locker room. *Playboy* magazine disregarded the severity of the incident when it published an article about the case and offered Olson a photo spread. The harassment of Olson brought attention to how all female reporters were treated and discriminated against. Olson was the object of much criticism; the media believed that football, like other

professional sports, was a man's domain and that women deserved what they
got. Olson was publicly slandered by many members of the Patriots and
received death threats for coming forward. Eventually, Olson settled her lawsuit with the Patriots, their owner, and several current and former employees. Her ability to do so demonstrated the importance of the movement
against sexual harassment as well as the ostracism and criticism that victims
experienced by coming forward.

In Carrie Baker's analysis of the legal system, grassroots movements,
and incidents of sexual harassment, she asserts that the legal system and
process was a powerful advocacy tool in late twentieth-century American
society, but it depended on receptive judges. Her analysis of the *Jenson* case
shows how a judge or justice could change the law according to their personal bias. Although the women in that case ultimately received monetary
compensation for damages and made history with the first class-action lawsuit, they also were let down repeatedly by the court system. The real social
change of the 1990s was not in the legal decisions that were made but in
the visibility that the sexual harassment movement gained by being placed
on the public agenda.

Throughout the 1990s, accusations of sexual harassment became more
and more prevalent. Previously, many cases were brought to public attention
in the 1970s and 1980s, but were not as socially prominent. The landmark
case of *Bundy v. Jackson* in 1981 was the first time the courts (the U.S. Court
of Appeals for the Second District) decided that Title VII of the Civil Rights
Act of 1964, which protects against employment discrimination based on
race, color, religion, sex, and national origin, could exist for sexual insults.
The case did not reach the Supreme Court and, according to Baker, it set limits on discrimination lawsuits by initially ruling that "sexual harassment did
not in itself represent discrimination absent any tangible economic effects."
However, a precedent was set for later in the 1980s when the court would
rule for protections against sexual harassment under Title VII. In *The Most
Exclusive Club: A History of the Modern United States Senate*, the historian
Lewis Gould attributed some of the progressive gains for women to 1992
being the "year of the woman." More women candidates were seeking seats
in the Senate than any other year so far, and four women were elected to the
legislative chamber, including Senators Barbara Boxer and Diane Feinstein.

Additionally, the beginning of the 1990s saw the passing of the Civil Rights Act of 1991 as an amendment to the Civil Rights Act of 1964. The new act allowed for the improvement and strengthening of federal civil rights laws to provide damages in cases that included intentional employment discrimination. These progressive changes were unparalleled and created a new frontier for women in the workplace. Sexual harassment was in the public eye for the first time in American history. Many of the men accused disparaged the character of their accusers; they argued that the women were after money or wanted to destroy the political careers of congressmen. Nevertheless, after Anita Hill, women across America had a face for their experiences and were more determined and confident.

The legislative branch experienced many scandals on both sides of the aisle. In 1992, Senator Brock Adams, a Democrat from Washington state, terminated his bid for reelection after the *Seattle Times* ran a story that eight women had come forward with allegations of sexual harassment and rape. Adams had first been accused of drugging and assaulting a House aide in 1987. He denied the accusations when the story broke and continued to serve his term, but eventually withdrew from the race as more women came forward and stories continued to break after he announced his bid for reelection. In the same year, Senator Daniel K. Inouye (D-Hawaii) and Senator Bob Packwood (R-Oregon) were accused of sexual harassment. The noted historian Lewis Gould contended that the context had now shifted, as compared with the 1980s, when "women were marginalized. Male condescension was routine. Sexual harassment flourished." Gould addressed sexual harassment and assault allegations as a larger issue within the elite gentleman's club of the Senate. Packwood proved that sexual harassment was a workplace issue with his advances on female staffers in his Washington and Oregon offices. The Senate Ethics Committee interviewed several witnesses, but ultimately it was the Senator's personal and detailed diary, subpoenaed by the committee, that revealed his inappropriate behavior. Packwood was forced to resign when the allegations of sexual harassment and his drinking problem were made public by the media. Gould also looked at senatorial culture in the 1990s and argued that the legal battle with Clarence Thomas was representative of how much the Senate remained a male preserve. Although there was an Ethics Committee, lawmakers avoided thinking about the prevalence of sexual harassment incidents within the halls of Congress. This workplace issue was evaded as a matter of political policy.

Hill and *Jenson* set precedents in the beginning of the decade; even if the law did not protect victims, it made sexual harassment in the workplace visible to Americans. At the close of the decade, the Rehnquist court decided on the logistics of liability in sexual harassment cases. In *Burlington Industries, Inc. v. Ellerth* the court ruled in a 7-2 opinion that under Title VII employers are liable for supervisors who create hostile working conditions for employees. However, with *Ellerth*, a new precedent was set; according to the Oyez Project, "in cases where harassed employees suffer no job-related consequences, employers may defend themselves against liability by showing that they quickly acted to prevent and correct any harassing behavior and that the harassed employee failed to utilize their employer's protection." The court decided that this defense could not be used by employers when the employee is forced to take legal action because of harassment—as in the case they were reviewing.

Congress, specifically the Senate, was in a precarious position regarding sexual harassment in the 1990s. Senator Inouye and Senator Packwood were exposed in the media for sexual harassment and rape, but simultaneously, the Senate was responsible for the Clarence Thomas hearings and the military scandal after the incidents at Tailhook. Congress was a disappointment to many citizens because of its responses to the numerous scandals that broke in the 1990s. Gould attributed this feeling to the elitist male culture of the Senate, which did not change even in the 1990s when more women were present.

In the 1990s women in the military were struggling for equality in the right to participate in combat, but were also fighting abroad in Operation Desert Storm and Desert Shield. This is not to use the term "women" monolithically. Lesbian and bisexual women experienced dual discrimination: from the laws banning them from serving because they were women and from the controversy surrounding DADT. The end of the Gulf War specifically created an interesting paradox for women. As the women's historian Linda Kerber observed in *No Constitutional Right to Be Ladies*, women pilots were demanding an end to the combat restrictions that had been in place for decades. Some interpretations of the Second Amendment claimed that only men had the right to join militias; this belief alone barred women from entering military institutions. Over the course of the last quarter of the twentieth century, this interpretation became increasingly contested. Kerber writes that women pilots were heading the efforts for equality in the military, not the enlisted women on the ground.

The 1990s saw changes in military culture, specifically, the U.S. Navy was influenced by the box office hit *Top Gun* and the implementation of DADT, which moved the conversation in a new direction. Kerber argues that when the categories "combat" and "noncombat" were eroded, that is, when women could participate in combat, a new context was created for the roles that men and women were expected to play in the military. The focus now shifted to strengthening the differences between heterosexual men and women in the military and a culture of hypermasculinity (top gun culture) became dominant. These institutional changes were occurring at the same time as the biggest sexual harassment scandals in American military history were aired by the media. Although the laws changed over the course of the 1990s, they continued to protect the male traditions of military culture.

The navy was influenced by pop culture in the 1990s. It saw a direct increase in enlistments after *Top Gun* was released in 1986. The carefree, egotistical attitude of the Tom Cruise character Maverick was appealing to American men. The story merged military culture with sex and celebrity culture, creating an image of military service as hedonistic: a way to obtain women as sexual objects and live on the wild side. Jean Zimmerman, in *Tailspin*, described Maverick as "something new for the military, an MTV hero." The *Top Gun* soundtrack rocketed to number one on the Billboard charts after the release of the movie and was popular even decades later. The only women in the movie are sexual objects and wives; the main female character, Charlie, is a conquest and lover for Maverick. The sexual focus and hypermasculinity of the film, it has been argued, faithfully mirrors the culture that newly enlisted servicemen were expected to participate in at the annual Tailhook Symposium, a three-day event with over five thousand navy and Marine Corp officer participants. A hypersexual, hypermasculine culture already existed before the release of *Top Gun* and the incidents at Tailhook were only about men getting caught for participating in the gauntlet. The

United States military has always preferred a solely male enlisted force since its creation. Women faced challenges on several fronts regarding protection and equality in the military. The Aberdeen scandal (to be discussed) and the Tailhook scandal created a unique opportunity for the military to address the issue of sexual harassment in the enlisted women's workplace. However, two servicemen, McKinney and Kelso, were allowed to retire with pensions and were not further reprimanded for their (different) roles in the sexual harassment charges. Military sexual harassment policies were a work in progress in the 1990s. The policies that existed revealed that rights were a myth and inspired hollow hope, but they also gave the furtive issue of institutional sexual abuse more public exposure.

Women were now coming forward and filing complaints against hostile work environments. Lieutenant Paula Coughlin is another example of a brave woman who spoke out against gender-based violence in the workplace. It was she who exposed the severity of the harassment that was occurring in the navy's Tailhook Association, "an independent, fraternal organization internationally recognized as the premier supporter of the aircraft carrier and other sea-based aviation." During the 1991 Tailhook convention at the Las Vegas Hilton, several instances of sexual harassment and assault took place against the women who worked in the navy as comrades of the men and women who had been invited to the elaborate party.

In the month after the assaults at the hotel during the symposium, Captain F. G. Ludwig Jr. stated in a debriefing document that the annual symposium had been predicted to be the "mother of all Hooks" and confidently assessed that "it was." The navy had racked up $23,000 in damages to the hotel, which included the replacement of carpeting and smashed windows that had been shattered when couches were thrown at them. There were reports made by five women who had been forced through the third-floor "gauntlet": they had drinks spilled on them, were verbally abused, physically abused, and sexually assaulted. According to Zimmerman, the feelings in the first weeks after Tailhook of the men who had participated were that it was "just about the best party ever." The women brutalized at the party would receive little legal protection.

In the weeks after Tailhook, Coughlin decided to take action. Her boss, Admiral John Snyder, dismissed her request for help on several occasions over the course of several weeks. He used victim-blaming language and told her that she should have expected this behavior; that's what she "got" for going up to the third floor. Coughlin filed formal charges through the navy, and only after she wrote formal complaints to navy headquarters in Washington, DC did she receive Snyder's support in a letter. The longer the military did not address her complaints, the more distressed Coughlin became. Eventually she decided that she wanted the men to pay and went public with details of the assaults.

The Naval Investigative Services (NIS) and the Navy Inspector General issued initial reports based on their investigations. By February 1994, 140 cases of misconduct had surfaced. Coughlin provided a face for the scandal, but there were up to ninety other women who had been violated by the servicemen, including six officers' wives. In the end, over fifty men were implicated for participating in the "gauntlet" and assaulting the women, including an underage girl from Vegas who had her clothes removed. Of the men implicated, six were accused of blocking the investigation by the NIS. The investigation was further hampered by the officers who chose to lie about the events or claimed that because of heavy drinking they could not remember anything. Some officers refused to speak about the events out of fear of implicating themselves or others. Coughlin identified the main person who assaulted her, but no one was willing to testify as a corroborating witness. During the pretrial hearing, the defense lawyer for the man accused of being the lead perpetrator presented a photograph that he claimed was from the Tailhook event. In the photograph, the man did not wear the clothing that Coughlin had described in her report. Because of this, the navy judge dismissed the case.

The course of the action taken by the NIS and investigators led to the same place that had heard evidence in the Anita Hill case years earlier—the Senate. In 1994, the Senate was once again faced with the responsibility of deciding the future of men who had been responsible for the harassment of women in the workplace. The main target of the Tailhook scandal on the Hill was the chief of naval operations, Frank Kelso. The hearings were to determine whether Kelso would be allowed to retire with four stars or be demoted to two stars because of his failure to maintain order and discipline within the navy. Eyewitnesses placed Kelso and the Secretary of the

Navy, H. Lawrence Garrett III, near the gauntlet, despite their testimony
that they were nowhere near the third floor. Unlike Kelso, Garrett decided
to resign from the navy immediately and not proceed with the Senate hearings. Despite outspoken opposition from some members of the Senate, the
decision once again sided with the man on the stand by a 54-43 vote. There
was no punishment for Kelso and in 1994 he was allowed an early retirement
with all four stars.

Infuriated by the outcome of the Senate hearings, Coughlin and six
other victims of the gauntlet sued the Tailhook Association and the Las
Vegas Hilton for lack of security. The Tailhook Association settled with the
victims of the assaults before trial. The Hilton, however, decided to go to
trial. As with Anita Hill, the "nuts and sluts" defense was used during the
trial. The defense argued that Coughlin was a party girl and attempted to
portray her as a bad girl who had voluntarily participated in events that made
her a sexual object. Unlike other court cases in American history, the jury
did not buy into the defense argument and awarded Coughlin $6.7 million
in compensatory and punitive damages, which was later reduced to $5.2 mil-
lion. Judge Philip Pro had to reduce the award because of a Nevada law that
limited punitive damages to a maximum of three times the compensatory
damages. Although Coughlin had been compensated monetarily, she still
felt the trauma of the assault and the case. Michael Boorda, who replaced
Kelso, transferred Coughlin to his office of naval personnel, but this solution
could not remedy what had happened. Because of the vast amount of hate
mail and her lingering distress, in February 1995 Coughlin resigned from
the navy.

As with many other workplace sexual assault cases, the Tailhook incident represents a twofold issue: women were looking for protection from
and retribution for sexual harassment and assault, but also wanted to eradicate their second-class status in the workplace and society. Some scholars
view Tailhook as a response to the shifts in military culture, which created
a backlash against the equality that women were gaining. As pointed out by
Jean Zimmerman, the legal ban on women serving in all positions in the
navy was linked to assaults and their second-class positions. In 1990 and
1991, there were approximately forty thousand women deployed in the military during the Gulf War. Although many women contributed in a variety

of capacities during the operations, they were still barred from serving on combat ships and as navy pilots. The Women's Armed Services Integration Act of 1948 was originally decided on as an order of Congress; it was a complex law because it gave women a permanent place in the military services but restricted their assignments. Specifically, navy women were prohibited from serving on navy ships with men. Additionally, women in the navy and air force were restricted from any aircrafts that flew in combat. Women were being restricted to noncombative positions in each sector of the military. The first steps to repeal the 1948 law started in July 1991, the month before the Tailhook scandal. Both legislative branches had voted to lift the discriminatory law banning women from warplanes and to create a commission to review the issue. However, it was not until November 1993 that Congress successfully reversed the 1948 decision as part of the National Defense Authorization Act of 1994. This decision also segregated women by mandating that the secretary of defense notify Congress ninety days prior to "clos[ing] to female members of the Armed Forces any category of unit or position that at that time is open to service by such members" or "open[ing] to service by such members any category of unit or position that at that time is closed to service by such members." There has been speculation that it was because of the shame associated with the Tailhook scandal that Congress reversed the law that banned hundreds of thousands of enlisted women from serving on combat ships.

The landmark year of 1994 saw a number of government decisions for women's rights. In addition to allowing women to take to the sky, the U.S. Department of Defense reversed the previous "risk rule" that restricted women from "noncombat units or missions if the risks of exposure to direct combat, hostile fire, or capture were equal to or greater than the risk in the combat units they supported." The risk rule was commonly cited as limiting to women; now women could not be excluded from positions simply because of potential danger. However, the new policy still did not allow women to serve directly in open-ground combat positions. In January, Secretary of Defense Les Aspin established that "service members are eligible to be assigned to all positions for which they are qualified, except that women shall be excluded from assignments to units below the brigade level whose primary mission is direct combat on the ground." This initiative did not change the role of women in the military overnight and it further institutionalized sexist policies, but it also opened thousands of jobs to women, including 32,700 U.S. Army positions and 48,000 Marine Corps positions. According to the Department of Defense, the decision to exclude women from ground combat was made based on the experiences of women during Operation Desert Storm; others have speculated that it was also rooted in the assaults on servicewomen at Tailhook and the subsequent attention on women in the military.

The army also experienced sexual harassment scandals in 1996 and 1997. In 1996, incidents of rape, sexual assault, and sexual harassment at the army's Aberdeen Proving Ground surfaced. Nearly fifty women made sexual abuse charges, and of these, twenty-six were rape accusations. The courts ruled in favor of most victims and convicted eleven drill sergeants of marital rape and sexual harassment; only one was cleared. Sergeant Delmar Simpson was sentenced to twenty-five years in prison and dishonorably discharged from the army. In response to the scandal, the army set up a hotline and reported getting nearly two thousand calls. The army was forced to take a stand on sexual harassment. As a result, the Senior Review Panel was created. The investigation by the panel created an opportunity for women who were previously too scared to report incidents to speak up. Twenty-two-year-old Brenda Hoster came forward with sexual harassment charges against the top-ranking enlisted man, Sergeant Major Gene McKinney, also a member of the panel. Hoster accused McKinney of sexually assaulting her in her hotel room during an official trip to Hawaii in 1996. Seven weeks prior, Brenda Hoster had reported the assault to the Pentagon but it had taken no action and suppressed the complaint. Hoster explained that when they ignored her request for a job transfer, she, like many other women, concluded that the only option was to retire early. The sergeant major denied all of the allegations, but excused himself from duties until the case was reviewed. After months of litigation, the decision was to demote McKinney to master sergeant and allow him to retire months later with a full pension based on his position as the highest-ranked man in the army. This slap on the wrist proved that rights for women in the military was a myth.

In the 1990s women in the military endured multifaceted discrimination and conflict. While the military fought abroad in the Gulf War, Somalia, and the Balkans, sexual harassment was brought to the attention of the people and gay, bisexual, and transgender women were navigating the new DADT laws. The institutional policies in place forced women to overcome two forms of discrimination. The assault charges made in Tailhook were as much about sexual harassment as they were about second-class status within the military and the rest of society. The fight for equality within the military was the underlining issue for the women who were banned from serving in fight planes and who were in need of protection from their male colleagues. Decades of discrimination sealed the second-class status of women and supported the dehumanizing physical assaults and the prohibition against women in combat positions. Progressive change occurred now and then over the decade. For example, on October 20, 1994, the USS *Eisenhower* made history as the first carrier to deploy with men and women crewmembers. Small changes in public opinion and policy were evident in the protest of women senators against allowing Kelso to keep his stars and the decision to allow women to serve on combat shifts. However, as events in the years since have shown, women still do not have full legal protection in the military; an official policy to support equality has not been fully implemented.

In the 1990s activists sought new legal protections for women. The Violence Against Women Act (VAWA) was constructed to respond to the fallibility of the criminal justice system. Legislatures and activists viewed the act as an opportunity to create a responsive criminal justice system that would hold criminals accountable and coordinate community response to violence against women (the first collaboration between the criminal justice system, the social services system, and private nonprofit organizations that responded to domestic violence and sexual assault). When the bill was introduced, there were approximately four million women suffering from domestic violence. The legislation was groundbreaking and has since impacted American legal and social culture by providing monies to domestic violence and rape crisis programs across the country. It is important to note that VAWA was not a one-size-fits-all answer to domestic violence, but it was landmark legislation that changed the nation's response to sexual and domestic violence. The challenge was implementing VAWA on the local level and holding police officers and judges accountable; even many justices on the Supreme Court were vocal about their opposition from the beginning.

Senator Biden and Representative Barbara Boxer originally introduced VAWA to the Senate and House in 1991. According to Gregg Ivers and David Kaib, the version that Boxer introduced was opposed by the Bush administration, which had been lobbying senators behind the scenes on a civil-rights remedy within VAWA, arguing that the legislation was unconstitutional. This proposed civil-rights remedy would authorize victims of gender-motivated violence to sue their attackers for compensatory and punitive damages in federal court. The Department of Justice submitted a letter to the House and the Senate Judiciary Committees imploring them not to approve the legislation. Ivers and Kaib explained that the Judiciary Conference of the United States, representing federal judges, passed a resolution opposing the bill. Although the language of the bill awarded new rights to victims, the Judiciary Conference concluded that this would increase lawsuits, and that the courts could not "handle such a burden." The struggle between the opposing groups continued, and resulted in a debate over states' rights versus federal rights, specifically the impact that the bill would have on interstate commerce. Ultimately, after the hearings, the Senate Judiciary Committee agreed to support VAWA, including the civil-rights remedy.

The other more important point of the controversial bill was how to define the term "gender-motivated" violence within domestic violence and sexual assault. The proposed legislation required that the victim prove that the crime was not random, but in fact gender animus. As with other crimes that are motivated by racism or homophobia, the challenge of the law was proving the discriminatory intent. This part of the law was structured around previous bills that had been designed in the late nineteenth century to protect black Americans from hate crimes. Debran Rowland noted in *Boundaries of Her Body*, "To many, the civil rights provisions of the Violence Against Women Act was supposed to be what the future held. It was supposed to do for women what the Civil Rights Act of 1964 did for minorities." When facing the opposition, Biden countered the criticism with the famous statement, "Theoretically, I guess, a rape could take place that was not driven by gender animus. . . . But I can't think of what it would be." When Boxer left the House for a Senate seat, Biden was faced with the challenge of finding a new cosponsor in the House. Representative Orrin Hatch agreed to cosponsor the bill with modifications.

The compromise bill was added as an amendment to the Violent Crime Control and Law Enforcement Act (VCCLEA). The bill was protected under the Commerce Clause and the Fourteenth Amendment of the United States Constitution. According to Legal Momentum, a legal and education fund for women, as stated in the Constitution, the Commerce Clause grants Congress the power to regulate activities that have a substantial effect on commerce (under a rational-basis test). This clause was applied to VAWA when Congress found that gender-based domestic and sexual violence qualified, given the extreme costs to taxpayers. In 1994, it was estimated that domestic violence cost between $5 and $10 billion a year to the health care system, the criminal justice system, and other sectors of American society. The civil-rights remedy in the civil-rights provision was the most controversial aspect of VAWA and the reason the bill took four years to pass. After many drafts and outside advocacy efforts from grassroots feminist organizations, the bill was passed and signed into law by President Clinton in 1994 with the civil-rights remedy included. For the remainder of the decade, the civil-rights provisions of VAWA brought trials to courthouses across America, until the case of *United States v. Morrison* challenged the constitutional legitimacy of VAWA.

The civil-rights remedy of VAWA had been challenged, specifically by the Supreme Court, since it was first introduced by Senator Biden. As described by Debran Rowland, the [inevitable] "Congressional-Supreme Court showdown" resulted in the case of *United States v. Morrison* and the striking down of the civil-rights provisions. The legal proceedings of the college student Christy Brzonkala demonstrated judicial activism and the priority of states' rights over federal law and over victims' rights. The legal question in this rape case was whether Congress should have the authority to enact the Violence Against Women Act of 1994 under either the Commerce Clause or the Fourteenth Amendment; *Morrison* demonstrated how fragile rights are and how fallible constitutional protections can be.

In the fall of 1994, Brzonkala was raped by two varsity football players, Antonio Morrison and James Crawford. Brzonkala filed a charge against the boys with the university and Crawford was released from the charges because of insufficient evidence. Morrison admitted to having sex with Brzonkala more than once but argued that the sex was consensual. Brzonkala would later use the language of the young men to prove the assault was motivated by gender animus. The language of the defendants during the assault was considered too vulgar and was omitted from the briefs by the Supreme Court for "reasons of decorum." The university sentenced Morrison to a two-semester suspension. Morrison appealed the charges but after a second review was found guilty again and sentenced to a two-semester suspension. Without notifying the victim, the senior vice president of the university disregarded the sentence to suspend Morrison and allowed him to return. Brzonkala responded by withdrawing from the university and bringing suit "against Morrison, Crawford, and the Virginia Polytechnic Institute [to the] United States District Court." Brzonkala charged her assailants under a clause of the Violence Against Women Act that "provide[d] a federal civil remedy for the victims of gender-motivated violence." The defense argued that this section of the act was unconstitutional; the court agreed with the defendants and Brzonkala appealed to the Fourth Circuit Court of Appeals. The ruling of the appeals court was divided on the constitutionality of the case and the protections afforded to her; although the evidence made it clear this was a gender-motivated rape case, the appeals court ruled that Congress did not have "the constitutional authority to enact" the protections specified in the act. Regardless of the reasons that Congress initially created protections for women victims of gender-based crimes, the circuit court ruled that "violence against women had only an attenuated and indirect relationship with interstate commerce." The case moved on to the Supreme Court, where many justices had been waiting for it.

When VAWA was initially introduced in Congress, many federal judges criticized it, specifically the Chief Justice of the Supreme Court. In 1998, Rehnquist spoke out against the bill, stating that it was "one of the more notable examples of laws that unduly expanded the jurisdiction of federal courts." Rehnquist also said on record that he believed the civil-rights remedy would increase the workload of the federal judiciary, which was already "overburdened." When *United States v. Morrison* was presented to the Supreme Court in 2000, Rehnquist had the long-awaited opportunity to state his opinion of the law and the Fourteenth Amendment. The Rehnquist court granted power to the states in a 5-4 ruling. Chief Justice

Rehnquist concluded in his opinion for the court: "under our federal system [the] remedy [for the rape of Christy Brzonkala] must be provided by the Commonwealth of Virginia, and not by the United States." The Supreme Court affirmed the decision of the Fourth Circuit Court of Appeals and changed the civil-rights provisions of VAWA. The civil-rights provision was first enacted under the commerce clause of the Constitution and argued that gender-based violence has an impact on interstate commerce. However, with a strict interpretation of the commerce clause, the Supreme Court affirmed the decision of the Fourth Circuit en banc, declaring that the civil-rights remedy was unconstitutional. Although the commerce clause had been applied in 1994, since VAWA did not regulate an activity that substantially affected interstate commerce or redress harm caused by the state, the 5-4 ruling stated that the civil-rights remedy was not constitutional, regardless of the impact of domestic and sexual violence on women's employment, productivity, health care costs, and interstate travel. Among the justices who dissented, Justice David H. Souter, George H. W. Bush's first nomination to the Supreme Court, argued that VAWA contained a "mountain of data assembled by Congress . . . showing the effects of violence against women on interstate commerce." In *United States v. Morrison: Where the Commerce Clause Meets Civil Rights and Reasonable Minds Part Ways: A Point and Counterpoint from a Constitutional and Social Perspective*, Marianne Moody Jennings and Nim Razook elaborated on the argument of the dissenting justices, which was that if Congress had provided information on interstate commerce activity, then the courts must defer to this conclusion.

The *Morrison* decision revoked many hard-won rights under the civil-rights remedy. Debran Rowland summed up the discrimination against women and rape victims by the legal culture: "In the end, women's rights gave way to states' rights and the court effectively—and perhaps determinedly—undermined the very purpose of law (i.e., to grant women a remedy in cases of rape and sexual assault because states have often failed to pursue cases of this sort)." The courts have the power to uphold the civil-rights provision of VAWA, yet the Rehnquist court stated that rape and violence against women was a states' rights issue and therefore commemorated rape and told men and women that rape is acceptable. Although the courts ruled otherwise, violence against women is a national issue and has been since before the founding of the colonies. Although legal institutions were addressing the issues that activists had been trying to bring to the forefront of American culture for decades, the result ultimately left women across America with different legal provisions under VAWA than they had been promised.

In the 1990s even the executive branch of the government was forced to address charges of sexual harassment. For the first time in American history, the president was called before the Supreme Court on charges of sexual harassment of an employee. According to the *Washington Post* and Oyez, in 1994, Paula Jones filed allegations against President Clinton that he had propositioned her, that she had suffered several "abhorrent" incidents, and that he exposed himself to her in a hotel room in Little Rock, Arkansas. Jones said that the event happened three years earlier when he was governor of Arkansas and she was a low-level state employee, and that her rejection of the governor's advances resulted in her punishment by state supervisors. Clinton rebutted her allegations by saying that she was attempting to harm his political reputation and make money off the story. He had support in June 1994 from the Arkansas state trooper Danny Ferguson, who went on record to dispute key allegations from Jones. As reported by the *Washington Post*, Ferguson claimed in court documents that Jones had "praised Clinton as sexy, volunteered her phone number and offered to be his girlfriend."

Clinton petitioned for the case to be suspended and dismissed under presidential immunity. The district judge denied the immunity request, but granted a stay until after Clinton had finished his term in office. When this decision was appealed to the Eighth Circuit, the court affirmed that the case should not be dismissed on the grounds of presidential immunity, but reversed the ruling to defer the start of the trial on the grounds that it would be "a 'functional equivalent' to an unlawful grant of temporary presidential immunity." In May 1997, the case was brought to the Supreme Court and the justices unanimously decided to dismiss the request to have the trial suspended. According to Oyez, the court decided that the Constitution "does not grant a sitting president immunity from civil litigation except under highly unusual circumstances." The court further asserted that the separation of powers and the need for confidentiality mandated by the Constitution did not qualify Clinton for immunity; Article 3 of the Constitution allows the court to exercise control over the executive branch and the legislative branch, if necessary.

The following month, Clinton offered Jones $700,000 to settle, but Jones wanted an apology in addition to the monetary compensation. The legal battle continued as Clinton's lawyers argued that there was no evidence of emotional distress or punishment in the workplace. Predictably, Clinton's lawyers investigated and interrogated Jones about her previous sexual history and job history. The second round of settlement negotiations began in the winter of 1998. The deposition on January 17, 1998 was the first time a sitting president was placed on the stand as a defendant in a court case. The perjuries committed by Clinton during this deposition are among the eleven counts of impeachable offenses that were outlined by the former federal judge and Republican attorney Kenneth Starr. Previously, women had difficulty filing suits for sexual harassment in courts, although less high-profile cases were being challenged and dismissed by the courts. Although the Jones case was given press time internationally, the popularity of the defendant, regardless of the decision to not grant presidential immunity, influenced the case in his favor. Faludi noted that the conservatives of the 1990s had "cast themselves as the feminist defenders of female dignity, the right-wing architects promised to emancipate the nation's women from the clutches of the Groper in Chief. And so it was that the greatest assault on liberalism in modern times would be mounted in defense of women's rights." Although the Republican rhetoric asserted that the condemnation of the president was in support of women's equality, the agenda of the party showed Americans that this was truly an issue of bipartisan politics. In November 1998, Jones and Clinton agreed on an out-of-court settlement for $850,000 and no apology, as she had previously requested.

As with the Hill-Thomas scandal, the Clinton-Jones case was complicated by bipartisan politics. Conservatives, including anti-choice activists and a coalition of Republicans, backed Jones as an attack on the president. BBC News reported that the conservatives were staging a "symbolic confrontation between working-class people and the intellectual liberal elite." The bipartisan issues of the Clinton-Jones case were different from the bipartisan issues in the Senate, but likewise resulted in divided political parties at war with each other. The Clinton scandal was important for continuing to put sexual harassment on public display, regardless of the complexity of the case. Whereas the Thomas hearings changed how Americans discussed sexual harassment in the workplace, the Clinton controversy took a new look at what checks could be placed on the power of the executive branch. The case of *Clinton v. Jones* protected the victim, as did the other cases, but defining the rights of the president under the Constitution complicated the process. The Clinton controversy is considered to be primarily representative of bipartisan politics. Those involved in the attack on Clinton had a political agenda and their tactics were part of the larger picture of conspiracies and scandals plaguing the Clinton administration.

Many court decisions in the 1990s did not support marginalized groups and victims, but did create visibility in the media and the public. Although the movement against sexual harassment, the LGBTQ rights movement, and the reproductive rights movement all engaged in grassroots activism before the 1990s, the backlash against progress at this time redefined the warring ideologies of the parties to these issues. Fifteen to twenty years after many of the restrictive and prohibitive laws regarding marriage equality had been passed, the gay rights movement successfully repealed almost all of the laws. The movement against sexual harassment has been strengthened by the antirape movement; however, the reproductive rights movement is arguably under more extreme attack than in any other time in U.S. history. The civil rights progress made in the 1990s was essential to the success of the movements that evolved in later decades.

Recommended Reading

The most comprehensive look at women's history in America from a legal perspective is Debran Rowland, *Boundaries of Her Body: The Troubling History of Women's Rights in America* (Naperville, IL: Sphinx Publishing, 2004). An analysis of LGBT legal history is provided in David A. J. Richards, *Women, Gays, and the Constitution: The Grounds for Feminism and Gay*

Rights in Culture and Law (Chicago: University of Chicago Press, 1998). A. J. Richards, *The Case for Gay Rights: From Bowers to Lawrence and Beyond* (Lawrence: University Press of Kansas, 2005), focuses exclusively on the evolution of LGBT law in America.

Conclusion

The Clinton Administration, 1996–2000

THE ECONOMIC RECESSION and the need for policy changes to help those affected were complicated by the at times negative image of the Clinton White House and the various scandals that preoccupied the media. Media stories had plagued the Clintons since the president's early years as a politician and he was inundated by scandal for the duration of his political career. The scandals were magnified when cable television began around-the-clock coverage. "Travelgate" was the first in a series of scandals. In 1993, an audit of the White House travel office discovered over $18,000 in mismanaged funds. The director kept an off-book ledger, which resulted in misused funds. Consequently, all seven travel office staff were fired and the FBI started an investigation of the travel office. There was pressure from the media and political groups to justify the firings, and critics claimed that the firings were to make room for "friends" of the Clintons. Seven separate, lengthy investigations were conducted by private counsel and others, up to the FBI, but no evidence was uncovered of wrongdoings, illegal activity, or illegal firings on the part of the Clinton administration. Investigators concluded that the firings were not illegal and were justifiable.

The investigations and media attention perpetuated the already adversarial relationship between the Clinton administration and the press. As described by Michael Takiff in *A Complicated Man*, the firings aroused a disproportionately hostile reaction from the media. Prior to the investigations and restructuring of the travel office, the media had benefited from its relationship with the office, specifically in the lavish accommodations that were arranged for the White House press corps. Were it not for the Clinton administration's contentious relationship with the press, the scandal around the travel office could have potentially dissipated; however, the media kept it in the spotlight.

"Travelgate" was only one of many scandals that plagued the Clinton administration; however, it was not the first. An investigation of the Clintons, and a forecast of what was to come, began in 1978 and was dubbed "Whitewater" by the media, after the plot of land in question. A series of investigations consumed seven of the eight years Clinton held office. In 1978, information emerged about a business deal that dated back to the Clintons' early days in Arkansas in the late 1970s. As a young attorney, Hillary began working for the Rose Law Firm in Little Rock. A few months before Clinton's election for his first term as governor of Arkansas, the Clintons partnered in a real estate deal with James and Susan McDougal, the future owners of the Madison Guaranty Savings and Loans. The project was to develop vacation homes on 230 acres of riverfront land along the White River. The investment proved to be a dud and in 1992 was officially dissolved.

The business venture left the Clintons with a financial loss of more than $40,000. Regardless of the loss, the Clintons remained close friends of the McDougals throughout the beginning of Clinton's political career. The McDougals were supportive of the Clintons financially and held a $35,000 fundraiser for the young politician. According to Jim McDougal, when Clinton was governor, he asked McDougal to give some of the legal work of the Madison Guaranty Savings and Loan to Hillary, who was an employee at the Rose Law Firm. In 1985, through a series of loans, the McDougals purchased property called the Castle Grande for $1.75 million. The following year, the money from the loans was used to pay both overdrafts for the Whitewater account and to purchase additional property for Whitewater Development Corp. In 1988, Hillary authorized the destruction of her working files on both Madison Guaranty and Castle Grand, as per protocol. In 1989, Jim McDougal was indicted on bank fraud and one year later acquitted by a jury. In 1989, when it appeared that Clinton would make a bid for the presidency in the 1992 election, Lee Atwater, the Republican political architect, took it upon himself to investigate the potential candidate. The information unearthed a scandal and a series of investigations that lasted ten years and cost $70 million in public funds.

Although the Whitewater investigations began after Clinton was elected president, the articles in the press began appearing in the spring of 1992. To manage press questions about Whitewater, the Rose Law Firm, and the mishandling of funds at Madison Guaranty, the Clintons created a "Clinton campaign Whitewater team." The attention of the public focused on the Clintons' initial investment and Hillary's legal duties in the Rose Law Firm. Despite the emerging scandal, the public gave Clinton the benefit of the doubt and elected him. Once in office, however, press questions regarding Whitewater gained more prominence. Although McDougal bought out the Clintons' share of the investment in Whitewater and the business partnership had officially been dissolved, the investigations continued to question the Clintons' initial investment.

As pressure from the press and independent nongovernment organizations to produce evidence grew, the Clinton administration decided to ignore the stories in the hope they would eventually dissipate. However, the opposite happened: the more the administration ignored the scandal, the more the press uncovered. As more information was unearthed, the press alleged that the Clintons were hiding information. A series of editorials was published in newspapers criticizing the administration's decisions and the aptitude of its attorneys. Hillary reflected in *Living History* that being seasoned in the world of politics, they understand the attacks and responded with an appropriate political strategy. Other members of the administration, new to politics and Washington, could not handle the constant public denigration, particularly the deputy White House council and close personal friend of the Clintons, Vince Foster. The media was especially critical of Foster. Attention focused on Foster, blaming him for his "carelessness" and many of the failings of the Clinton administration. Eventually the weight of it all became too much for him.

The scandal became deeply personal when the Clintons suffered the devastating loss of their colleague and close friend. On July 20, 1993, Foster told an aide he was leaving the office and never returned. That night, in a park approximately ten minutes from the White House, Foster's body was found with a fatal gunshot wound. A few days passed with no report of suicide; many news organizations speculated foul play. Later in the week, a suicide note was found in the bottom of Foster's briefcase, which enumerated his frustrations with politics and the scandal and revealed his belief that he was not cut out for the Washington lifestyle. Foster's suicide and the removal of files from his office after his death revived the media's interest in the Whitewater investigation. It was not long before the news outlets ran conspiracy stories that blamed the Clintons for his death and speculated that it was a cover-up for other issues in the administration. Even after an official report was released ruling Foster's death a suicide, the media continued relentlessly to question his death.

Federal investigation into the bad business deal continued into the following year, when in January 1994 Attorney General Janet Reno appointed the former U.S. attorney and prominent trial attorney Robert Fiske as an independent counsel to investigate the Whitewater scandal. The following year, Kenneth Starr was appointed by a panel of conservative judges to be Fiske's successor as the independent council continued investigating the case. Starr was known for being meticulous in his work at any cost, even if taxpayers were footing the bill. The journalist Max Brantley asserted in an interview with PBS that Starr was looking for a crime, not looking for the answers to the investigation, and that this was "persecution, not a prosecution." Into 1995, the House and the Senate congressional committees held hearings on the Whitewater scandal that lasted into the next term of the Clinton administration.

After a few years, the media focus on Whitewater abated as the administration gained public support and initiated successful domestic policies. However, in January 1996, after two years of subpoenas for the billing records from the Rose Law Firm, the records appeared. Carolyn Huber, the First Lady's assistant, had turned over copies of the Rose Law Firm's billing documents to the investigation. Media attention to the case revived when Huber testified that she had found the records among papers in the First Lady's book room six months prior, but it was only in January that she realized which papers they were. Three weeks later, Hillary Clinton became the only First Lady to testify before a grand jury. After forcing the First Lady to testify at the courthouse in downtown Washington, DC, the records and her testimony merely showed that she had worked for Jim McDougal, but there was no conclusive evidence that she had any knowledge of his fraudulent work.

After Hillary's testimony, Starr decided to continue the investigation, more determined than ever. Many of the files that Fiske had closed before leaving the investigation were reopened and reexamined. Upon Starr's request, both those who had already testified and new witnesses were called to testify. In April 1996, David Hale testified that Bill Clinton had inquired about the $300,000 loan to Susan McDougal and was aware of the situation. Clinton then testified on video camera that he had no involvement or knowledge of the loan transaction between McDougal and Hale. The next month the grand jury portion of the investigation came to a close as both the McDougals and Governor Jim Guy Tucker were convicted of bank fraud. Jim McDougal agreed to cooperate with the investigation and began to state new information that implicated the Clintons in the dishonest scheme. He went on record for the first time in the investigation to collaborate Hale's allegation that Clinton had known about the fraudulent bank loans, thus changing his previous testimonies. The American public generally agreed that this new information was sporadic and nonsensical. Susan McDougal refused to cooperate and was jailed for contempt. With the investigation still underway, Starr stayed on as independent council. Relations between the investigators and the White House intensified as Starr became more convinced the Clintons were guilty of a crime and the White House believed it was being subjected to a residential witch-hunt. In four years, the cost of the investigation had exceeded more than $30 million and would continue to rise. Wanting to focus on issues other than the exhausted Whitewater scandal, Clinton worked to refocus his administration on policy-related issues crucial to the American people.

In 1998, scandal would engulf the Clinton administration again, this time focusing on the president's personal indiscretions with a twenty-one-year-old White House intern, Monica Lewinsky. The news of the affair broke to the public in 1998, but the transgressions began during the government furlough in November 1995. Although full-time government employees had been temporarily laid off, interns were still allowed to come to work. The affair began when only Clinton and Lewinsky were in the office and continued for years after. In early 1996, White House staff began to notice the visibly close and flirtatious relationship between Clinton and Lewinsky and had her transferred from her White House internship to the Pentagon. Nevertheless, Lewinsky continued to visit the White House frequently. While working at the Public Affairs Office of the Pentagon, Lewinsky met Linda Tripp, who was stationed a few cubicles away from her. Tripp had also transferred from the White House to the Pentagon after serving the Bush and Clinton administrations. Although Tripp had worked for the Democrats, she was one of many extremely anti-Clinton people in Washington. She was specifically looking for a weakness in the administration or the president's personal life to bring the family down. Some have attributed Tripp's desire to hurt the Clintons to her resentment about her own career and her own mistreatment as a government employee by the White House. Tripp acted as an older sister or maternal figure for Lewinsky, and the young former intern confided the details of the affair to her. Unbeknownst to Lewinsky, before the two had met, Tripp had already approached publishers about writing a "tell-all" book to slander the Clintons. Now with a real story and all of the confidential details, she once again looked for an agent.

Tripp located a literary agent willing to pursue the story. However, the agent told Tripp she would first need to produce evidence, so in the fall of 1997, Tripp proceeded to tape her phone conversations with Lewinsky. The audio recordings gathered Lewinsky divulging her feelings of adoration and confusion about the president. Much like Starr, who had spent the majority of the Clinton presidency investigating the family, Tripp wanted to expose Clinton and began to share the information with Starr. There was no one more invested in exposing the dirt on the Clintons than Starr; he was especially interested in a scandal that would provide more concrete evidence, since his investigation into Whitewater had hit a dead end. In the meantime, Clinton had secured a job for Monica in the private sector with help from his friend Vernon Jordan. This was later questioned: was this Clinton's way of buying her silence? Other inquiries into Clinton's relationships with women began to come to light and Lewinsky was subpoenaed to testify in a sexual harassment case against the president brought by the former Arkansas employee Paula Jones.

In the lawsuit, Jones alleged that Governor Clinton had propositioned her sexually in a hotel in Arkansas and she had declined his advances. In later years, Jones restated the allegations as part of a civil-action lawsuit against the president. The case of *Clinton v. Jones* stemmed from another Clinton scandal known as "Troopergate," which alleged that when Clinton was governor of Arkansas, state troopers had arranged sexual liaisons for the politician. That story had broken in 1993. When Clinton's lawyers learned of the *Jones* case, they attempted to suppress, or at least curb, the ensuing publicity. His lawyers argued that a sitting president was immune from private lawsuits, but this reasoning would not protect Clinton from what was to come. Initially his lawyers were able to defer the case from going to trial until he left office. However, in *Clinton v. Jones* (1997), the Supreme Court ruled that the president was not above the law and the case could not be deferred. The lawyers representing Jones sought to establish a pattern of sexual predation on lower-level young female employees. It was at this time that they discovered Lewinsky's story, with help from Tripp. On January 16, the day before the president was to testify in the *Jones* case, Lewinsky was first set up by Tripp. At one of their arranged meetings, the FBI showed up and begged her to cooperate and give them her story against the president. Despite their pleas, she refused to provide any information. Meanwhile, the First Lady was still in the dark about the president's infidelity with Lewinsky and she stood by her husband as he prepared to testify.

When Lewinsky was subpoenaed, Starr already knew about the affair. Starr saw an opportunity for a perfect storm in which the *Jones* case, Whitewater, and the Lewinsky scandal could potentially come together in one case against the president. Starr anticipated the testimony and waited to play his hand and see if Clinton lied about his affair with Monica on the stand under oath. He knew that the affair itself was not an impeachable offense, but if the president was questioned about his affair with Lewinsky and perjured himself, Starr had a case. Additionally, Starr believed that Clinton would tell Lewinsky how to testify when called to the stand. January 17 was the opportunity Starr and his team had been waiting for since the start of the Clinton administration. Starr was not the counsel on the case and the lawyer representing Jones took the lead. He used the federal legal definition of "sexual relations" to establish a concrete definition for acts that take place in a sexual relationship: A person engages in "sexual relations" when the person knowingly engages in or causes (1) contact with the genitalia, anus, groin, breast, inner thigh, or buttocks of any person with an intent to arouse or gratify the sexual desire of any person; (2) contact between any part of the person's body or an object and the genitals or anus of another person; or (3) contact between the genitals or anus of the person and any part of another person's body. 'Contact' means intentional touching, either directly or through clothing. The definition did not cover the activities of the Lewinsky-Clinton affair, giving the president a loophole to wiggle out of the charge. He denied the affair, but the plaintiff's lawyer pressed for information about gifts and the details of their relationship.

After the testimony, as the story quickly became international news and the alleged affair went viral, Clinton turned to his old confidant Dick Morris. Morris told PBS that he ran a poll to see how the American people would respond and the data concluded the American people would forgive him if he came clean. The issue that most concerned the public was that he had already lied to his family, his staff, and the country. Although Clinton heard the advice, he decided to continue to lie to Hillary and to the people. Two days after his testimony, the tapes of Tripp and Lewinsky's conversations were made available to the public. Clinton stood by his story, and he went on television to state that he was not having an affair.

Throughout the initial scandal and the trial, Clinton's staff and family stood by him and he continued to declare his innocence and lie to them. In a television interview, Hillary defended her husband, just as she had during the initial campaign to get him elected to the White House. She was an impassioned defender of Clinton's fidelity and stated that the Starr and Jones investigations were a continuation of the "right-wing" conspiracy against Clinton. The administration had been plagued with scandals since his presidential inauguration; Clinton had promised his wife he had been faithful and this was simply another attack on the president. As the media covered the scandal around the clock, Clinton's advisers, believing he was innocent, encouraged him to more aggressively deny the affair. He gave another press conference, at which he famously stated, "I never had sexual relations with that woman. . . . These allegations are false and I need to go back to work for the American people," while shaking his finger and banging the podium. This adamant denial of the affair became the most iconic moment in the case after the truth was revealed.

The president attempted to compartmentalize the publicity about the affair and resume his executive duties. On January 27, 1998, he was schedule to give his annual State of the Union address. Clinton decided to move forward and focus not on the scandal, but rather on the impressive budget surplus of the administration and that government could use this money to protect Social Security in the next round of budget negotiations. The media still covered the speculations about the affair, and it was only a matter of time before hard evidence surfaced. Lewinsky produced a blue dress that had the president's semen on it, making it hard for him to continue denying the allegations. The president had no other choice but to stop lying and come clean to Hillary, his daughter Chelsea, and the people. Hillary appeared utterly humiliated that she had publicly defended him.

The scandal moved to trial when Starr promised Lewinsky immunity if she testified against the president. Based on her testimony, Clinton was immediately subpoenaed, becoming the first president in American history to testify before a grand jury in his own defense. He gave his grand jury testimony from the White House on August 17, 1998. Clinton's lawyers negotiated that the interrogation could last for only four hours; Clinton's strategy was to run out the clock. He nitpicked the language and most famously told the lawyers, "it depends on what the meaning of the word 'is' is." Regardless of his elaborate stories and attempts to evade the questions, he was finally forced to admit his "inappropriate intimate contact" with his intern. The next step was to address the American people he had lied to in a live press conference; he came clean to not only his constituents but also to his staff. He had lied to people closest to him who had defended him.

The day after the press conference, the Clintons left for their annual family vacation on Martha's Vineyard. His staff and the media waited for his return, anticipating that the remainder of his presidency would go one of two ways: he would either resign or be impeached. Clinton already had a complicated relationship with his own party; there was speculation that the Democrats would abandon their own president as they had done with Nixon. When Clinton returned, he gave an impassioned press conference, telling the American people he would never resign from the position to which he had been elected. When the U.S. embassies in Kenya and Tanzania were bombed by the terrorist organization Al-Qaeda, Clinton responded by bombing known terrorist locations in Afghanistan and Sudan. Many criticized the bombing as an attempt to distract the American people from his indiscretions.

On September 9, Starr released details about the investigation as it pertained to Lewinsky in a 453-page report to Congress. He stated eleven counts of impeachable offenses against the president. The Starr report explicitly advocated for impeachment and argued the reasons for it. However, Clinton had the support of the American people. Regardless of the scandal, he had managed to maintain his popularity. When polls were conducted to see where the American people stood on the issue, many believed that the push for impeachment was because Starr and his team were simply after the president. On the same day as the report, Clinton appeared in the Rose Garden at the White House to publicly apologize for the first time since the affair was exposed. After months of press coverage, he fully apologized for lying to the people, the Congress, and his family.

Clinton quickly proved that he was still the "Comeback Kid" and so was the Democratic Party. In October 1998, the economy experienced its first budget surplus in nearly thirty years. The American people were forgiving enough to give the Democrats another chance in the 1998 midterm election and continued supporting the president. The Democrats were able to pick up five seats in the House. It was the first time since the Civil War that the opposing party was unsuccessful in gaining seats in the sixth year of a presidency. Most important, after the election the Republican Speaker of the House Newt Gingrich announced his resignation. Other politicians and the public blamed him for the Republican loss. However, the Clinton scandal was not over. On October 5, the Judiciary Committee of the House voted 21-16 along party lines to pursue the impeachment hearings. Three days later the House voted to open the inquiry for impeachment. Clinton had been hounded by gossip and investigations since before he took office; it was the affair with an intern that would bring him and his administration down. The Republicans wanted to see the president held accountable. Although the charge was perjury, it was apparent that the move to impeach the president was about a deep and long-standing adversarial relationship between Clinton and the 105th House of Representatives. The impeachment process began and asked the question, what "misconduct" is a violation of the presidential oath?

Clinton faced impeachment on four counts. On December 19, before the new Congress was sworn in, the House voted along party lines in a 228-206 vote to impeach him for two of the counts: obstruction of justice and perjury. Clinton was the first president in a century and only the second in American history to be impeached by the House. When Clinton's impeachment moved to the Senate, the debate continued for three weeks. The Senate was placed in a precarious position because they only had two options, to either remove the president from office or grant an acquittal. Les Benedict explained that this created resentment among Senators of both parties: many did not feel he deserved removal, but could not rationalize acquittal, and there was no middle ground or alternative options. After much deliberation, forty-five Senators voted "guilty" on the count of perjury and half voted guilty on the count of obstruction of justice. However, neither vote was enough to secure the two-thirds majority required and the Senate acquitted the president. Clinton had always been protected by public opinion; the Senators were aware that constituents did not want him removed from office.

The Lewinsky affair cast a permanent shadow on the Clinton presidency. The Clinton administration is often not discussed without reference to his infidelity and impeachment. Scandal had plagued the administration from the beginning, but this time Clinton was undoubtedly guilty. As in the Watergate or the Iran-Contra scandals, the president would never be able to escape the consequences of his actions. Unlike the discredited behavior of former presidents Nixon and Bush, Clinton's misconduct resulted in deeper questions about the role of the presidency. The intersection of dishonest behavior and politics surprised no one in the 1990s, but now all three branches of government and the American people were forced to address the issue in a way that had not previously been relevant. Like other presidents who had had extramarital affairs, the Lewinsky affair would become part of Clinton's social legacy; however, his political legacy would always include the House impeachment. Although an affair with an intern is not an indication of a person's political talents or abilities, it did impact the politics in Washington: the trial and hearings consumed millions of dollars and much time, specifically that of politicians, who could have focused on other social, domestic, and foreign issues.

Regardless of "Monicagate," Clinton served his last year as president and continued to make policy changes domestically and abroad. The gun control debate was reopened when tragedy struck on April 20, 1999. Two high-school students in Littleton, Colorado, went on a shooting spree at Colum-bine High School before killing themselves. The nation was in shock as it tried to understand the violence. Clinton stepped forward, as he had with the Oklahoma City bombing years earlier, to comfort the American people. The debate about weapons control domestically extended to foreign policy as well. In October 1999, the U.S. Senate refused to ratify Clinton's bill for a Comprehensive Nuclear Ban Treaty, which protected citizens around the world by forbidding nuclear weapons testing. Those against the bill argued that the ratification would not protect the United States because it would not prevent other countries from engaging in nuclear testing or war. Other nations responded negatively to the Senate's decision and believed that non-ratification was an act of aggression. Regardless of Clinton's efforts, the treaty remained signed but not ratified. Clinton did make progress before leaving office in the Middle East peace process between Israel and Palestine. In July 2000, Clinton convened a summit at Camp David to bring together leaders to devise a solution to end the hostilities permanently. Israeli Prime Minister Ehud Barak was willing to compromise on the return of 90 per-cent of West Bank territory to Palestine and a shared control of Jerusa-lem. When this compromise was presented to the Palestinian leader Yasser Arafat, he refused. Although the meeting did not result in the agreement that was hoped for, the preliminary meeting between the two leaders was historic and lay the groundwork for future negotiations. Clinton left office with a 66–68 percent approval rating, depending on the polling, even after the *Jones* case, the Monica Lewinsky scandal, and the House impeachment (though acquitted by Senate vote).

Both First Lady Hillary Clinton and Vice President Al Gore now had the opportunity to further their own political careers. After much debate, Hillary announced her campaign for the Senate seat in New York State. Democratic Senator Daniel Patrick Moynihan had decided to leave office after serving twenty-four years in the Senate. Running against Republican Representative Rick Lazio, Hillary won 55 percent of the votes, becoming the First Lady to be elected to the Senate. The Clintons settled in Chappaqua in Westchester County, New York, and began the next phase of their lives. Al Gore campaigned for the presidency against Governor George W. Bush, son of the former president. Gore won the popular vote, but lost the election after suspicions of ballot fraud sent the case of *Bush v. Gore* to the Supreme Court. The Rehnquist court ruled in a 5-4 decision that Florida's order to recount ballots was unconstitutional, therefore giving the presidency to the Republican candidate George W. Bush.

The Clinton legacy was secure, not as he had envisioned it, as a result of health care reform, but with the unemployment rate at its lowest to date, as well as the lowest inflation rate in three decades. The home ownership figure was the highest in American history and crime rates had declined in many cities. Regardless of scandals, impeachment, and a precarious eight years, after a series of Republican presidents and the Reagan legacy, Clinton's moderate politics allowed him to leave office with the highest rating of any president since World War II.

The terrorist attacks of September 11, 2001, ended the decade of the 1990s. As described by Walter LaFeber in *Michael Jordan and the New Global Capitalism*, the hijackers were products of post-1970s capitalism and technology. The attack on the World Trade Center was in part successful because Al-Qaeda utilized "the newest computer, earth satellite, aircraft, and other technologies. They turned these technologies into deadly weapons against Americans, whom they saw as the source of the technology, new capitalism, and globalization that Bin Laden and his followers hate . . . the terrorists blamed the new capitalism for corrupting their homelands and, above all, Saudi Arabia, the center of Islamic religion." The attacks of September 11 forced Americans to reconsider national security issues and globalization.

In the late 1990s and early 2000, the world was turned on its head by one financial crisis after another. The financial crises were exacerbated by the already downward trajectory of the economy and the fall of the World Trade Center. September 11, 2001, changed the laws regarding technology and spying. Airport security increased and the Orwellian USA Patriot Act of 2001 gave law enforcement officials the right to tap phones and track the Internet activities of citizens. September 11 affected how people moved in the world. LaFeber made a connection between the rise of the United States as the leader in global financial markets, communications systems, marketing networks, and innovative technology and the security risks that cultural imperialism invited. Cultural imperialism and globalization created "explosively dangerous challenges and high costs to Americans . . . in the newly wired world's new century."

On the morning of September 11, 2001, the U.S. war on terror unofficially began when terrorists flew two planes into the World Trade Center Towers. In addition to the airplane passengers killed in the hijacking, over 2,700 people were killed in the Twin Towers and an estimated 400 police officers and firefighters were killed as they raced to save lives. The third plane was crashed into the Pentagon, killing 184 people in the building and all passengers aboard the plan. The fourth plane was crashed into a field in Pennsylvania as the passengers attempted to regain control of the plane. The loss of American lives devastated the country. As the decade of prosperity was declining and the millennium was beginning, Americans prepared for the next decade of war in the Middle East.

Recommended Reading

Haynes Johnson, *The Best of Times: The Boom and Bust Years of America before and after Everything Changed* (Orlando, FL: Mariner Books, 2002), specifically analyzes the "scandal times" of the 1990s. It gives one of the most in-depth looks at the Monica Lewinsky scandal and the impact of the terrorist attacks of September 11.

Index